DISRUPTING THE CENTER

DISRUPTING THE CENTER

*A Partnership Approach to Writing
Across the University*

REBECCA HALLMAN MARTINI

UTAH STATE UNIVERSITY PRESS
Logan

Published by Utah State University Press
An imprint of University Press of Colorado
245 Century Circle, Suite 202
Louisville, Colorado 80027

 The University Press of Colorado is a proud member of
the Association of University Presses.

The University Press of Colorado is a cooperative publishing enterprise supported,
in part, by Adams State University, Colorado State University, Fort Lewis College,
Metropolitan State University of Denver, Regis University, University of Alaska Fairbanks,
University of Colorado, University of Denver, University of Northern Colorado,
University of Wyoming, Utah State University, and Western Colorado University.

∞ This paper meets the requirements of the ANSI/NISO Z39.48-1992 (Permanence of
Paper).

ISBN: 978-1-64642-176-3 (paperback)
ISBN: 978-1-64642-177-0 (ebook)
https://doi.org/10.7330/9781646421770

Library of Congress Cataloging-in-Publication Data

Names: Hallman Martini, Rebecca, author.
Title: Disrupting the center : a partnership approach to writing across the university /
   [Rebecca Hallman Martini]
Description: Logan : Utah State University Press, 2021. | Includes bibliographical refer-
   ences and index.
Identifiers: LCCN 2021036992 (print) | LCCN 2021036993 (ebook) | ISBN
   9781646421763 (paperback) | ISBN 9781646421770 (ebook)
Subjects: LCSH: Writing centers—Administration. | Strategic alliances (Business) |
   Educational change. | English language—Rhetoric—Study and teaching (Higher)
Classification: LCC PE1404 .H338 2021 (print) | LCC PE1404 (ebook) | DDC
   808/.0420711—dc23/eng/20211122
LC record available at https://lccn.loc.gov/2021036992
LC ebook record available at https://lccn.loc.gov/2021036993

The University Press of Colorado gratefully acknowledges the support of the University
of Georgia toward this publication.

Cover illustration: "From Morning 'til Night," © Karen Schulz, [2019],
www.karen-schulz.com.

For my family.

CONTENTS

ACKNOWLEDGMENTS

This book would never have been possible without the smart, thoughtful, and creative input from many people.

First and foremost, I would like to thank the University of Houston Writing Center and its disciplinary partners, the writing consultants, and the student writers for their time and willingness to talk with me about their experiences with writing and teaching writing. From our first conversations, they challenged me to rethink all that I knew about writing centers. Years later I am still learning from them.

I am also eternally grateful to the wonderful teachers and writing center directors I have had over the years. Scott Whiddon, at Transylvania University, was my first writing center director. He introduced me to the work of tutoring and showed me the kind of teacher I wanted to be. I feel lucky to have met so many colleagues and friends during my time in the Rhetoric and Composition program at the University of Louisville. Mary Rosner, Karen Kopelson, Stephen Schneider, Mike Sobiech, Caroline Wilkinson, Matt Dowell, Simon Sangpukdee, Matt Wiles, Harley Ferris, Jennifer Marciniak, Adam Robinson, Megan Bardolf, Amy Luek, Hannah Harrison, Shyam Sharma, Brice Nordquist, and Nancy Bou Ayash have influenced how I see the work of writing centers. Joanna Wolfe has continued to be a mentor and a friend. Bronwyn T. Williams spent time talking through the major ideas in this book as well as mentoring me through the process of writing.

At the University of Houston, I greatly appreciate the support from mentors Paul Butler, James Kastely, Nathan Shepley, Chatwara Suwannamai Duran, and Jennifer Wingard. Carl Lindahl taught me more about how to understand and represent people on their own terms than anyone. James T. Zebroski has been the most important mentor and friend. His wisdom, insightfulness, honesty, and support made this project possible. Among my fondest memories of graduate school (and in academia thus far) are those many early mornings spent at the Blackhole, talking about writing, teaching writing, the politics of English departments, the job market, and the work of this book. I continue to learn from him and cherish our relationship.

I am indebted to the friendships that formed during my time at the University of Houston with J. P. Gritton, Maurice Wilson, Mark Sursavage, Clay Guinn, Liz Blomstedt, Zack Turpin, Conor Bracken, Katie Condon, Sarah McClung, Jonathan Richards, Adrienne DeLeon, Danny Wallace, Larry Butz, Enrique Paz, Soyeon Lee, and Michael Reich. I cannot imagine my time in Houston without the friendship of Erin and Thomas Singer. Erin was my closest friend in my cohort at Uof H, and I'm sure I wouldn't have made it through the program without her. Thanks especially to Rachel Bracken for all our long runs together and for being one of the most thoughtful friends I've had. Thank you to Michael Miller for his support and friendship. I will never forget his presence at my dissertation defense and his deep interest in talking about the project afterward, which meant more to me than he knows. Special thanks to my two dearest friends from my time in the program: Michelle Miley and Sara Cooper. I am so in awe of you both as colleagues, friends, teachers, and mothers. I'm also very excited about our collaborative projects in the works.

At Salem State University, Tanya K. Rodrigue and Alexandria Peary were supportive partners during my time there. Tanya has been a wonderful friend, collaborator, and mentor. She was one of the first to show me how academia and motherhood could be done together. Thanks to my colleagues in the English department: Theresa DeFrancis, Nancy Schultz, Elizabeth Kenney, Roopika Risam, Sandy Fyfe, Bill Coyle, Jan Lindholm, Amy Jo Minett, Scott Nowka, Pierre Walker, Meg Anderson, Michael and Claudia Jaros, J. D. and Eileen Scrimgeour, Keja Valens, Stephenie Young, and Elizabeth McKeigue. All the brilliant writing consultants and graduate students with whom I was lucky to work in the Mary G. Walsh Writing Center have helped me think about the important work we do in writing centers, especially Dorothy Calabro, Liz Soule, Pamela Leavey, Kelci Johnston, Mollie McDonald, Kate Parsons, and Ali Shirazi.

I am grateful to my colleagues and mentors at the University of Georgia, especially Michelle Ballif, Roxanne Eberle, Nate Kreuter, Richard Menke, Christine Lasek-White, Nancee Reeves, and Casie Legette. Isiah Lavender III has been an invaluable mentor, friend, and writing partner. If it hadn't been for him and Heather, we would have taken much longer to feel at home in Athens and at UGA. Lindsey Harding has been a generous, supportive, collegial, and administrative-savvy friend, as she has helped me learn how to navigate collaboration at UGA. The fabulous graduate students and writing consultants I've had the pleasure to work alongside in the UGA Writing Center have been particularly helpful. Paula Rawlins and Emma Perry have both served as assistant directors in the writing center. I always thought of them as co-directors and never could have managed directing the UGA Writing Center and writing this book without their support and brilliance. The graduate students in ENGL 6880: Composition Theory and Pedagogy have helped me think about familiar texts in new ways. I am always learning from the graduate students I work with closely: Sierra Diemmer, Mikaela Warner, Chanara Andrews-Bickers, Megan Fontenot, Savannah Jensen, Elizabeth Wayson, and Saurabh Anand.

This research was supported by two important grants: the International Writing Center Association's Ben Rafoth Graduate Research Grant and Salem State University's Summer Research Grant. Kevin Dvorak was an invaluable friend and mentor during my time as a graduate student and still today. Jackie Grutsch McKinney's research on writing centers helped me understand the limitations of our ways of talking about writing centers and encouraged me to ask the first questions that began to shape this research. No other scholar has been more influential in shaping how I think about writing centers.

There were many gracious scholars who offered their time and energy to me as I worked through the material of this book. R. Mark Hall read and responded to an early draft of this book with encouragement and critical engagement. Randall Monty was interested in this project before it was a book. His superb research also helped me contextualize this project among writing centers nationally. Rachael W. Shah was unbelievably generous to me when I cold-called her and asked to talk about her forthcoming book on partnership when I was still trying to figure out exactly what the term meant for me. Cassie Book has been one of my most constant and insightful colleague-friends since I started graduate school. She is one of the sharpest minds in the field.

I cannot imagine this book without regular, meaningful feedback from my dear colleague, Travis Webster. I am certain he read as many versions of this book as I did in the over five years we've spent writing together. Not only was Travis a generous reader, but he was also writing a book alongside me, which made the experience something shared. Academia would be a far less livable place for me without him. I am forever grateful for his mentorship, ongoing support, critical eye, and, above all, friendship.

Many thanks to the entire Utah State University Press team. Michael Spooner heard this project's first "pitch" and requested a book proposal. Rachael Levay offered generosity, encouragement, and professionalism. She has made this by far my best experience with academic publishing. I feel so fortunate to have had the opportunity to work with her so closely as a junior scholar with lots of life stuff happening along the way. Others at Utah State UP have been critical to getting this book finished: Laura Furney, Dan Pratt, Darrin Pratt, and Beth Svinarich, as well as copyeditor Steve Grinstead. Two anonymous reviewers have offered invaluable commentary that reshaped this manuscript into a much better version of itself.

Finally, I am most grateful for my family. This book would have never made it here without their support and kindness. The Hallmans, the Campbells, the Martini Paulas, and the Lara Nettos offered support from afar. I'm thankful for our Athens friends who have become family: MJ, Eva, Leo, and Phillip Elliot. My greatest gratitude goes to my mom for teaching me compassion, my dad for teaching me work ethic, my Aunt Karen for sharing her art and her processes with me (and for everything else, really), and my sister, Jamie, for teaching me humility and for always listening to me even when no one else did. I cannot imagine making it through this process without ongoing support from my partner and most important reader, Rodrigo Martini. Thank you for your generosity, encouragement, tough love, and many, many, many wonderful meals you've cooked me over the years. Your love and food have always sustained—and continue to sustain—me, no matter what. And of course, thank you to the joys of my life: Esme Grace, whose willingness to arrive a little late made the first draft and submission of this manuscript possible, and Maya James, whose anticipated arrival motivated me to finish. Their curiosity, love, and humor gave me the energy and grounding necessary for writing this book.

DISRUPTING THE CENTER

Introduction

WHY A STRATEGIC PARTNERSHIP APPROACH IN THE WRITING CENTER?

On June 7, 2016, a fraught colleague of mine at New Jersey City University (NJCU) contacted me about a callous dean's unchallenged decision to "dissolve the writing center" by moving it out of Academic Affairs and into Student Support Services. As part of that move, her colleague, who was a PhD in English, would also be "removed" from her directorship, along with the elimination of thirty other people. The "new writing center" would become part of a general tutoring center, where writing tutors would not receive training in rhetoric and composition as they were currently. My colleague was writing to share the petition to keep the writing center open and to ask for my support, as the projected close date for the center, June 30, was fast approaching.

The petition, written by the then writing center director, explained the administration's decision to close the center as "the latest 'cost-saving' action," meant to "save money by substituting top-quality tutors with lower-paid, less-qualified tutors." In other words, all current writing center tutors were fired; some tutors were invited to apply for positions at the general tutoring center, without any information about wages or hours, while all of the professional tutors permanently lost their jobs. Despite having their strongest year yet, with a 68 percent increase in one-on-one tutoring sessions in a single year and over 1,110 signatures on the petition, the administration closed the center in just three weeks' time. From the administrators' perspective, this move was meant to "end duplication of tutoring services and save money" (McDonald 2016). The provost claimed, "No one is losing their jobs, no full-time employee is affected," yet it was unclear whether or not the many adjuncts who worked as professional tutors would be hired by the student-only staffed tutoring center, as indicated by an email from the interim dean. The NJCU Writing Center shut its doors on June 30, 2016.

The NJCU Writing Center represents just one of several writing centers that have come under attack over the past several years.[1] Unfortunately, upper administrators seemingly do not understand or value writing

https://doi.org/10.7330/9781646421770.c000

studies and the work of writing centers. This problem continually pervades the modern academic world—it's not new. Nor is their willingness to make quick decisions for and about writing instruction without consulting writing studies experts.

And yet, our tendency to quickly assume that the administration works in a singular, consistently problematic way may also be unfair and limiting. For example, in another recent attempt to reposition a writing center as a "student service," thereby removing the qualified director of the Centre for Writers at the University of Alberta, a past director at the university spoke out on the WCenter listserv. Roger Graves, a past director of both the Centre for Writers and Writing Across the Curriculum and also the current director of the Centre for Teaching and Learning, admitted in response that he was "concerned" about "some of the comments that characterize 'the administration'" in the email exchange. He then attempted to rationalize the position from which "the administration" was working, as they tried to systematize how multiple writing centers on campus were positioned and how they reported. He also explained that conversations surrounding this particular writing center's repositioning "did not involve a budget cut, a change in services to students, or a physical change" and noted the administration's willingness to meet with and listen to the University Writing Committee, despite the fact that they did not act in the way the committee would have liked them to act. Graves acknowledged that there are indeed some "well-intentioned administrators" who simply do not understand writing center work, the implication here being that, rather than paint them as the ultimate bad guys, perhaps we should find ways of better communicating our work to administrators.

While we must learn to clearly describe our work to a broader university audience, writing center administrators also need to build strong relationships across campus. Part of why some writing centers close or lose their autonomy may be a lack of what Mark Hall has called "social capital," which is rooted in the ability to create and maintain relationships that involve the exchange of resources in a mutually beneficial scenario across a network of respected participants who often hold similar values and principles. This concept accounts for both the resources that a group accrues through institutional relationships (Bourdieu) and the "reciprocal nature" (Coleman) that develops through "extensive networks of people brought together by shared values, assumptions, and beliefs," which ultimately lead to the development of trust. By developing social capital, writing centers can make themselves valuable to the university while also challenging marginality. Even in 2010, Hall recognized budget cuts and noted that an important response is to position the writing center as a fundamental university resource, a move he highlights by describing a "partnership" between his writing center and the school of social work.

I agree with Hall's argument, especially his emphasis on social capital and cognition, which recognizes the importance of creating a shared vision. I also think we need to more closely examine how the language we use to describe our work across the university signifies one crucial way of building the kind of social capital for which Hall calls. This requires us to be more cognizant of how those outside our centers, including the administration, understand the teaching of writing, and it sometimes requires a willingness to change and adapt our language. Thus, instead of determining collaboration by identifying similar goals and values, we must also be willing to create new visions *with* others.

Within this context, and oftentimes alongside humanities disciplines and English departments more generally, writing centers find themselves working under increasingly difficult university climates as the reallocation of resources continues to suggest the national and local value placed on education and areas within it. Thus, we must proactively respond to whatever "crisis of education" arises. Recently, such crises have included high dropout rates (Douglas-Gabriel 2016), increasing tuition prices (Seltzer 2017), low employment (Hennelly 2016), and the increase of contingent faculty who are not fairly compensated for their work (Chen 2017). These "crises" provide the opportunity for change and, particularly, for what can be thought of as "disruptions" in higher education.

In *The Innovative University: Changing the DNA of Higher Education from the Inside Out* (2011), business scholars Clayton M. Christensen and Henry J. Eyring argue that traditional universities have the potential to respond to these interruptions in education through "disruptive innovations," which occur when a new approach, often presented as either cheaper or more user-friendly than what already exists, challenges the dominant educational paradigm. Identified by some as the most influential business idea of the early twenty-first century, disruptive innovations are initially considered to be inferior, yet over time their emphasis on functionality and their ability to improve the services or product eventually catch on with mainstream customers, rather than solely meeting the needs of "low-end" customers, or those previously considered to be "non-consumers" (Bagehot 2017; Wolfe 2016). In this case, the concept of disruption is a "positive force" that has the potential to alter the university context and its services, making them more simple, convenient, accessible, and affordable (Christensen, Horn, and Johnson 2008, 11). Further, disruptive innovations interrupt the traditional educational trajectories by changing the very nature of how we understand quality and improvement. In this way, that which was once deemed "inferior"—the disruptive innovation in its early development—becomes the preferred approach, thus redefining the practice and its context.

In the current climate of higher education, universities must react quickly when likely disruptions present themselves. While disruptive innovations in higher education often come from outside the university, this book makes the case that writing centers can effectively respond to—and counter—these external disruptive innovations through their own internal innovative practices that ultimately lead to positive change. For example, despite the assumption that instructor-to-student is the ideal or preferred educational environment, writing centers work from the idea that valuable learning occurs in peer-to-peer scenarios. This kind of education also happens to be more accessible to student writers and less expensive than hiring full-time instructors. In this way, writing centers themselves work as a kind of disruptive innovation to the traditional, classroom-based, instructor-student educational standard.

When writing centers can find ways to respond innovatively to potential disruptions in higher education, they increase their chances to build social capital. And the more social capital they have, the more likely opportunities to be innovative present themselves. For instance, developing a course-embedded tutoring program to support a writing-intensive art history course when university budget cuts lead to increased class sizes, if done through strategic partnership—the primary response to disruptive innovations described in this book—will likely increase social capital for the writing center. Not only will this create a meaningful relationship between the writing center and the specific course or department (in this case, art history), but it could also help establish a writing center identity with increased social capital (in the College of Arts and Sciences more generally, and beyond). Likewise, if the writing center has a good partnership with a particular department already and has established social capital, then when budget cuts impact curriculum, departments may approach the writing center for help in creating an innovative solution to support writers and teachers of writing before looking externally.

Alongside the need for a timely response to external disruptions, and in order for their responses to work, universities often have to change their inner structure (or DNA) to meet new higher education demands. Christensen and Eyring (2011) explain that a university's

DNA consists of deeply rooted, historical, institutional traits that seem innate or natural within particular institutional types. Of course, there is nothing natural about institutional structures. Yet, such traits that seem to be commonly present include procedures like face-to-face instruction, departmentalization, long summer recesses, competitive athletics, a tenure and promotion process, and a general education curriculum alongside a chosen major (135). Currently, Christensen and Eyring argue that online education is the most prominent disruptive innovation because it directly challenges the face-to-face trait that so many universities express as an essential element of institutional DNA. In their response to external online education products and services then, universities face the challenge of creating a response that simultaneously makes space for some kind of online (or hybrid) models for learning and alters the university's traditional, face-to-face instructional practice that makes up part of their institutional DNA. Michael B. Horn and Heather Staker present one such approach in a K–12 context in *Blended: Using Disruptive Innovation to Improve Schools* (2015), where they argue for an approach that combines in-person and online learning methods that allow some degree of student control over time, place, path and/ or pace (34). While this approach alters the DNA of a primarily face-to-face instructional environment, it also does so intentionally, from within, incorporating elements of both in-person learning and online models via a new, hybrid, or blended approach.

In this book, I argue that writing centers in particular can respond to crises of higher education and the disruptive innovations that challenge university practices through their own innovative approaches to writing instruction. We can (and must) find ways to work both within and against a current political climate driven by college administrators who are strongly influenced by a business-model mentality, corporate interests, and post-Fordist values, including privatization, efficiency, cost-cutting, and mass production. Our ability to develop partnerships with colleges and departments across campus presents one successful strategy for doing so. Rather than focusing on what we will or will not do and insisting on singular visions of writing instruction, I argue that writing centers need to start thinking more strategically and creatively about how we can work *with* departments across campus to support student writers, and simultaneously about how those departments can help provide support for writing and the work of writing instruction. Given the rising value of writing in the workplace and the expectation that college graduates have writing proficiency (Association of American Colleges and Universities 2015), more universities have initiated quality enhancement plans that emphasize writing. Departments from art history to math have grown increasingly concerned with the quality of writing instruction that students receive in their majors.[2]

As extracurricular learning spaces that primarily work through peer-to-peer instructional approaches outside the traditional instructor-student classroom scenario, writing centers are well positioned to challenge dominant educational paradigms through localized disruptive innovations. Similarly recognizing the potential writing centers have for responding to change in higher education, Joe Essid and Brian McTague argue in *Writing Centers at the Center of Change* that, within the corporate university, writing centers will likely face challenges from or related to private firms or artificial intelligence that offer tutoring or writing support services, the cutting of additional tenure-track lines as certain majors and programs are eliminated, curricular changes especially to general education requirements, additional "writing-focused" services appearing on campus without communication with the main writing center, students engaging in more writing including multimodal and multimedia composition, and concerns related to job security (2020, 11–12). In this book, I present a strategic partnership framework as one response to current or potential disruptions such as these, and I include three partnership case studies that inadvertently respond to current or potential "disruptive innovations" in our educational paradigm: online education, outsourcing to public-private partnerships (P3s), and career readiness initiatives like the "Go Pro Early" model. My argument is that through intentional use of the strategic partnership framework, we can directly intervene before disruptive innovations change a university's DNA in ways that threaten ethical teaching and learning.

Within the context of "disruptive innovations," I use the case studies to explore the role of the writing center in the twenty-first-century university. I intentionally use the term *twenty-first-century university* to acknowledge a current university climate that requires an awareness of the challenging job market and the need for students to be well prepared for the workforce, in addition to the way that universities operate as businesses and have been doing so for a long time. In using *twenty-first-century university*, I mean to move beyond arguments about the "neoliberal university" and the "corporate university," which bring with them problematic ideologies that conflict with humanitarian ideals about higher education and often accompany a "fight the man" mentality. In some ways, picking this fight becomes imperative because writing centers are well positioned to engage in it (Monty 2019). Yet, this book operates from the premise that, administratively, we must work within as well as against the business mentality of the twenty-first century, and that we can ethically do both. In other words, we can be spaces that "incorporate frameworks of social and restorative justice . . . in response to the neoliberal academy" (Monty 2019), while also adopting administrative practices and terminologies that speak across departments. In a sense, to survive and sustain writing center practices, we must.

Within this context, I explore the following questions:

1. How can writing centers actively respond to disruptive innovations in ways that support their survival and prosper, and as a result continue to support writers and the teaching of writing?

2. What do sustainable writing center practices require in terms of our administrative work?

This book argues that writing centers and other key stakeholders in the teaching of writing across the university benefit from a strategic partnership approach to leadership. Strategic partnership involves intentionally creating relationships with multiple parties by establishing a shared vocabulary around the teaching of writing that encourages mutual benefit and stakeholder engagement within a negotiated space. This is a book primarily for writing center administrators, but also for administrators of writing across the curriculum and writing programs who are interested in networking across a wide range of departments, colleges, and administrative units. Although this book focuses on academic partnerships, this approach could also be adapted to work with student life, first-year experience programs, and public-school systems, among others.

Ultimately, this book makes a case for the valuable role that extracurricular centers and programs can play in twenty-first-century higher education and uses the writing center as an example. When a partnership framework is spearheaded by a program or center that has been historically marginalized, like the writing center, the program must begin by creating a sense of agency, both internally and externally. Thus, agency has become a central concept in this book and for the development of strategic partnerships.

ESTABLISHING WRITING CENTER AGENCY: RESPONDING TO DISRUPTIVE INNOVATIONS IN HIGHER EDUCATION

As I mentioned earlier, the establishment of a writing center demonstrates a disruptive innovation. In particular, a writing center staffed by undergraduates who provide peer-to-peer writing support proves to be both cheaper and more user-friendly than reducing class sizes and hiring well qualified writing instructors in full-time positions. The idea of peer-to-peer learning also challenges the dominant educational paradigm of teacher/student. However, there is also pedagogical value in peer-to-peer learning and support, especially when learners work with those who are operating at only a slightly higher level than they are (Vygotsky 1962; Zebroski 1999). Even though writing centers primarily hold a history of remediation and marginalization (North 1984; Carino 1992), they also fit within the definition of disruptive innovation. Thus, the navigation of disruptive innovations in higher education feels like familiar territory for writing centers that can present themselves as both an internal response, or "smart solution," to a disruptive innovation while also engaging in pedagogically ethical and sound practices.[3] Yet, writing centers still need to establish their own sense of agency by first owning the perception that they can act and make meaningful decisions about the teaching of writing and, second, by showing that they are well positioned to respond to disruptive innovations, specifically related to writing instruction, in ways that other departments and units are not.[4]

Developing a sense of agency enables writing centers to be more creative and innovative because they have more autonomy to make decisions based on their own values and needs or those they perceive, rather than simply to appease a parent department or administrator. While *innovation* as a keyword truly befits the twenty-first-century university, I define innovation in writing instruction as that which disrupts, revitalizes, or reinvents traditional approaches to writing, which are often rooted in current traditional curricula, textbook method(ologie)s, and face-to-face best practices. In using the term *current traditional,* I mean to evoke Berlin's (1996) description of current traditional rhetoric (CTR), which includes still-common composition pedagogies such as teaching modes (Ramage and Bean 2012; Seyler 2014) and presenting writing as formulaic and thesis-driven (Birkenstein and Graff 2016; Bartholomae and Petrosky 2010). With the exception of a more recent focus on argument (Lunsford and Lunsford 2008), CTR has for the most part persisted despite our belief that other approaches have threatened it (see Zebroski's 1999 "The Expressivist Menace").

Market values are equally significant to this definition of *innovation,* especially in terms of how upper administrators use the word to represent educational designs that seem new. Within and among writing teachers, *innovation* can mean a new and/or subversive approach to writing instruction, especially an approach that upsets traditional argument genres.[5]

But not always.

In his important book *The University in Ruins* (1996), Bill Readings claims that institutions work from a "discourse of 'excellence'" that replaces earlier notions of the university as the place that operates according to the language of culture. I contend that in the twenty-first-century university, innovation can be thought of as the new "excellence." In particular, Readings argues the following about "excellence" that I believe also holds true for "innovation" in today's university:

> "Excellence" is like the cash-nexus in that it has no *content*; it is hence neither true nor false, neither ignorant nor self-conscious. It may be unjust, but we cannot seek its injustice in terms of regime of truth of self-knowledge. Its rule does not carry with it an automatic political or cultural orientation, for it is not determined in relation to any indefinable instance of political power (13).

Thus, the word *innovation*, like *excellence*, does not necessarily carry any specific content, but is rather used as an adjective to describe the next best thing in pedagogy worth selling. Readings further notes that this "concerns the question of how the University is to be evaluated" (18). This notion means that, in order for work to be recognized as successful and especially for it to be recognized as exemplary, it must have some connection to innovation.

This book accepts the dual meaning of innovation as both potentially creative and part of a larger corporate terminology and framework. Embracing the idea of innovation in writing instruction and programming allows us to work with, within, and against business-model approaches to education. For writing centers, this adaptation means recognizing our history as a kind of disruptive innovation and using our experience and knowledge about operating effectively on the margins of the university to disrupt other innovations in higher education.

"A LIKELY PARTNERSHIP SUGGESTS ITSELF . . .": PARTNERSHIPS IN/AND THE UNIVERSITY

Although little empirical research exists that explicates what writing center partnerships look like and how we can create them, the term *partnership* is familiar in writing center studies. Data from a 2016 writing center website corpus sample of 1,298 individual institutions indicates that nearly 25 percent (n = 322) of writing centers are using the term *partner* (n = 167) in some way, while only 13 percent are using *partnership* (Monty 2016). The use of these terms varies, as some writing centers define what constitutes a partnership and others simply use the word without explaining the kind of relationship it indicates. Some universities even use *partnership* to refer to a business relationship with an outside, third-party company. This was particularly common at community college writing centers.

The earliest significant mention of *partnership* in scholarship appeared more than thirty years ago, in a 1989 *Writing Center Journal* article titled "Writing Centers and Writing-Across-the-Curriculum: An Evolving Partnership" by Susan Dinitz and Diane Howe. In this article, Dinitz and Howe discuss writing centers, and the work of peer tutors in particular, as being an obvious approach to integrating writing into the curriculum, explaining that following an increase in faculty workshops around writing across the curriculum (WAC), "A likely partnership suggests itself: professors can require students to meet with peer tutors to work on drafts of papers" (45). However, as these authors point out, such requests often come in large numbers, for huge numbers of students, with little attention to the resources and funding necessary to meet these needs. Dinitz and Howe present three models for these partnerships that sound all too familiar still, and the problems that emerge from them: (1) required sessions at the writing center; (2) assigning tutors to classes; and (3) peer group critiques, the most promising of the three, according to the authors, because this approach provides a "more manageable and economic model" (49) that involves the writing center director providing peer review guidelines to students and facilitating an in-class peer review workshop. The hope in this scenario is that "some professors eventually feel comfortable taking on some or all of these roles themselves" (50).

What strikes me about this idea of partnership is the lack of stated collaboration, a central tenet of writing center partnership literature beyond this piece (Eodice 2003; Fitzgerald and Stephenson 2012; Hall 2010; Myatt and Gaillet 2017; Beason-Abmayr and Wilson 2018). While *collaboration* has a long history in writing center scholarship that recognizes its potential drawbacks (Clark 1988; Lunsford and Lunsford 1991; Harris 1995), the term still gets used often, as if we have an agreed-upon understanding of its use. One notable exception is *Writing Program and Writing Center Collaborations: Transcending Boundaries*, in which Alice Johnston Myatt and Lyneé Lewis Gaillet (2017) complicate the term by arguing that we should think about collaboration as existing along a continuum of complexity, approaching it "by design and with a sense of the entrepreneurial" (2). My development of a partnership framework expands on this element of collaboration by engaging directly with the term's business undertones that administrators and faculty across the university (in terms of both disciplines and positions) use as they discuss their work with the writing center. While collaboration is an element of the kind of partnership I argue for here, the term does not adequately account for the complexity and challenge involved.

Unsurprisingly, I have found that many of the concerns Dinitz and Howe raised in 1989 in regard to scheduling; faculty development; communication; tutor qualifications, recruitment, and exploitation; student-centered learning; and expense still remain critical concerns for establishing successful writing center partnerships and must become part of the conversation among all parties involved. Perhaps we miss collaboration as part of Dinitz and Howe's notion of partnership because of how this approach was developed and then delivered by writing center administrators, rather than created in early conversation *with* faculty. In other words, there was nothing really collaborative about Dinitz and Howe's partnership. I do not mean this as a criticism, but rather as an observation that raises a couple questions: How have writing center/program administrators positioned themselves (and how should they) in relation to partners across campus? And how often are partnerships or collaborations named as such simply to indicate an interaction between two offices or educational spaces?

Dinitz and Howe point out how these partnership "problems" were then handled and solved internally, rather than being recognized as programmatic, university-wide concerns worthy of support and brainstorming across stakeholders outside the writing center. This practice of developing university-wide writing support structures from within is another trend across writing center/program administration literature (Harrington, Fox, and Hogue 1998; Barnett and Blumner 1999; Cox, Galin, and Melzer 2018). While we may be well positioned to lead these kinds of projects, we may also miss opportunities to establish joint responsibility early on, which is necessary for both building trust and establishing respect.

One thread of scholarship that seems to avoid this misbalance is writing center/library collaborations. Not only are such partnerships especially prevalent, with 65 percent of respondents in a recent 197-response survey indicating a "collaborative relationship" between the writing center and library, but they also work from a clear alignment of goals, including a focus on student success, and often co-located services (Ferer 2012; Jackson 2017; Deitering and Williams 2018). Scholarship surrounding these partnerships often involves researchers from both positions. In other words, both the physical and philosophical positionalities between writing centers and libraries make them compatible. Such is not always the case across disciplines.

If we move beyond writing program scholarship around partnership, two additional areas of partnership literature emerge: academy/community partnerships and academy/industry partnerships. In her seminal text *Rewriting Partnerships: Community Perspectives on Community-Based Learning*, Rachael Shah looks to community partners as valuable knowledge makers who have much to teach academic instructors about how to engage in community-based work. By establishing critical, community-based epistemologies based primarily on more than eighty interviews with community members, Shah argues that partners' experience, participation, and assets make them valuable "holders and producers of knowledge" (30). Despite the vastly different context for her study of partnership, Shah's emphasis on partner knowledge and how that knowledge should inform and shape our institutional work aligns with this book's attention to how the perspectives of Southern Research University Writing Center (SRUWC) partners, who exist primarily outside of English and writing studies, can inform our administrative, pedagogical, and curricular approaches to writing programming and instruction.[6]

Working at the crossover between community partnership and writing centers, Tiffany Rousculp's valuable book *Rhetoric of Respect: Recognizing Change at a Community Writing Center* (2014) uses the phrase "writing partner" to define the role of consultants in the Salt Lake Community College's Community Writing Center. For her, a rhetoric of respect requires an awareness of one's values, strengths, and limits while simultaneously recognizing another person's contribution. She argues:

> Respect implies a different type of relationship, one that is grounded in perception of worth, in esteem for another—as well as for the self. Even so, respect does not require agreement or conciliation—as "tolerance" suggests: rather, it entails recognition of multiple views, approaches, abilities, and importantly, limitations (especially our own). In other words, respect needs flexibility, self-awareness. Engaging within a rhetoric of respect draws attention to how we use language in relation with others; how we name and classify, how we collaborate, how we problem-solve. Whereas respect itself may exist as a feeling, a rhetoric of respect requires discursive action. (25)

What I find valuable about Rousculp's work is her direct recognition of the need for respect, rather than simply "tolerance or acceptance" of another person (24) or an assumption that respect is established simply due to the seemingly comforting nature of collaboration. Because of this, Rousculp's "rhetoric of respect" becomes an important lens for understanding how the strategic partnership approach I set forth in this book can work across disciplines.

Similarly, Brizee and Wells (2016) use "partners in literacy" to describe their community engagement work rooted in a writing center that develops online resources for an adult literacy program. These authors emphasize engagement as a necessary component for creating sustainable relationships, rather than a focus on "serving" a community, which often follows a "volunteerism or charity model" (128). Finally, McCleese Nichols and Williams (2019), in their article "Centering Partnerships: A Case for Writing Centers as Sites of Community Engagement," point out that writing centers are in a strong position for community engagement work in part because their values and practices are compatible, given approaches like "meet[ing] writers where they are" (95) and "thinking strategically, and often, about our position within a larger institution" (98). In these four pieces that emphasize academic/community partnerships, the concept of partnership and the specific role of partner is never recognized as an intentional language choice for naming this kind of collaboration. Yet, this language still does important work in establishing a relationship between the university and the community.

Likewise, texts that explore academy/industry partnerships rarely elaborate on the significance of using the term *partner/partnership*, perhaps because this language is common in the business world. In Bridgeford and St. Amant's 2015 book *Academy-Industry Relationships and Partnerships: Perspectives for Technical Communicators*, the term *partnership* suggests a general working together with those outside the university. More recently, some higher education experts have recognized the role of public-private partnerships (P3s) in the twenty-first-century university (Marks 2019; Carlson 2019). As Carlson notes in his *Chronicle of Higher Education* report, "The Outsourced University: How Public-Private Partnerships Can Benefit Your Campus," P3s often allow institutions to focus on the "academic core—teaching and research" while "transfer[ring] much of the rest of their operations to companies that specialize in those relationships" (4), a concept academics tend to call "outsourcing." Although he highlights the importance of the term *partner* in this relationship, Carlson does not explain how to create a partnership or what qualities make for a successful partnership.

In contrast to most academy/industry literature, Clare Banks, Birgit Siebe-Herbig, and Karin Norton (2016) focus on explicating partnership in *Global Perspectives on Strategic International Partnerships: A Guide to Building Sustainable Academic Linkages*. Focusing specifically on global education and cross-institutional partnerships that span across different countries and languages, these scholars identify strategic partnership as a particular kind of partnership that, when successful: (a) requires more preparation and forethought than most institutions expect; (b) is rarely bilateral (between two universities), and instead requires support from third parties; (c) works from a recognition of the vocabulary around partnership, arguing that "the more we can adopt globally agreed-upon definitions of different types of partnerships, the clearer expectations will be for potential partners"; (d) involves more creative thinking about *mutual benefit*; and (e) necessitates consideration of ethical issues (ix).

These characteristics of successful *strategic* partnerships align with the concept of internal, academic writing center partnerships I identify in this book. My research suggests that *strategic* partnerships often depend on strategic discourses that help create the relationships and the resources necessary for sustaining writing center work. At the same time, partnerships allow for writing center activity that is tactical, "determined by the absence of power" in unofficial places (de Certeau 2011, 34). This approach enables plenty of opportunities for "trickster" moments and unconventional responses to the unexpected in the writing center (Geller et al. 2007), especially between writers and consultants.[7] Furthermore, developing strategic partnerships also creates an environment for the kind of subversion Harry Denny (2010) talks about in *Facing the Center*. In reference to Cal Logue, Denny suggests that although "a subversive position might appear as assimilationist, involving what on the surface might be interpreted as a tacit acceptance of institutional protocols . . . it actually involves manipulating discourse and populations in ways that advance individual needs while undermining the status quo" (53). This kind of subversion also involves "the use of language in coded ways that inform insiders and manipulate those in positions of dominance" (54). While I do not consider strategic partnerships to be manipulative, they do involve using language that appeals to university administration, often a kind of language that we would likely not use otherwise.

In this book, I establish a process for building writing center partnerships as a way to sustain, enliven, and protect writing centers in the twenty-first-century university. Given that partnerships must fit within the local circumstances, I offer an in-depth look at one writing center and its variety of partnerships across the university. Drawing on Banks et al.'s concepts of negotiated space, mutual benefits, stakeholder engagement, and transformational partnership, as described later in this chapter, as well as on site-based data collected from one university writing center rooted in strong, cross-disciplinary partnerships, this book presents primary values, strategies, and recommended actions. To get a sense of how partnerships work, I practice a qualitative replicable aggregable data-driven (qual-RAD) method that adapts traditional RAD writing center research (Driscoll and Wynn Perdue 2012) to fit an anthropological, human-centered, ethnographic design that seeks to understand the science of writing center administration. Although they are not officially part of the strategic partnership structure, using qual-RAD methods to understand the culture of writing at a university by observing, interviewing, and listening to how writing happens across campus—especially through Geertz's "thick description"—would be an exemplary first step toward laying the groundwork for agency and respect.

After setting a context for developing strategic partnerships rooted in agency and respect within the SRUWC via interviews with the writing center staff and its key disciplinary partners, this book investigates how three partnerships work in response to disruptive innovations. Each case study considers one or more of Banks et al.'s key concepts in light of partnership engagement. Rather than attempting a perfect and replicable model, I aim to demonstrate and reflect on partnerships in practice, with all their complexity, and to offer both strategies for establishing successful partnerships and problems/pitfalls to anticipate and avoid.

KEY ELEMENTS IN STRATEGIC PARTNERSHIP

The framework offered in this book depends on several concepts that work together to create a necessary foundation for strategic partnership and the ongoing development vital to sustainability. These concepts are defined below. Figure 0.1 provides a visual representation of how some of these terms work together in a strategic partnership approach.

- **Disruptive innovation**: A new approach, often presented as either cheaper or more user-friendly than what already exists, that challenges the dominant educational paradigm. Presents the opportunity for internal university programs (like writing centers) to create strategic partnerships and to build social capital in lieu of using external higher education services.
- **Social capital**: A relationship-based resource that enables a respected and trustworthy identity established via a shared vision in a mutually beneficial scenario. Often created by building strategic partnerships that increase the likelihood for localized responses to disruptive innovations in higher education.
- **Agency**: The belief that one can act and make meaningful decisions about the teaching of writing.
- **Rhetoric of respect**: A way of acting and speaking that recognizes and values multiple viewpoints, positionalities, abilities, and limitations with a high degree of flexibility, self-awareness, and the

willingness to change or alter one's preferred method or vocabulary to make space for another.

- **Negotiated space**: The shared space in which a strategic partnership exists. Requires openness, honesty, and collaboratively developed, ethical frameworks with attention to weak elements, despite sometimes differing worldviews across partners and/or stakeholders.

- **Mutual benefit**: A situation in which all partners gain value via an emphasis on equity (fairness and justice), rather than equality (sameness). Recognizes three benefit types (direct/indirect, material/nonmaterial, and immediate/long-term) and their potential negative consequences.

- **Stakeholder engagement**: A collaborative approach to project management that requires identifying all potential stakeholders and the various roles they might play as the strategic partnership develops over time.

- **Transformational partnership**: The most radical and successful kind of strategic partnership through which change occurs at both the individual and the institutional or community level. Often involves combining resources, developing collaborative curricula, and dynamic growth over time.

METHOD(OLOGY)

For this project, I needed a method(ology)[8] that acknowledged the value of rich, site-specific research, participant voices, and the subjectivity-bound perspectives that individuals offer, leading them to tell stories that are simultaneously representing and misrepresenting the realities of a situation. In other words, I rejected entirely the notion of an objective research study or unbiased researcher, both assumptions from which replicable, aggregable, data-driven (RAD) writing center research seems to work. Instead, this research method(ology) aligns with others that center narrative voices through in-depth study (Simpkins and Schwarz 2015; Reich 2018). Alexandria Lockett gives us an important warning in "A Touching Place: Womanist Approaches to the Center" when she argues that "the language of RAD tends to strip the human experience of its nuance and may risk diminishing the various ways we might interpret experience as data" (33). Lockett urges us to recognize that "qualitative, artistic investigation about the human experience is a legitimate form of data collection" (33). Writing center research has begun the important work of including the voices missing from our scholarship by recognizing connections between writing centers and social justice (Hallman Martini and Webster 2017; Greenfield 2019), race (Riddick and Hooker 2019), class (Denny,

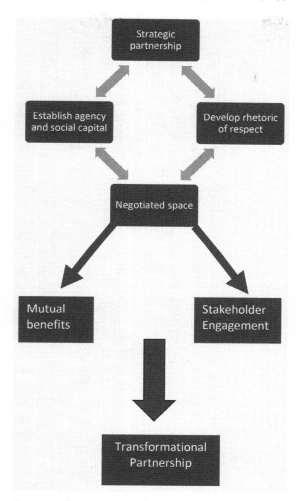

Figure 0.1. Strategic partnership framework

Nordlof, and Salem 2018), and identity (Denny et al. 2019; Webster 2021). In all of these studies, careful attention to human experience(s) within a historical, social, political, and cultural context is central; it is the researcher's responsibility to recognize how that context shapes the stories that emerge.

To follow this trend of writing center research while simultaneously working from an explicit method(ology) that could be adapted and used by future researchers to understand the administrative processes through which writing centers work, I used critical ethnographic methods to develop a qualitative-RAD method (qual-RAD). I worked primarily

Table 0.1. Definitions for RAD and qual-RAD Writing Center Research

RAD WC[a] Research (Haswell 2005; Driscoll and Wynn Perdue 2012)	Adaption[b]	qual-RAD (extensions)
A best-effort inquiry into the actualities of a situation	A best-effort inquiry into the **complexities** of a situation	Inquiry into the complexities of a situation with an awareness of how the researcher's ever-present perspective and those provided by participants are partially (in)accurate (Heath 1983; Brodkey 1987; Chiseri-Strater 1991; Mortensen and Kirsch 1996; Kirklighter, Moxley, and Vincent 1997; Cintron 1998; Cushman 1998; Brown and Dobrin 2004).
Explicitly enough systematized in sampling, execution, and analysis to be replicated	Explicitly **defined research methods and at least partially** systematized in sampling, execution, and analysis to be **adapted**	Clearly defined and adaptable methods for data collection and analysis (Bishop 1999; Cauthen 2010; Heath 1983; Seidman 2012).
Exactly enough circumscribed to be extended	Exactly enough **described** to be extended.	Specific and reasonable scope appropriate for the study's context and purpose with attention to possible extensions (Beaufort 1999; Bowie and McGovern 2013; Lillis 2008).
Factually enough supported to be verified	Enough **concrete data provided to** support **claims**	Concrete data provided through "thick description" that determines the research narrative's form (Brandt 2001; Cintron 1998; Cushman 1998; Geertz 1973; Heath 1983; Lindquist 2002).

[a] *The abbreviation* WC *is used interchangeably with* Writing Center *and* Center *throughout this book.*
[b] *Bold font indicates changes from the original language.*

from a critical ethnographic approach rooted in the tradition of ethnographic research developed in the field of rhetoric and composition (Brodkey 1987; Brown and Dobrin 2004; Chiseri-Strater 1991; Cintron 1998; Cushman 1998; Heath 1983; Kirklighter, Moxley, and Vincent 1997; Mortensen and Kirsch 1996). These scholars establish critical ethnographic research as a qualitative, empirical approach that uses rigorous research methods including interview, observation, field notes, reflection, and textual analysis; moves beyond description towards critique/action; maintains an awareness of ethnographic text as constructed under the influence of social, economic, political, material, and academic pressures; and requires deep self-reflexivity and awareness of the constructedness and limitations of the ethnographic text itself. This critical ethnographic approach works both within and against writing center studies' commitment to RAD research. Thus, my qual-RAD method differs from traditional writing center RAD research in the ways listed in table 0.1. Since this book offers a new methodology and one helpful for those interested in creating strategic partnerships, I describe the four major components of qual-RAD below and provide an entry point into the book's method/ology through each.

Component 1: Inquiry into the Complexities: Setting a Context

Inquiry-based research often requires a formal investigation motivated by specific research questions to which the researcher does not already know the answer. The researcher is open to what they may find, and knowledge is co-created with others. Hence, hypotheses may be noted as the researcher's expectations and assumptions, but they are secondary to the study. Research questions evolve as the researcher engages with the subject matter and participants. Yet, there are no "actualities," as traditional RAD might suggest, in this kind of inquiry-based research because the research deals with people. Further, site-based studies are by nature situational and contextual, so there are no actualities. This also complicates any idea of replication in the strict sense of the term.

Rather than attempting to understand the "actualities" of a research situation, qual-RAD seeks to better understand the *complexities*. Complexities remain particular to each study but often involve a close eye toward similarities and differences that emerge in the data: The major themes and the outliers in terms of participant perspectives are equally valuable and worth serious investigation. In addition, the researcher is aware of their own stakes in the project and that their perspective ultimately shapes how the study unfolds. In their 2010 edited collection, *Writing Culture: The Poetics and Politics of Ethnography,* James Clifford and George Marcus argue that we must recognize the always obtrusive voice of the writer and how both the speaker and their construction of culture via written text complicate ethnography (and I would argue other site-based research with people). Given the awareness of multiple perspectives that are always by definition partial, we cannot inquire into the "actualities" of a situation at all.

Instead, we must recognize that a situation's "complexities" require attention to moments of tension and resistance as they emerge both within the researcher and among participants. While our instinct may be to overlook or move on from these moments, they often lead to the most important complexities in qualitative research. Thus, throughout this book, I pay close attention to moments of tension and try to explore them without minimizing perspectives that do not align. Although my goal is to provide a usable framework for establishing strategic partnerships, the

ability to adapt this framework for a particular context involves acknowledging and learning about its limitations, failures, and inconsistences.

Before beginning to understand the complexities of a research situation, the researcher must closely consider the research context. For me,
this meant attempting to step back from my familiarity with the research
site so that I could observe and describe it in concrete terms. I did this
early on in my project and include the narrative below primarily drawn
from observation notes taken in September 2015.

To get to the Southern Research University Writing Center (SRUWC),
you have to really want to go there. Because it's physically located on
the exact opposite side of campus from the largest student commuter
lot, on a hot day in the South it can easily take thirty minutes to walk
from the back of the student lot to the front door of the building that
houses the center. It almost feels like a crime to walk into such a new,
clean building drenched in sweat. The distance from the lot is in part
because the writing center is on the newer side of campus, within one of
the business school buildings and surrounded by other business school
buildings and new student dining areas. The University and Classroom
Building, also known as the Insperity Building, houses the writing center
on the second floor. The floor is split between the writing center and the
university-wide testing company, the Center for Academic Support and
Assessment (CASA), where nervous students line up outside the door
with number 2 pencils and thumbprints, waiting to prove their identities
so they can take exams.

The writing center has no center. It does have two large writing
center–like rooms with small round tables and chairs, and computers
outlining the room's border. It also has a series of individual offices,
several group conferencing rooms, a room for English TAs, and an
office suite area with a front desk, a kitchen, and the offices of the upper
administrators.[9] The wall and carpeting are in neutral shades with no
color, signage, or expression of any kind, with one exception: a small
suite that includes several Mark Rothko prints, a front desk/waiting
room area, a kitchen with two refrigerators next to an almost always
fresh pot of Starbucks coffee, and the office of the executive director,
the associate director, and one of the lead project managers. Tutors
sometimes gather for lunch behind the kitchen in the storage closet,
where there's a table inside a small room that holds broken computers
and extra paper towels. The large tutoring rooms and small conference
areas have clean white walls and some have windows. They are sterile.
New. Professional. There are no traces of couches or hominess or comfort. Nothing indicates that when you enter one of the rooms you are in

a writing center. A nervous test taker could easily end up in the wrong place, as could a student writer looking for their writing consultant. It seems like you should whisper there.

All of the SRUWC administrators and full-time consultants are staff members who have little communication with the Department of English and little, if any, formal education or training in the professional field of rhetoric and composition or the sub-specialty of writing center studies. Despite this lack of formal scholarly professionalization, the SRUWC has an impressive campus presence. In its 2015 annual report, the SRUWC documented 22,928 student interactions, collaborated with faculty across campus in fifty-seven writing in the disciplines (WID) partnerships, and led more than thirty workshops. In particular, the SRUWC developed new projects with Science, Technology, Engineering, and Math (STEM) students, created a new online writing center with synchronous writing support, and developed more support for graduate-level writing.

In fall 2015, the SRUWC staff included an executive director, an associate director, four assistant directors, a technology director, four program managers/coordinators, two part-time web developers, three graduate student writing center fellows, and approximately twenty-two peer/professional consultants. Of these staff members, eleven were full-time and many of the others worked at least twenty hours per week. In particular, the SRUWC set its mission as shown in table 0.2, per the SRUWC website. As shown, the SRUWC's mission includes assessment, writing instruction, curricular innovation, community outreach, professional development, and research in the teaching of writing. It does not mention improving student writing. Both student writers and consultants are nearly absent.

In terms of demographics, SRU was among the most ethnically and linguistically diverse universities in the country, both in terms of students and faculty. In 2015, over 70 percent of the student population at SRU identified as non-white, and nearly 10 percent were international students from more than 150 different countries. Faculty at SRUWC were also diverse, with less than 50 percent identifying as white. A more complete breakdown of ethnicity is presented in figures 0.2 and 0.3.

Concept 2: Defined and Adaptable Research Methods
Clearly defined research methods make adapting and extending research studies possible and remove the need for exact systemization or replication. Since qual-RAD works under the assumption that replication is neither possible nor desirable, methods for both data collection

Table 0.2. SRUWC mission statement

Writing is thinking. It is an indispensable activity for every discipline conducting research within a university setting and an essential component of a university education. Ongoing instruction in writing helps to initiate students into the changing intellectual demands of university life and introduces them to the complexities of their chosen disciplines and professions. Because writing provides the tools to discover and articulate solutions to intellectual problems, improved writing remains a continual goal of university education.

To address these concerns, the mission of the University of X Writing Center includes the following activities:

Assessment: developing effective means of evaluating student and institutional writing needs that promote curricular innovation and provide informative directions for both students and teacher.

Writing Instruction: providing instruction in writing that meets the diverse needs of a student population at undergraduate, graduate, and professional level.

Curricular Innovation: promoting the creation of new writing curricula to meet changing student and disciplinary needs, reexamining present curricula to respond to new practices in the field of writing instruction.

Community Outreach: establishing outreach programs and partnerships that make available the results of the Center's inquiries and activities in the teaching of writing and foster collaboration with the region's educational and professional communities.

Professional Development: encouraging the ongoing professional development of faculty and staff across the full spectrum of disciplines.

Research in the Teaching of Writing: fostering the creation and dissemination of new knowledge about the teaching of writing in a large public institution serving an urban, multiethnic, multilingual community.

---

and analysis must be made explicit for both validity and adaptability. One example of clearly defined research methods for data collection in the field of writing center studies is Jackie Grutsch McKinney's *Peripheral Visions for Writing Centers*. As mentioned in the acknowledgments section of this book, Grutsch McKinney's text provided the exigency for this project, as I was interested in better understanding what I knew was a counternarrative to the writing center grand narrative: the story and workings of the SRUWC. Thus, I designed my qual-RAD study by replicating and adapting Grutsch McKinney's online survey questions for a face-to-face, audio-recorded interview.[10] Yet, these questions had to be expanded for a different setting that was synchronous, face-to-face, and verbal, rather than asynchronous, virtual, and written. Thus, I worked from a semi-structured, in-depth interview format and included additional questions to try to get at more nuanced answers, such as: (1) How long have you been working at the SRUWC and what is your role? (2) Describe your writing center and how you perceive the culture there. (3) Describe yourself as a writing center professional. (4) How do you approach the teaching of writing? (5) What projects and duties do you

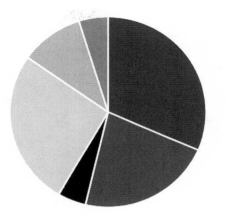

■ Hispanic/Latino 31.5% ■ Asian 22.2%   ■ Non-resident Alien 4.7%

▨ White 26.3%   ▨ Black or African American 10.5% ■ Ethnicity Unknown/Other 4.8%

Figure 0.2. Ethnic diversity of undergraduate students at SRU

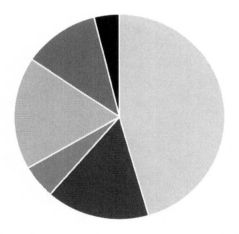

▨ White 47%   ■ Hispanic/Latino 16.4%   ▨ Non-Resident 5.5%

▨ Black or African American 18.2% ■ Asian 12.1%   ■ Ethnicity Unknown/Other 4%

Figure 0.3. Ethnic diversity of faculty at SRU

have at the SRUWC? In addition, some interviewees told stories that moved away from a particular question or topic, even though each interview was coded and analyzed for evidence in its entirety for what Grutsch McKinney identifies as the writing center grand narrative.[11]

Although qual-RAD requires the researcher to make their methods explicit, there is still room for divergences to emerge as the study develops in real time. For instance, although I went into each interview with the same set of questions, sometimes the order in which the questions were asked changed, and additional follow-up questions were added in conversation with individual participants. Not every person was interviewed for the same amount of time or the same number of times, and had I sought to make the interviews more uniform I would not have been able to center the participants' voices. I also shared interview questions in advance and told interviewees that anything they wanted to tell me was more important than the questions I had to ask. Offering this statement is one technique I used to challenge the power dynamic inherent in most interviewer/interviewee relationships: The interviewer has the power, thus controlling and dictating how the interview unfolds. Instead, I wanted interviewees to decide what we talked about and to determine their own sequencing and telling of their SRUWC experiences.

This approach to data collection, or qualitative interviewing, draws on the work of ethnographer-folklorist Carl Lindahl (2004), who argues for working from the assumption that the interviewee is always right and that the goal of the researcher is to do their best to represent people on their own terms. While I was upfront about my interest in how participants understood their writing center work, I tried not to let my own agenda determine how our interview unfolded.[12] Another way that I got at this was by reserving interruptive questions I had for the end of the interview. For instance, if an interviewee mentioned a term or an event that they did not explain, rather than interrupting and asking for clarification, I made a note of it and waited until the interviewee was finished talking to bring up my questions. My intention was not to conduct identical interviews with each SRUWC administrator, but rather to understand and represent them as individuals on their own terms.

Much like my approach to interviewing, my observations focused on representing participants on their own terms. In order to do this, I focused on describing and understanding conversations, focus groups, and writing center sessions in the moment. When I had analytical thoughts, I either jotted them down in the margin or tried to reserve them until later. I often took copious notes before and after sessions so that I would understand my own expectations and reactions immediately before and after data collection. Rather than working from a set of specific questions, I primarily focused on describing what I saw and heard. Nearly all observations that included a conversation were audio-recorded, logged, and analyzed according to the methods below.

Some elements of my data collection and analysis were more systematic while still allowing for variance. Rather than fully transcribing and analyzing each interview through the use of software, I used a logging method developed by Lindahl, who describes logging as a detailed table of contents for the entire interview. The logging method enables the researcher to summarize and paraphrase the interview with attention to key words, while reserving transcription for only the most significant moments. Although some researchers, such as Irving Seidman, warn against selective transcription, the thorough logging and noting of the interview still requires careful listening, documentation of the entire interview, and a fair amount of selected transcribing. This logging method/ology aligns with qual-RAD writing center research because it works from the assumption that a neutral, objective log/transcription is neither possible nor preferable. Thus, interview logs/transcriptions are informed by the researcher's perspective and are deeply interpretive and selective (Riessman 2007). To maintain consistency, the logging should be done by the same researchers who conduct the interviews whenever possible, not outsourced to research assistants, outside agencies, or computer programs. According to Lindahl (2003), interview logs should: (1) follow the order of the interview; (2) focus on the interviewee's words rather than on the questions of the interview; (3) begin a new entry when the topic changes (approximately every one to four minutes or when the interviewer poses a new question); (4) mark each new entry with the time so that the researcher can go back and find the section easily in case they wish to return to it; and (5) use short sentences to describe what is said, along with brief quotations when preserving the language choice of the interviewee is necessary.[13]

When site-based research is approached through inquiry-based methods, the kind of systematization traditional RAD calls for becomes difficult. For a study to be systematized, it must execute a preconceived plan. This kind of structure makes flexibility and adaptability difficult, all the while emphasizing the researcher's plan rather than allowing the participants' voices and knowledge to impact the direction and ultimately the findings of the study. A common practice in qualitative interview research is to give the interviewee an opportunity at the end of the interview to add anything they did not have a chance to mention (Lindahl 2003, 2004; Seidman 2012). Although this material is often positioned as secondary to the researcher's questioning agenda, some of the most insightful knowledge emerges from these moments or others that are similarly unstructured.

For instance, it never occurred to me in my ethnographic study of SRUWC to ask participants about their first sessions, in part because few of them were meeting with student writers directly at the time of my research. Yet, when those stories became important to several participants, I adapted my interview questions to include one about first consultations. Careful study of these stories indicated a survivalist mentality in the writing center that became an important element of the business-minded culture. Some of these stories are expanded as a part of "thick description" in chapter 2 of this book.

Component 3: Reasonable and Clear Scope with Contextual Awareness

Setting boundaries around qualitative research can be tricky. Given the wealth of data possible through site-based research with people, researchers may struggle to get a sense of a study's scope prior to data collection. Further, the idea of "exact circumscription" that traditional RAD calls for may never be possible in some qualitative research, since even after the scope is established, the boundaries may be justifiably messy and inexact. Thus, the scope of a qual-RAD study should be determined through inquiry and the complexity of the research situation. Sometimes, a small-scale, in-depth study addresses research questions more fully than a broad sweep with random sampling, although both are valuable to knowledge-making. Explicitly setting a reasonable scope with direct consideration of how future researchers might build from the current study makes extension more possible.

Throughout this project, I regularly had to cut back on the scope because I was getting so much rich material. Although I originally envisioned a multi-institutional study, I quickly realized that I had enough data to tell a rich and complex story of a single site, the SRUWC. Then, within this site I had to narrow my scope even more. While my three years' experience as a rhetoric and composition graduate student and tutor influenced my understanding of the research site, I conducted formal qual-RAD critical ethnographic research in the SRUWC from fall 2015 to spring 2016 that engaged in several modes of data collection, including over thirty hours of interviews with writing center administrators and disciplinary partners; over forty hours of observation of WC program meetings, professional development activities, and orientations; one focus group meeting; analysis of hundreds of pages of online writing studio consultations for the WC/first-year writing program partnership; and the observation of twelve face-to-face partnership meetings for the WC/engineering partnership. In addition, participants shared numerous documents with me that informed this research, including annual reports, budget data, writing assessment data, assignments, and syllabi. My data included observation notes; textual analyses of recent annual reports, assignment designs, and memos; audio-recorded reading groups with peer tutors; audio-recorded group tutoring sessions; and audio-recorded interviews with SRUWC consultants, university administrators, and disciplinary faculty.

Within this context, I originally wanted to conduct in-depth interviews with undergraduate peer tutors and students, as well as look at several partnerships in-depth. I knew my project was going to be a critical ethnographic study of a writing center, but I did not realize it would be an administrative-focused project, nor did I know it would focus on theorizing and establishing a partnership approach to writing center work until well into my interviews. Of the thirteen writing center partners Sam (SRUWC administrator) suggested as possible interview participants, twelve agreed to talk with me. I expected to hear from only half. Furthermore, several of them shared syllabi, assessment data, and budget spreadsheets, all materials I did not expect to receive. This wealth of information shifted the scope of my project because I realized that, to best tell an in-depth story well with all the information I had unexpectedly received, I would not be able to extend data collection to as many additional participants. Already, an important story to follow was emerging.

This research narrative includes many participants whose roles vary from significantly prominent and recurring to brief encounters, including sixteen writing center administrators, eight writing center consultants, fifteen university administrators or disciplinary faculty members, eight graduate teaching assistants, seven graduate students, twelve undergraduate students, and, of course, myself. These sixty-seven writers and teachers of writing provide a single yet significant slice of the writing culture at SRU, and of the SRUWC in particular.

Although narrowing a study's scope can be seen as a limitation, it is often necessary in qual-RAD research. This constricting risks a study becoming too localized and larger implications beyond a single site become harder to determine. Yet, researchers must acknowledge these limitations as areas for future research and possible extensions. Most importantly, researchers can justify the narrow scope by providing "thick description" of data (Component 4). Thick description requires close attention to both the big and small "gestures" that occur within a research site so that the researcher notices and is nearly able to interpret data as if they were an internal member of the community under study. The emphasis falls on intricate representation through description, rather than on creating a unified and rational narrative.

Component 4: Thick Description of the Particular

Qual-RAD research emphasizes a deep look into complexities but often within a somewhat narrow scope. So rich data, rather than facts, determine its worth. A combination of fact and verification, as called for in traditional RAD, is not the focus of qual-RAD because this method assumes a research scenario in which fact and verification are subjective.

Clifford Geertz offers a more useful way of thinking about data collection for qual-RAD with his concept of "thick description": a method that requires the ethnographer to determine the particular context of a culture through a participative and interpretive approach to research that attempts to think and make meaning with, not just about, the members of the culture under study.[14] Geertz recognizes the heart of "thick description" in a moment from Gilbert Ryle's work where he describes "two boys rapidly contracting their eyelids" (1973, 6). Upon simple observation, the boys' movements look the same, but closer analysis and interpretation suggest that one boy has an "involuntary twitch" while the other is intentionally "gestur[ing]." Thus, the central question for anthropology is "whether it [can] sort winks from twitches and real winks from mimicked ones" (16). For Geertz, the aim in understanding a culture should be "inspecting events, not . . . arranging abstracted entities into unified patterns," and thus "coherence cannot be the major test of validity" (17). The practice of "thick description" and the knowledge it produces is meaningful because of its "complex specificness, [and] circumstantiality . . . [which] makes it possible to think not only realistically and concretely *about* [participants], but, what is more important, creatively and imaginatively *with* them" (23). Thus, the research narrative itself cannot be expected to fit into a routine format. Instead, the data drives the story.

Geertz's concept of "thick description," carefully applied to interview-based ethnographic research and other kinds of site-based research with people, proves useful to a qual-RAD method/ology. Rather than simplifying similarities by way of coding and counting, "thick description" encourages a more nuanced look at differences across similarities, too. Thus, "thick description" in qual-RAD is (1) *specific and circumstantial*; (2) *participative*; (3) *interpretive*; (4) *imaginative*; and (5) *collaborative*.

For this book and the development of a strategic partnership approach to writing center administration, engaging in thick description means emphasizing the site-based research first and foremost over outside research and/or theoretical frameworks. It means that my first commitment is to sincerely represent my research site and the people acting in it, with all of their complexity, regardless of how messy that project may become. Although interviews and observations are the primary sources of data in this book and factor into each chapter, I also used a range of additional protocols in one or more chapters, which included conducting one focus group; analyzing online studio conversations; studying writing assignments, syllabi, and writing assessment data; and analyzing student surveys and tutor notes. The collection and analysis of these materials were a valuable part of this book's "thick description," because they often enabled me to better contextualize and understand the participants' stories and the cultures in which they worked. These additional materials were also often shared with me during interviews and observations and/or explained to me by participants who explicitly brought them into their stories. It was often through supplemental material or discussions outside of the research scenario I created with my requests and questions that I learned the gestures of the culture, which helped me understand the mindset necessary for creating partnerships.

* * *

Like all research projects, this one began from a particular point of view, and thus with a few biases and assumptions. When I conducted research for this book, I was a fourth-year PhD student in the English Department focusing on rhetoric, composition, and pedagogy, who had roles both within the SRUWC and as a first-year writing instructor in the English Department. I was also a participant-observer in two of the partnerships I describe in this book, as well as a mentor to some of the new hybrid first-year writing instructors I interviewed. My position in relation to both the SRUWC and the participants is complex and varied.

In addition, I recognize that I communicated with the participants and interviewees in multiple settings, multiple ways, and from multiple positionalities.[15] For instance, several of the SRUWC administrators and the English Department hybrid instructors are my friends, who I spoke with informally about their administration and tutoring outside of the formal interviews during conferences, over lunch, and in between meetings. Thus, while I do draw on the formal interviews, I also draw on unrecorded conversations that occurred in more relaxed settings. Finally, I recognize that the project of this book is not only the stories as told by my participants and their work, but it is also a story filtered through my perspective and told by me.

As the writer of this text, I also had to make a few choices that will impact your reading and understanding of this book. First, as most ethnographic studies do, I used pseudonyms in place of participants' names. Given the diverse context in which this research took place, I took special care to choose pseudonyms that were compatible with participants' real names. Second, I included a participant matrix at the end of chapters 2 through 5 to provide some context for and description of the primary participants in each.[16] In the cases where significant participants had already been described, I noted which chapter included their short bios. I did not provide a participant matrix for chapter 6 because all of the participants had already been included in previous matrices.

Finally, I made the conscious choice to bring in other literature around partnership, specifically Williams's definition of agency, Rousculp's "rhetoric of respect," and Banks et al.'s framework for global strategic partnerships. I found these texts helpful in providing an important structure for understanding participant narratives within a context beyond a single writing center at a single university. They also helped me recognize some of the implicit concepts that emerged by giving me a more intricate terminology through which to think about this research.

CHAPTER OVERVIEWS

In the chapters that follow, I present a strategic-partnership approach to writing center administration. By looking closely at a writing center with a strong awareness of its place in a twenty-first-century university, I show how internal narratives about writing in chapter 1 (among writing center staff) and external narratives about writing in chapter 2 (among university administrators and disciplinary partners) develop and shape strategic partnerships. In chapter 1, "Establishing Agency: Laying the Groundwork for Strategic Partnership," I provide a more detailed account of the research scene, including a short history of the writing center and its split from the English Department, which was critical in its ability to develop partnerships across the university. Drawing primarily on interviews with writing center staff, this chapter shows how the SRUWC creates a strategic consulting firm environment rooted in agency (Williams 2017) that still enables tactical development among peer undergraduate tutors.

In chapter 2, "Counselors, Tsunamis, and Well-Oiled Machines: Partners Defining Their Writing (Center) Partnerships," I draw on interviews with university administrators and disciplinary partners to show partner perceptions of a twenty-first-century writing center rooted in respect. Looking specifically at the use of metaphor in talk about writing (centers) and the teaching of writing, I show how and why establishing respect (Rousculp 2014) and agency (Williams 2017) in writing center partnerships is critical for building sustainable relationships across the university. Despite the often-asymmetrical power dynamic between writing centers and partnering departments/colleges, analysis of metaphor use suggests that writing centers provide an invaluable resource.

In chapters 3–5, I use case studies to showcase important partnership concepts: mapping mutual benefit and stakeholder engagement in chapter 3, creating negotiated space in chapter 4, and building transformational partnerships in chapter 5. These chapters are also directly connected to current or potential "disruptive innovations" in higher education and thus show how a writing center might act in direct response to online education, the use of public-private partnerships through outsourcing, and career readiness initiatives.

Chapter 3, "Reworking with the English Department: Partnering Online with a First-Year Writing Program," focuses on a writing center partnership linked to first-year writing that responds to the disruptive innovation of online education. Given the precarious relationship between the English Department and the Writing Center, I consider how early acknowledgment of mutual benefits across stakeholders leads to the partnership's quick growth. Yet, uneven stakeholder engagement and a lack of communication also creates an unequal distribution of labor in the development of the hybrid first-year writing/online studio partnership. After presenting data surrounding the value of online writing studios from three key participant groups—graduate teaching assistants (English Department), online studio facilitators (Writing Center), and student writers—I argue that the writing center can effectively and ethically respond to the push for online education through a strategic partnership approach that involves mapping out mutual benefits (Sutton 2016) and a plan for varying levels of stakeholder engagements (Proctor 2016) over time.

Chapter 4, "Engaging Challenges: Partnering as a P3 with the College of Business," provides an example of the writing center engaging in a small-scale P3 in which, through conversation with the business school, a third party was invited into the partnership. I examine how the writing center took a misstep in its response to the disruptive innovation of P3s by exploring a public controversy connected to outsourcing writing evaluation and (eventually) instruction. By looking closely at the impact of a third-party company on two business college partnerships—one that resulted in total outsourcing and another where the writing center continued to play an integral role in the development of writers—I consider how creating a negotiated space (Helms 2016) early on can help in planning for and anticipating ethical dilemmas in partnerships.

Chapter 5, "Navigating Workplace Realities: Partnering with STEM in the College of Engineering," shows how the writing center, through partnership, can respond to an overemphasis on career readiness (specifically, the potential disruptive innovation of the "Go Pro Early" movement) by expanding its definition of writing in the university to make room for writing in the profession (WIP). In this partnership, the writing center provides an important role in supporting students who are engaging in multimodal project designs, writing in teams, attempting a kind of clarity that communicates across contexts, and writing for outside (and multiple) audiences. With a close look at this integrated writing curriculum across four core writing courses taught within the college of engineering, I argue for a more cross-disciplinary understanding of writing as WIP that enables the kind of transformational partnerships that are the most sustainable.

I conclude by offering specific action steps for establishing agency, developing a rhetoric of respect for building relationships, and creating strategic partnerships.

* * *

The concept of partnership in general has much to offer writing center administrators, and how partnership works at the SRUWC provides meaningful insight into what such partnerships might look like. Yet, I want to forewarn readers who may be coming to this book for a step-by-step, how-to guide about creating partnerships in their own writing centers. The very method through which this book was created makes such an approach both unlikely and undesirable. Instead, I hope to emphasize the value of creating unique relationships built through mutual recognition of agency and respect. I hope you will find concepts and suggested actions that make you rethink your approach to collaborative, administrative work. And, finally, I hope to offer a language for communicating our invaluable, innovative writing center work across the university.

1

ESTABLISHING AGENCY
Laying the Groundwork for Strategic Partnership

Near the end of our interview, Jeremy, a SRUWC program coordinator who had also become a friend of mine, talked nostalgically about the "old days" in the SRUWC,[1] when consultants stayed in their positions longer and lived closer to campus. Jeremy had trouble articulating what he meant, but he noted a recent "difference in attitude and mentality." Then, he explained what he meant by telling me two stories. The first began in response to my question about why the scheduler only included consultants' initials rather than their names. Jeremy explained that it used to be something that consultants had strong feelings about, but that it no longer seemed to bother them. I asked Jeremy if he knew why, and he made this distinction between present-day consultants and consultants from the "old days":

> I think they wanted their names [on the scheduler]. I think they were tired of being numbers, quote-unquote, because it's like you go through the system and sometimes it feels like you're nothing but a PeopleSoft number. And so, just to have yourself reduced to initials on a website might come across as being locked into that same train of thought. . . . I guess I don't have strong feelings about it, though, because I feel like your entire life you're a number, or you're initials, or you're something along those lines, so is it any different? Nope. Is it just the way it is? Yup. So [laughs] I mean, I would venture, though, to say that there are people who probably don't have strong feelings and there are probably people here that are consultants that do have strong feelings about it where they . . . don't like it, or maybe they do like it.[2]

As he continued comparing the "old days" with the present, Jeremy told a second story about a conversation he had with a new consultant during orientation:

> I think, for example, one of our consultants said something in orientation this year, like, "Oh, I was expecting to come in and just [say] like, 'This is wrong, this is wrong, this is wrong. Okay, goodbye. And this is wrong, this is wrong, okay, goodbye.'" And it's kind of like this conveyor belt of students coming in and you're just checking things off and then the next one comes, and the next one comes, and the next one comes, and when she realized that's not really what we do and that's not really what we're about, then it kind of changed. And, I think in the old days when we hired people it was more understood that that's not what we do. I don't

https://doi.org/10.7330/9781646421770.c001

know, again, . . . how that happened; I just know that that's kind of what seems to be the perception.

Jeremy was careful to qualify this as "what seems to be the perception," explaining that other staff members might not see things that way.

If these two stories represent differences in terms of attitudes and mentalities among consultants, then they may also suggest a shift from feelings of frustration with the sometimes reductionist effects of the push toward efficiency (e.g., new consultants who want their names on the SRUWC scheduler and are tired of being reduced to initials and numbers) to an expectation of efficiency and willingness to partici-pate in it (e.g., from new consultants who conceive of their work as a conveyor belt of students who need to be checked off). Although their meaning is somewhat unclear, even to Jeremy, these stories also align with the twenty-first-century corporate mindset that emerges again and again in stories told by other SRUWC administrators and consultants. Yet, Jeremy simultaneously challenges this approach when he explains that the conveyor-like way of working with students on their writing does not adequately represent the kind of work they do.

Jeremy's sense of the kind of work the writing center does and does not do with student writers reflects his perception of the writing center's agency. He recognizes misunderstandings of the writing center's work as such, and he knows how to challenge them on behalf of the writing center at large. In this chapter, I show that developing, recognizing, and encouraging agency is a crucial administrative move that creates a strong foundation for building strategic partnerships. Through analysis of interviews with the SRUWC staff, I use the SRUWC's history, structure, and language choices as an example of how to encourage agency, not only in the center itself but also within consultants and student writers.

Despite his agency, Jeremy still struggles with how the twenty-first-century university has changed consultants' approaches to their work in the writing center. Many scholars have recognized this link between the university and a business-model approach to higher education, both in general terms (Barrow 1990; Bok 2003; Giroux 2002; Nelson and Watt 1999; Slaughter and Leslie 1997; Slaughter and Rhoades 2004) and also within the field of English studies in particular (Bousquet, Scott, and Parascondola 2004; Downing, Hurlbert, and Mathieu 2002; Ohmann 1976; Readings 1996; Rose 2012). Similarly, Daniel Mahala (2007) notes how writing centers in particular are shaped by pressure from the "managed university" that "has favored the growth of user-friendly innovations . . . [and] also undercut writing instruction" (7). These texts all seem to agree in two ways: The corporatization of the university describes our current moment in education, and thus we must exist within it. And the business-like mentality with which the university (and especially administrators) operates is in conflict with student-centered pedagogies in ways that can damage students, despite the positive connotations of words like "innovation" and "entrepreneurship."

In the twenty-first-century university, the writing center has great potential to support writing across the university and to be a kind of disruptive innovation itself. Not only does a writing center offer a "cheaper and more user-friendly" approach (Christensen and Eyring 2011) through peer-to-peer tutoring, but it also challenges traditional classroom spaces and hierarchal structures between students and teachers. Thus, writing centers must find a way to both exist as a space that supports student writers and make the case more broadly that the space can play an integral role in the teaching of writing across campus. In fact, our ability to do one of these things effectively depends on our ability to do the other well too.

Both a student-centered and a cross-departmental writing support approach require the writing center to act with a certain degree of agency, something that will likely take a conscientious effort given the marginalized history of writing centers. Although conversations about agency in writing studies tend to focus on how writing centers can support students in developing agency (Alvarez et al. 2016; Gordon 2014; Paiz 2018), writing centers themselves should also be aware of how they can establish and act with agency, and how those abilities shape both the space of the writing center and the ways students exercise their agency as writers. Stephen North, in "The Idea of a Writing Center," recognizes how perceived agency shapes understandings about writing centers. After identifying Maxine Hairston's critique of "writing labs" for their skill and drill mentality and agreeing that these kinds of writing centers are understandably written off, North notes that the reason such perceptions of writing centers exist is because of their lack of agency. North writes,

> Where centers have been prohibited from dealing with the writing that students do for their classes—where, in short, writing centers have been of the kind that Professor Hairston is quite correctly prepared to write off—it is because the agency that created the center in the first place, too often an English Department, has made it so. The grammar and drill center, the fix-it shop, the first aid station. . . . They are, instead, the vital and authentic reflection of a way of thinking about writing and the teaching of writing that is alive and well and living in English departments everywhere. (1984, 437)

For North, the agency (or lack thereof) that created the writing center in the first place made it into a basic, drill-based center. Rather than establishing their own sense of purpose and agency from the beginning, writing centers were likely created to work on elements of student writing with which English professors did not want to deal. Thus, North recognizes that initially and historically, writing centers were not created as places with their own agency, but rather in pursuit of someone else's agency.

What does it mean for a writing center to have agency? In *Literacy Practices and Perceptions of Agency: Composing Identities*, Bronwyn T. Williams provides a definition of student agency that is useful for thinking about how writing centers can develop their own agency too. Williams defines agency as "the perception, drawn from experiences and dispositions, that the individual can, in a given social context, act, make a decision, and make meaning" (2017, 9). Applying Williams's definition of agency to the writing center means that a writing center is aware of its own autonomy and can thus take action and make meaning on its own terms, rather than needing to seek approval from a domineering department, college, or unit. While this does not mean that writing centers require no oversight, it does suggest that, in order for writing centers to have agency, they need some degree of independence.

Agency is an essential characteristic of the twenty-first-century writing center. Not only does it enable the writing center to act widely across campus, but it also means that the writing center can exercise choice about what projects it takes on and how those projects unfold. The SRUWC establishes itself as a twenty-first-century writing center with a strong sense of agency reflected in its administrators and consultants. This sense of agency determines how the SRUWC staff interacts with both faculty and writers across campus and ultimately leads to its ability to work by way of strategic partnership while still maintaining a commitment to student writers. The SRUWC is an example of how a space can be both student-writer focused and cross-disciplinarily savvy, working both within and against twenty-first-century university frameworks.

THE WRITING CENTER "RESURRECTED": A CONTEXT AND HISTORY OF THE NEW WRITING CENTER

My research for this project began with nearly three hours of interviewing Melissa, the executive director of the SRUWC. She has a PhD in English from SRU, and her background is in British literature. She admitted that she only agreed to direct the center when, as she said, "all of my options had run out." Yet, Melissa grew to love her work because of its dynamism and the way that "every day is different." In particular, Melissa described her own approach to writing center work as "open-minded" because she is willing to try anything: "I never say no to anything. . . . There's just not anything that involves writing that we don't do." That being said, sometimes when faculty approached them, the writing center would have to "sway them [faculty] to try our [the SRUWC's] method, and then they stay." Part of Melissa's role, as she described it, was to "sell our idea" to university administrators and disciplinary faculty.

Already in these early moments of the interview, Melissa's sense of agency is strong, as is her awareness of how the twenty-first-century university functions and what kind of work is involved in collaboration. While she may agree to all departmental requests, Melissa's work still involves "swaying" faculty to use the SRUWC's approach, something that most of them are willing to do. Despite her entrepreneurial willingness to experiment and try new things, Melissa still balances this approach with some hard boundaries. For instance, she mentions that the writing center would not be involved with grading, even though other departments put a lot of pressure on them to do so. Melissa explains:

> So, [some departments] think teaching writing, sometimes . . . is having someone who knows how to grade a paper, grade the paper, and that someone is the writing center. Well, we just don't. We're not going to go there, and we might set up a rubric, grade a couple of papers according to the rubric, and give them back to the department, and that generally works.

Here, Melissa suggests a few ways that the SRUWC helped change the way faculty taught writing. Rather than simply refusing to help with grading, the SRUWC aided faculty in creating tools for evaluation (rubrics) and even gave them examples of how to apply the rubrics to student writing. As she continues to talk about the history of the SRUWC, Melissa's stories reveal that its ability to act with agency results from its split from English, its transactional approach to college-level partnerships, and its risk-taking practices rooted in a privileged, entrepreneurial mindset.

Before I spoke with Melissa for this project, I was under the impression that she was the founder and the first director of the SRUWC. Having been in and out of the writing center over the past four years, I had the sense that she built the center from the ground up. In a way, she did. There were no traces of previous directors or leadership in the stories told among staff or in documentation, and hardly any mention of its split from the English Department. For instance, the website provides the following SRUWC history.

SRUWC HISTORY

HISTORY OF THE WRITING CENTER

The Writing Center began humbly in 1999, in the basement of XX Hall. It employed ten writing consultants who did walk-in tutoring only. Its two classrooms were a hodgepodge of salvaged computers from the English Department and two brand-new video projectors, with which innovative faculty and TAs taught the first technology-enhanced humanities courses at SRU.

On June 6, 2001, tropical storm Allison hit the Gulf Coast, killing four people and causing billions of dollars in damage. Along with other vital parts of the UofX, the Writing Center's basement facility was completely flooded. Everything—records, computers, furniture—was lost. For the next school year, the Writing Center struggled to survive in various temporary locations across campus, while insurance claims were filed and a new space was sought. Finally, in the fall of 2002, the Writing Center opened its doors to the public on the second floor of AA Hall.

In the fall of 2012, the Writing Center made yet another move in order to accommodate its continued growth. Leaving aging computers and many happy memories behind, the Writing Center relocated to the second floor of the new Classrooms and Business Building. There, with spacious consulting rooms and up-to-date computer labs, it continues to service the writing needs of SRU students and faculty members.[3]

Yet when I ask about its history and beginning, Melissa explains that the SRUWC "was conceived in the English Department," where it started out as tutoring for students taking first-year composition courses under someone else's directorship. When that director left, the dean of the College of Liberal Arts and Social Sciences approached Melissa and asked her to take over as director. Shortly after Melissa took over, tropical storm Allison hit in 2001, filling the SRUWC with two feet of water. The university administrators at the time "weren't sure if they were going to resurrect the writing center or not," so the center "conducted business" in temporary trailer houses.

When administration decided that they would indeed reopen the writing center, now on the second floor of a different building, Melissa's exchange with someone from the provost's office caused her to envision a new kind of center. She explains:

I said, "I suppose that means that we'll continue to tutor freshman comp and students in the English Department." And he looked at me and said, "You can do whatever you want to do. If you don't want to do that, you don't have to do that," and I said, "No kidding?" He said, "You can recreate the writing center," so that's when it really started.

To start this new writing center in 2002, Melissa was given a budget of $800,000 that partly came to her from the computer company, since the computers ruined in the flood had been insured. She used the funds in part to bring writing studies experts from composition and writing across the curriculum to help create the new center. Another important early move was hiring more tutors by "narrowing down" the staff of techs, who primarily helped with operating the computers and outnumbered the consultants eight to two. The administration at the time was "pro–writing center," and the associate dean who oversaw the writing center was, according to Melissa, their "good angel" who "funded everything that I asked for . . . [and] came to meetings and knew what was going on, which was key as we were first getting established," even though that associate dean "wasn't always an easy sell."

Melissa speaks quite directly about the writing center's split from English, explaining that, "the difference [for the SRUWC] came when the English Department cut us loose." Once that occurred, the SRUWC began to hire tutors from various majors outside of English and to work with students and faculty across the university. Melissa credits the English Department chair at the time with signing off on the "separation" that enabled the SRUWC to become an "independent entity." Although Melissa believes that there are still, nearly fifteen years later, some faculty in English who are angry about the split, she argues that "it was the right thing to do."

Despite the long and complicated history in the field about where writing centers should be located, for Melissa the separation from English was integral to establishing a new kind of center. The most recent results from the Writing Center Research Project indicate that this kind of freedom is rare; fewer than 20 percent of centers reported an "independent" affiliation, while more than 30 percent are associated with the English Department or a rhetoric/composition program. The remaining 50 percent are affiliated with learning skills centers or student services or had "other" affiliations. This lack of commonality in writing center location aligns with the writing center's "history as not a place but a method" (Boquet 1999, 466) and as "a gap in the university structure" (Hemmeter 1990, 42). This is significant since, as Haviland, Fye, and Colby (2001) point out, "location is political because it is an organizational choice that creates visibility or invisibility, access to resources, and associations that define the meanings, uses, and users of designated spaces" (85). Such locations are usually influenced by the writing center's proximity to certain departments, writing programs, campus-wide tutoring centers, student service organizations, second-language learner programs, residence halls, or libraries. Because of their lack of locatedness, writing centers must establish themselves via networking across departments and within various student services. Building these kinds of relationships often benefits writing centers (Macauley and Mauriello 2007), and, in Melissa's case, her independence was necessary for expanding her vision beyond first-year writing.

By 2003, the SRUWC was a new place. The university noted this new identity in an article released by the Office of Internal Communications, referring to the SRUWC as "entrepreneurial" and "pro-active."[4] Although praised by some, Melissa's entrepreneurship was also considered "controversial" because it sometimes involved charging university administrators and disciplinary departments fees for SRUWC services. Melissa speaks about this element of the SRUWC at various times during our four interviews, yet the first time it comes up is about five and a half minutes into our first one, as part of her story about the history of the SRUWC and its new beginning. After her exchange with the provost described above, Melissa explains:

> And so, we built a writing center. What was controversial at the time, that someone who is no longer here at SRU said, "you're going to get in trouble for that." We charged for our services. Not everybody, you know, students could come in, walk-in consultations, but, for example, if a large college wanted to have their students come to the WC, we said, we will develop a program with your faculty and work with your students. Now, I'm talking about a lot of students—Law, College of Business—but you have to pay us, because we'll have to pay the writing consultants who will work with them [students]. And, nobody was doing that at the time, and you know, it worked. And now, we're still doing that and, what's interesting about it is, the College of Business, for example, likes to say that they outsource the teaching of writing to the writing center. And that makes it a more objective kind of process. . . . First customers were the Law School and Business, other than the students who would drop in for walk-ins.

Since this seemed central to the SRUWC's approach, I asked Melissa how colleges like Business respond to being charged for partnerships. She explains that, for the larger colleges, this financial element seemed normal, and they "don't mind [paying] at all" because they think of their work with the SRUWC as a kind of "outsourcing . . . [to] writing experts" that "gives them more legitimacy." Melissa says that a "cost estimate" is part of some partnership processes in that when they begin conversations with university administrators and disciplinary faculty, the SRUWC administrators explain up front the money needed to carry out the project, which requires the hiring/paying of more consultants at a particular hourly rate. When potential partners from large colleges approach the writing center after the semester has started, they have already planned the semester and thus the additional project is not in the SRUWC's budget. Thus, the SRUWC would have to hire additional consultants, and that is what they charged departments for: "We're not making any money, we're just paying for the people who are going to be in charge for that project—the writing consultants—and they [the partners] accept it."[5]

When smaller colleges with fewer students and less money approach the SRUWC, Melissa still tries to work with them, supporting the projects with grant money and endowments since "there's a lot of areas that just don't have any money so we'll do it, you know, gratis. But the big schools, the big colleges who do [have money], and have 800 students, let's say, in a class, like the General Business class, they don't mind paying." In some of these large, college- or department-level partnerships, the SRUWC has more than 600 student interactions in a single semester.[6] Even now, Melissa recognizes why this practice seems controversial to some, yet she also explains, "I don't know many writing centers that see the number of students that we see either." Other writing center administrators off the record explain this practice as a kind of "Robin Hood–like" mentality: Take from the richer departments and provide for the poorer.

Melissa's historical telling of how she inherited the SRUWC and her vision for its revival, its move outside of the English Department, and its entrepreneurial model led to its continuing growth over the next decade.[7] Midway through her story, Melissa's language shifts from religious to corporate. Early on, she tells a kind of rebirth narrative beginning with the SRUWC's "conception" in the English Department followed by a physical—and perhaps metaphorical—flood that wiped out the writing center and provided the opportunity for a "resurrection," which was then made possible by an upper administrator who served as the writing center's "good angel" and supported Melissa's new vison. This language acknowledges the element of luck that helped everything fall into place. For example, having a "good angel" who supported Melissa's vision as well as an English Department chair who was willing to "let go" of the writing center, seemed to happen, in part, by chance. Melissa indicates that, without these two supportive moves, her vision for the writing center would not have had the space to grow.

Once she has her independence from the English Department and the monetary support from the dean's office, Melissa's description becomes corporate, as she explains an "entrepreneurial" approach that enables her to attract "customers" from across the university. Although Melissa acknowledges this as "controversial" to some, she also notes that those with whom she worked who are paying the bill do not have a problem with it; they find value in "outsourcing to writing experts." While "outsourcing" is another cringeworthy word for writing centers and most humanities-based disciplines in general, Melissa understands that those who "outsourced" also considered the writing center staff to be the writing experts. While writing centers are often perceived as free university services and the SRUWC continued to be free for students, Melissa's approach places a monetary value on large-scale, customized writing support. Upper administrators at the college level who are willing and able to provide money for writing acknowledge the work involved and provided support for that work. Yet, rather than only work with departments who have money, Melissa also works with those who do not and tries to find other ways of supporting those partnerships.

Melissa's privileged identity as a white, upper-class woman with substantial business experience that predates her time in graduate school and her writing center directorship clearly influence her willingness to engage in these somewhat controversial practices and her confidence in requesting a split from English. Melissa regularly reminds me that she sometimes thinks about retiring so she can spend more time golfing and playing bridge with her friends, all of whom are already retired or do not work. As the wife of a prominent businessman in the area, Melissa's livelihood does not depend on her job in the writing center, which makes her well positioned to take risks. Although these risks would not necessarily seem so possible for someone whose livelihood depends on keeping their job, the value and payoff of taking them is worth consideration.

Further, Melissa's willingness to take risks is directly influenced by her sense of agency: The more agency one has, the more likely they are to take risks, and the more risks one takes, the more agency they likely feel. Within a strategic partnership framework and in thinking about international higher education partnerships, Naureen Madhani connects agency with power, since power requires "having something that someone else wants or needs, and being in control of the performance or resource" (2016, 218). Since the support for teaching writing was in high demand, the writing center was a highly desirable resource once its scope became campus-wide rather than based in a single department. Melissa, as a savvy administrator, recognizes this early on and exercises her agency to increase resources for the writing center that she then uses at her discretion.

THE MAKEUP OF A TWENTY-FIRST-CENTURY WRITING CENTER ENGAGED IN STRATEGIC PARTNERSHIP

In practice, the SRUWC functions like a twenty-first-century writing center. By this, I mean the writing center seems aware of the larger, corporate university structures in place and finds methods of working within and against them in ways that make sense to administrators and faculty across the university as well as to students. The SRUWC staff describes the writing center and the work that goes on there in ways that conflict with familiar writing center narratives. For example, the writing center grand narrative that Grutsch McKinney's (2013) seminal text uncovers includes defining the writing center as a "place where all students go to get help with their writing," an element that was present in the SRUWC. Yet, this center was rarely described as comfortable, homelike, or iconoclastic, all of which are also components of Grutsch McKinney's grand narrative. Instead, there is a more professional, workplace feel, and staff members describe the writing center with business terminology. For example, when I ask Max (project manager) to describe the culture of the writing center, he says the following:

> Individualized, meaning that the staff works separately, without a lot of administrative control. . . . [T]he university's corporate approach seeps into how the writing center operates. . . . [They use] an administrative approach that depends on independent producers who work from their own values in numbers. They're constantly trying to put things into numbers and measure that way.

Jeremy also acknowledges this "corporate model," explaining its existence through the language used in the SRUWC: "It's very much like we call our tutors consultants, they make an appointment and you can cancel and reschedule and it just kind of sounds like a doctor's office. That's not necessarily a bad thing because it's very efficient and it works very well for what we do here." Jeremy's decision not to judge this practice as good or bad is an example of how one can work in the twenty-first-century university without having to fully agree or disagree with how it shapes the environment.

The use of these business terms by SRUWC staff aligns with Melissa's language. In her story about how the SRUWC came to its new version, she describes her disciplinary partners from the law and business school as the writing center's "first customers" and attributes the separation from the English Department as that which allows them to "expand our customer base." She speaks of the need to "sell our ideas" to other departments, describes students who made individual appointments outside the partnership structure as "independent agents who need help with a paper," and refers to consultants themselves as "independent contractors."

Considering consultants to be "independent contractors" rejects any kind of micromanaging, which in turn permits the consultants to develop on their own terms. This independence, although initially challenging, eventually contributes to consultants' sense of agency, too, as described more fully below. Similarly, seeing student writers as "independent agents" suggests autonomy; they choose to come to the writing center on their own volition. The SRUWC creates the schedule with these kinds of students in mind: they require students to make appointments at least forty-eight hours in advance and do not offer any walk-in tutoring anymore. This means that their sessions are rarely panicky, last-minute attempts to wrap up an essay minutes before its deadline. A closer look at the SRUWC's structure and description of space, culture, and work across administrators, consultants, writers, and disciplinary partners reveals a twenty-first-century writing center well positioned to operate as a hub for writing support across campus.

The Administrators

In addition to the use of corporate language, the SRUWC's structure also contributes to its business-model environment. In particular, the unique structure of having eight full-time middle administrators who work as project managers, in addition to an upper-management team (including the executive and associate directors), one full-time technology director, and two part-time technical assistants, and a large staff of twenty-two peer consultants, suggests a very capitalist structure.[8]

Figure 1.1 presents the SRUWC's organizational structure. The upper-management team (Melissa, Sam, and Hannah) does the work of locating potential university/disciplinary faculty partners, negotiating the terms of work, and developing cost-estimate plans. The project managers (Max, Brad, Lindsay, Dan, Warren, Jeremy, and Anne) are the ones who maintain relationships with university administrators and disciplinary partners. These project managers communicate with the university administrators or disciplinary faculty, train and prepare consultants to work with student writers in the partnerships, supervise and advise the interactions between consultants and students, and keep track of

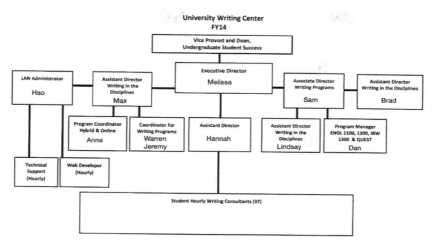

Figure 1.1. 2015 SRUWC organizational chart

assessment and follow-up reflections. Although they rarely work directly with students themselves, project managers are essential to making the SRUWC work. Highly important to the work of the SRUWC is the technology team, led by Hao, who maintains internal operations and archives assessment data and helps create and organize online spaces to support writing partnerships.

Sam (associate director) describes one particularly useful way of thinking about how these various tiers of writing center staff work together. First, he characterizes the SRUWC as a "hybrid or heterodox of a service center, a program development center, project management, almost like a consulting firm for faculty and administrators, and we also contribute to curriculum development." He then extends this idea to include the following:

> Especially in terms of the WC professional, I think a lot of times in terms of engineering, and how an engineer basically looks at systems and functions. The function that we're trying to accomplish is student education and development in terms of writing. And, that's kind of the easy part. The hard part is to allocate limited resources and use the existing systems in order to achieve that outcome, and a lot of times, it's because our students are limited in the time that they can devote to things, they're limited in their motivation. . . . [W]riting is not always a high priority for them, so one thing creative administrators do is try to create a motivational structure to try and get students to commit as much as possible. So, thinking of things like incentives and requirements, you know. Connecting the writing program to the existing requirements so that there's an efficiency to the system, so there's a lot of administration that sort of functions like

engineering, especially where we're dealing with relatively large numbers of students. And there are, literally, systems that have to get integrated. Our WC relies especially on the online scheduling system, but then also local area network resources for file management and web-based databases, we have an intranet. All of those things are [ways we] try to use the systems to create efficiency so that our most valuable resource—which is the writing consultants—spend most of their time in contact with students. Again, that's kind of the engineering function of trying to use as many systems as possible to enable the one function that has a really hard limit on it—the hourly workers, we can only work them so many hours, and there seems to be a natural limit in terms of how many students we can find who are suited to the work.

Sam argues here that an effectively functioning writing center depends on a kind of administrative engineering that goes into creating a supportive environment for the work of writing consultations. Alongside the technological supporting structures, the upper-management team and the project managers work to create this backdrop that allows for the "efficient" use of the SRUWC's "most valuable resource . . . the writing consultants." Sam recognizes that administrative work involves figuring out how to best utilize limited resources and motivation, which he links to work with student writers. Yet, some of what he says seems better geared toward partnering with faculty, such as "connecting the writing program to the existing requirements." Further, Sam emphasizes integration and efficiency, but ultimately circles back to the issue of supporting the most student writers as possible with a finite number of qualified consultants who are also limited in terms of time and money. Good, "creative" administration, then, according to Sam, involves a kind of behind-the-scenes engineering aimed at preserving and supporting the work of writing consultants.

The Consultants

From their first sessions in the SRUWC, consultants are expected to operate as "independent contractors." In other words, there is no coddling or team tutoring or assigning of first-year writing students to new consultants. Instead, new consultants are expected to work with whoever made an appointment with them, just the same as those who have years of experience. Although I rarely asked directly for first-session narratives, all but three staff members shared them with me. These detailed stories were surprisingly consistent in how they used survivalist terms to describe the new experience. For example, Dan explains his first writing center consultation as being "thrown to the wolves." Rather than teaching in a traditional one-on-one environment, Dan led a small group of developmental writing students through a weekly, semester-long mini-course. He says:

> I remember, I had the whiteboard and I was looking back and forth, and was like, "we're going to talk about this, we're going to talk about that, here are these concepts," and I remember turning around and they were just wilting. Just wilting, and I was like, oh man, they don't want to hear this. It's not going to work. I'm just fishing in dirt if I think I'm going to teach them writing concepts like this, because they're just dying in front of me.

His continuance as a consultant depended on his ability to figure out how to work with these students. Dan does figure it out, and eventually takes on a leadership role within this particular partnership. Other SRUWC consultants speak of being "thrown right into the fire" (Jeremy), getting "thrown in there" (Warren), and feeling like they had to "just stick it through" (Hannah).

In a different kind of survival story, Lindsay compares her struggle with figuring out how to work with students who had more limited writing abilities than she imagined with trying to navigate an icy road:

> I need to do a big gear [shift]. . . . I felt like . . . I was driving an 18-wheeler, it was a full, icy highway, and I've got to make a quick left turn, how am I going to do that, you know? Because I couldn't . . . see an easy way to do that, not just for myself but for the people I was working with.

While these survival metaphors are not explicitly explained as part of the SRUWC's corporate influence, they contribute to its culture. Becoming a consultant in the SRUWC involves this almost violent experience of being "thrown" into consulting before being ready and finding a way to survive the experience. Then, in working through this experience, the consultant's agency shifts, as they go from being passively "thrown" into the consultation, to coming out on the other end of things, and making it through.

For new consultants, the environment of the writing center is not a comfortable, homey place, but one where challenging, serious work happens.[9] Oftentimes, consultants feel unprepared, in part because the student-writer population is primarily first-generation and multilingual. Not only are writers linguistically and ethnically diverse, but they bring in work from across the disciplines, including dissertations. For instance, Jeremy's first session as an undergraduate consultant is with an international graduate student in biology who brings in a dissertation chapter. After feeling like he is "kind of thrown right into the fire, right away," he also explains: "But, I thought it was good too and that I handled it well and that the student was pleased so I was fine with it." Most have similar stories of overcoming the challenge in some way that makes them appreciate the challenge and gain confidence, upon reflection.

Similarly, Hannah experiences what is initially a stressful first day of tutoring that eventually makes her realize that she can help writers. She describes her first session this way:

> My first consultation was a BWT [business writing tutorial] consultation and most consultants are assigned to other projects, they aren't assigned to BWT because of scheduling, but because of my scheduling they put me on BWT. . . . It was the afternoon, everyone was home already—just the consultant night manager [was there]—and I came in and I met with a student and had no idea that when I looked at the student's name that they would be non-native, that they would have a name that I couldn't pronounce or even know the gender of the student, and then I met with the student and remember that their ability to communicate in English was very broken and I thought, what did I get myself into? I'm not a language teacher, so why am I here? Because this person obviously needs a language tutor. But I stuck it through the thirty minutes that I had to meet with him and said I'll see you next week even though I didn't probably expect to see him because I was going to tell someone that they made a mistake. And then I had another student come in an hour later and it was the same thing. The same experience. And then I saw another consultant having a similar experience at a different table and I had a conversation with them after everyone left and asked if this is what it's like and they said, yes, this is what it is, and I said, well, I don't think I can do that, and they said, yeah, you can, you're doing fine, just stick with it, so I did.

The "mistake" Hannah refers to is the decision to hire her. The story begins with a sense of isolation, as she's nearly the only one in the writing center at the time. Her assumptions about what she thought the writing center would be are laid bare when she notices the student's name on the scheduler and comes to terms with the language and cultural differences that will likely play out in her session. Although she feels out of her comfort zone and not adequately prepared, Hannah "stuck it through" and is further encouraged to "stick with it" by another consultant. These lived experiences of tutoring in the writing center strongly conflict with the conveyor belt metaphor Jeremy described from orientation.

As time progressed, I saw how first sessions are, in a sense, part of an initiation process that leaves consultants with a sense of pride after they make it through. While one way of reading these first consultation stories suggests that the SRUWC operated from a "survival of the fittest" business-like mentality—where upper administrators only step in to help when a "lifeline" is truly needed—there is another way of reading them. If we think about agency and helping consultants develop a sense of confidence, then giving them the experience of a challenging first session without filtering who consultants work with provides them an immediate sense of the student writers who use the writing center. Not only this, but once consultants realize they can get through their challenging first sessions, they also learn that they can, ultimately, help writers, and that struggling in new writing scenarios is part of the ongoing work of tutoring. From their first sessions, SRUWC consultants begin establishing their own independent tutoring personas, influenced primarily by how they work through their early sessions. The consultants who will eventually make up the majority of the administrative staff come from these experiences, a factor that further contributes to a twenty-first-century writing center that functions with agency and confidence.

As a result, consultants dispute the assumption that writing centers "just tutor" and strongly prefer to be called "writing consultants." According to Jeremy, *consultant* "adds some kind of professional air to the job," while Melissa preferred *consultant* because it "implies that there's a give and take," in contrast to the way that *tutor* suggests more of a one-sided give on the part of the tutor. She explains:

> It's more than just tutoring writing. It's hard to get that concept shunted aside and then talk about the other concepts, but it's a lot more than that. . . . I feel really comfortable in saying that we have done a pretty good job teaching writing on campus.

For Melissa, "tutoring" does not adequately describe what it means to "teach writing." This preference for *consultant* over *tutor* also fits with the business-like mentality of the SRUWC, yet the reason the SRUWC prefers this language seems to involve establishing respect, authority, and independence around the work of teaching writing in the center.

Much of how consultants function in the SRUWC described thus far has drawn on interviews with the SRUWC staff. This approach works in that most of the staff were previous consultants, and during the year of my ethnographic study nearly all of the consultants were new and still getting a sense of the writing center. Still, it was a goal of mine to find, explore, and participate in the unofficial culture of the SRUWC, which meant interacting with the consultants outside formal meetings and structured sessions. However, the organization of the space made doing so a challenge. Figure 1.2 shows a map of the SRUWC, with labels for (1) upper-administrator offices, (2) project-manager and tech-team offices, (3) consulting/group conferencing rooms, (4) the English TA/

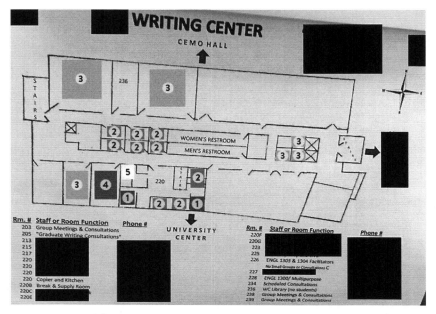

Figure 1.2. Map of the SRUWC space

online studio facilitator room, and (5) the undergraduate writing consultant's break room/storage. As figure 1.2 indicates, there is no office for the consultants. Instead, they have a "Storage Closet/Breakroom" in the main office right next to the front desk and behind the kitchen. This tiny space, which includes broken computers and a small table, is always quite public, and is hardly used. Otherwise, the consultants gather at a long table in the back of the main consulting room but usually talk in low whispers, if at all, since multiple consultations with students are going on around them. Given that the majority of the tutoring staff was new to the SRUWC, I only conducted a handful of consultant interviews, primarily with those involved in the case study partnerships discussed in chapters 3–5. Thus, the best opportunity I had to explore the SRUWC peer consultant "unofficial culture" was by attending the Reading Group gatherings.

When I interviewed Jeremy (project manager), he showed the most excitement when he spoke about the Writing Center Reading Group that he had begun as a senior consultant several years earlier. "Reading Group" was designed in part to supplement the project manager–led "In-Service" professional development sessions overseen by Linda (project manager). Jeremy described in-services as being cut-and-dried, practice-based, longstanding, hourlong lecture/presentations that were rarely interactive, with the exception of an occasional short activity or writing task. Full-time SRUWC staff members take turns leading them, yet tend to repeat the same topics and lessons over and over again. In-services cover familiar topics such as the resistant writer, strategies for working with English-language learner students, writing center work and hospitality, and learning from failure.

In contrast, Reading Group is conversation-based and changes every semester. Its purpose is to "offer consultants what we would be offering if they had to take a writing center class . . . because they are reading more about writing center theory." Jeremy leads Reading Group, along with another recent consultant-turned-project-manager staff member, Anne. Reading groups occur between four and six times every semester in an informal, book group–like setting with snacks and conversation over short pieces of writing center scholarship that rotate each semester. In preparation for fall 2015 reading group sessions, we read essays by Lester Faigley, Barbara Schapiro, David Bartholomae, Muriel Harris, Bonnie Devet, and John Nordlof published in journals such as *The Writing Center Journal, Praxis, Pedagogy, College English,* and *College Composition and Communication.* Eventually, Reading Group became a more formalized part of consultant training, in that consultants could attend either Reading Group or In-Service sessions to meet professional development requirements, for which they are also paid.

As part of my research and also as part of my assigned work as a Writing Center Pedagogy and Program Development Fellow, I attended most in-services and all reading groups in fall 2015 and immediately understood Jeremy's distinction between the two.[10] When I attended Reading Group, I began to understand the consultants as a community by way of hearing them interact with one another in a group setting. Thus, I heard them raise questions, challenge one another, and speak from their own experiences, pointing out connections and conflicts along the way. Although I still found this to be a bit of a constructed setting, it was my best opportunity to gather with them and listen to them without much oversight from the SRUWC administrators or senior staff members. Jeremy and Anne, both project managers, took on nondirective roles, raising questions and encouraging participation, but ultimately left the direction of the conversation up to the consultants themselves. These consultants, who are primarily undergraduate students but include some recent graduates, bring a critical eye to these texts and challenge claims made by writing studies scholars using their own experiences.

For example, consultants criticize the idea that students cannot create their own knowledge in classroom spaces and that consultants can (and should) debunk the assumption that they are writing experts (Harris 1995). As we continue our discussion about when consultants might embrace the role of expert and when they might distance themselves from it, a new consultant (Claire) offers another way of thinking through the expert/nonexpert (or, perhaps, peer) role:

> It seems difficult to imagine us [consultants] as a bridge. Instead, maybe the bridge is like the writing process: Even if it's rickety and not as functional, the consultant is making it a little more concrete and safer to cross. [The consultant is] not really a bridge or a translator but fills in the gaps that people don't have the knowledge for yet.

Here, Claire describes the consultant's work as a kind of scaffolding that centralizes the writer's process, rather than the consultant's expertise. She does not simply resist the role of expert but repositions it to be more about "filling the gaps" that students need, rather than providing a sturdy kind of support that writers rely on to move their writing forward.

During another reading group, consultants discuss Devet's (2012) "Using Metagenre and Ecocomposition to Train Writing Center Tutors for Writing in the Disciplines." Tania, an experienced graduate student consultant, explains that she has "a problem with seeing that the discipline accommodates the writer—instead, it's usually the writer who has to accommodate to the discipline, but the discipline does not accommodate to the writer." As she argues, assuming that the writer shapes the discipline (and thus, genres) is a "romanticized" way of understanding disciplines, because "when new students come to the university, they don't necessarily feel that they can contribute. Instead, we as tutors can help them find their own voices—'you can be a good writer if you know how to express your thoughts clearly.'" Tim (recently graduated professional consultant) then chimes in, asking, "Is [contributing to and shaping disciplines/genres] really the job of the student at the undergraduate level?" Sydney (recently graduated professional consultant) responds by sharing what she often tells students:

> I tell [students] a lot that it isn't necessarily their job to be perfect. They don't have to contribute hugely groundbreaking ideas. Instead, it's about developing skills more so than aiming for a product. It's more vocational than we want to admit. And, genre expectations are primarily constrained by professors.

As the conversation continues, the consultants question the extent to which nontraditional students, in particular, are really trying to master a discipline or genre or if they are "just trying to finish" their degree, whether or not the idea of metagenre can be multidisciplinary, and how tutoring from a metagenre approach may reinforce formulaic, rather than creative, approaches to writing.

During the best moments, which are frequent, consultants are a little subversive. For instance, after reading Bartholomae's (1986) "Inventing the University," consultants question the use of the term *basic writer* as a label for student writers, raise concerns about how academic discourse relates to privilege, ask how students are expected to contribute to the university when the system itself is so focused on the quantifiable, argue about how contributing to the university by replicating it is an "act of violence" for those who do not come from privileged backgrounds and instead want to offer new discourses (informed by fields like queer theory), and question whether or not teachers can read as audience rather than as intellectual/academic critics. By the end of the group meeting, consultants seem to agree that "butting heads with professors" is valuable and at times necessary. This concept is in direct conflict with SRUWC policy, referred to informally by both Melissa and Lindsay during interviews, and stated clearly in the SRUWC Consultant Handbook:

> We retain a strict policy of neutrality in the Writing Center. *Do not under any circumstance criticize or undermine an instructor, teaching assistant, course, grade or assignment.* If a student starts in that direction, remain objective and refocus the student to what he/she can do to improve the piece of writing at hand and him/herself as a writer.

However, in Reading Group, consultants point out that instructors sometimes commit "acts of violence" by expecting students to replicate the university's own language. While some consultants speak from their own positions as student writers who experience this kind of violence, others speak about the stories student writers share with them. Through the telling of these stories, consultants also point out how listening to and responding with both sympathy and frustration can help consultants and student writers "bond over shared attitudes," even when that means disagreeing with the instructor.

Rather than simply functioning as part of the larger writing center system and despite their low position in the organizational hierarchy, consultants act with independence and agency. They are deeply committed to questioning corporate pressures even if doing so conflicts with SRUWC policy. Here, consultant agency seems to manifest in the willingness to unapologetically raise questions about how writing center studies describe the practice of tutoring, especially when it conflicts with their own experiences as both consultants and writers alike.

They acknowledge the value of, and the need for pushing back on, institutional and faculty expectations and remain, above all, focused on supporting the student writer. Finally, they recognize their work as intellectually complex, so they create a community around investigating the work of tutoring in a scholarly way. Even within an "independent contractor" mindset, consultants still build a community of practice in which to explore their work with writers.[11]

The (Student) Writers

Just as a sense of independence and agency seemed to trickle down from the upper administrators—and Melissa in particular—to the project managers and consultants, it also impacts how the SRUWC staff perceive student writers. The clearest instance of this is in how staff members intentionally refer to student writers primarily as writers, not students, who have a future well beyond their role of student in the university. For instance, Anne explains how the writing center supports students as developing writers in a way that differs from other university spaces:

> The writing center functions as a third space—a voluntary interaction where students can focus on writing as a discipline. Writers don't often get to work on writing when they aren't in the classroom [and] the classroom isn't very focused on student writers' writing. Instead, in the classroom, they are students and it's hard for them to get out of that role, but in the writing center they are writer, not student. Thinking of them as students can be limiting. At the writing center, you can focus on writing as a discipline, or writing as its own discipline.

Anne speaks about the writing center as a place for writers who are not constrained or defined by the classroom or their role as students of other disciplines. Instead, she suggests that the writing center functions as a space where writers can choose to act as writers who focus specifically on writing. Similarly, Jeremy connects the shift from student-as-writer to writer-as-developing-professional. He explains that the WC's central mission is to help writers think about their future working lives beyond the university. He claims that:

> Regardless of what the student is working on, even if only implicitly, we work from an awareness that the student will have to write in the future, regardless of discipline or major, and thus the writing center is always helping students with their academic and professional goals in some way.

Thus, Jeremy imagines his work with student writers as having a reach beyond a single classroom or a particular writing assignment. This concept comes up during reading group discussions, project team meetings, and even group consultations with students (see Tim's exchange with student writers in chapter 6).

To work from a recognition of student-as-writer in preparation for a professional life that will include writing requires an acceptance of student agency, especially through the building of confidence and autonomy. This also supports students' level of motivation because it makes the writing center into a space that can provide a different emotional experience with literacy, one that is more formative and less evaluative (Williams 2017). Although she used language different from Anne and Jeremy, Melissa also recognizes the SRUWC's role in helping student writers grow professionally. Melissa considers confidence-building to be part of the consultant's responsibility. She explains:

> You don't want to take ownership of their paper. They want you to take ownership of the paper because they lack confidence in their writing. And if somebody asked me, "What do you think is the best thing you do?" I think the best thing we do is help the students who come to us gain confidence in their ability to write well, or to at least write coherently.

Thus, refusing to take ownership of student writing and instead working with the student writer to help them write more coherently is one of the "best" practices at the SRUWC. Dan also describes the importance of working with students so that when they leave the writing center they "feel empowered and more capable of accomplishing tasks in writing effectively overall."

The emphasis on the writer's long-term professional development, in part through establishing agency and confidence in writing, is also reflected in the SRUWC's primary philosophy. In particular, the center emphasizes metacognitive awareness above all other approaches. When she first discusses how the SRUWC works with writers, Melissa does not mention grades or number of appointments or faculty expectations or lack of ability. Instead, she explains that the work of consulting involves "showing [writers] how to think about writing and talk about writing." Melissa calls this method "the talking cure," which she describes in the following scenario:

> We call it the talking cure, like Freud. And, the writing consultants, part of their training [is learning the talking cure]. I'll give you an example. One of the things that they're told is not to hold the students' paper longer than a minute or so. To take a look at it, hand it back to the student, and say, "What is it that you're trying to say?" . . . And that works, because then the student gets engaged and tells the writing consultant what he or she is trying to say, or needs to say, or wants to say. And the writing consultants

will very gently say sometimes, "Well, what you just said now, to me, verbally is not what you wrote on this paper. Write it like you just said it." . . . [O]ftentimes [students] have problems between the thinking and the putting down of what they're thinking.

While "the talking cure" may sound like a common approach to tutoring, Melissa's emphasis on the metacognitive here makes the method more nuanced. For instance, before the conversation even begins, Melissa acknowledges the subtle power relations that often precede the start of the session itself via the student writer handing the paper over to the consultant and the consultant looking at it briefly, handing it back, and then engaging the student writer in conversation about the writing itself. Then, the work of the consultant involves trying to determine whether or not the student writer's verbal ideas are represented clearly in the student's writing. The consultant then reaffirms the student writer's spoken ideas and tells them to rewrite or revise based on how the ideas were presented verbally to the consultant.

This process is different from text-based tutoring that emphasizes reading the paper out loud in that it begins and ends with conversation about intended meaning. The "talking cure approach" further emphasizes writer ownership, confidence, and agency by suggesting that writers have the main ideas for their writing and are capable of articulating them or figuring them out through discussion, even if their writing suggests otherwise. In this approach, consultants ask questions to help guide students, rather than generating the ideas or materials themselves. The emphasis is on talk about writing, not on the writing itself. This approach moves beyond common writing center focal points like directive/nondirective, generalist/specialist, and higher-order concerns/lower-order concerns to emphasize the writer's articulation of their project. While there are times when writers do not have ideas in mind, or may not know how to approach project revision, this is not the default assumption at the SRUWC.

The Partners

Despite the agency with which SRUWC administrators and consultants work and their efforts to recognize and encourage agency in student writers, when they spoke about disciplinary faculty partnerships, the SRUWC suggested a total lack of agency around teaching writing. At least initially, the writing center staff took on an informant-like, leadership role in initiating partnerships. For example, Hannah describes the partnership work of the SRUWC like that of an adoption agency:

It's very much like an adoption agency, you know? They come in and they're like, "This is what we're looking for." And we're like, "Okay, yes, we can do that, no we can't, yes we have a child that fits that. Okay, we do, okay, here's your match. I'm going to stay here for a week just to make sure everything is going okay. And then, this person is going to be your foster parent or your adopted parent." And so, then I step out and the only time I come in again is as the administrator, collecting money from that person each semester after we work with that person for billing . . . and then also, I'll come in at assessing how well the project went, and then also recording the data from the project into the report—number of students we met with, how we interacted with them—so that we can include that in our annual review. . . . [I]t's like [the SRUWC is] the mom, the partners are the dad, and the students are the kid. They need us to organize everything and don't usually listen.

In Hannah's explanation of how partnerships begin and get organized, no one seems to have much agency except for the SRUWC. Somehow, the SRUWC also becomes the "mom" in the relationship, once the "match" occurs. Although this description of all roles is problematic and seems to conflict with how partnerships unfold in practice, it does emphasize one primary element: layered relationships. Since partners often begin their work with the SRUWC with little confidence, experience, or agency surrounding the teaching of writing, the relationship the writing center builds with instructors and administrators is crucial to each partnership's sustainability and ongoing collaboration. Figure 1.3 displays the SRUWC's partnership process and the multiple relationships encouraged across SRUWC administrator, project manager, consultant, and partner.

As figure 1.3 indicates, each partnership works via an initial conversation with an upper administrator in the writing center. Then, projects are assigned a project manager and a team of writing consultants who will work with student writers. A third meeting among all participants occurs before consultants and writers meet, as well as a post-partnership meeting after the project launches. Perhaps some of Hannah's familial language in her description of the adoption agency is indicative of the guidance partners often need from the SRUWC, especially in terms of helping instructors articulate their expectations for student writing, and in terms of sharing those expectations explicitly with students. For instance, Hannah says that, at first, most instructors are not clearly communicating what they want to their students. However, during early writing center partnership meetings with administrators and peer consultants, faculty listen to consultants when they voice confusion over an assignment prompt because they are consultants who are also student writers. For example, Hannah explains the value of having bookend partnership meetings with the project manager, faculty, and consultants. Part of the value lies in the ways that the consultants point out where assignments are confusing, which in turn helps instructors. Hannah says:

> [Consultants] tell the truth about how the students seemed. . . . It's better to have the consultants because they don't have the fear, "Oh, this is my partner [and] they're paying us," so it becomes less of like a consulting firm and more of these consultants, who really don't have any direct tie to it, other than that they work with the students, any direct tie, I guess, to money . . . so they feel a bit more comfortable speaking the truth.

Hannah recognizes how these multitiered relationships function to make the partnership work. While her upper-administrative role requires her to think about making sure the partner's needs are met and to worry about cost and assessment, the project manager and consultants are

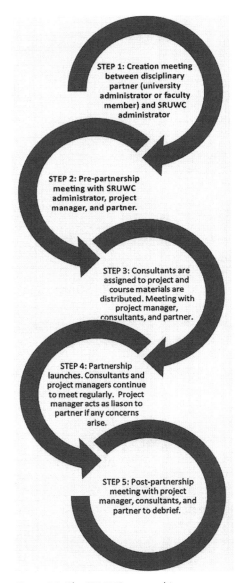

Figure 1.3. The SRUWC partnership process

focused solely on the teaching of writing and supporting student writers. Thus, they could perform different kinds of roles in the relationship. Hannah also explains that the SRUWC helps instructors develop rubrics and tells them how and why they should share them with students prior to grading, which is a foreign idea to most instructors. She tells them,

"You can know what you want and tell them too," joking that she would love to have the saying on a bumper sticker to hand out to faculty.

All SRUWC staff members describe collaborating with faculty/administrators as part of their writing center work and include one or more of the following: assessment of student writing, assignment design, development of rubrics and evaluation criteria, and/or assignment scaffolding via breaking a single major writing assignment into smaller parts. For instance, Max suggests that the writing center is a place where "there are a variety of approaches to teaching writing that complement writing instruction." Like Melissa, Max sees writing centers as places where the "teaching of writing" occurs. Sam explains part of the writing center's work as "curriculum development and faculty development," thus making the writing center "function as a program development resource."

Because of their emphasis on working with faculty in the disciplines, Sam explains, "We go beyond standard practice [of tutoring] by transcending the three standard concepts of university education: faculty, course, and semester." For him, "beyond standard practice" also means beyond common approaches to university educational structures. Sam suggests that the SRUWC's collaborations with faculty across campus upsets the traditional teacher-student dynamic, challenges the concept of course or classroom as site of instruction, and extends support beyond a single semester timeframe. In this way, the SRUWC lays the foundation for the work of disruptive innovation, particularly due to its ability to be flexible and extracurricular. For example, the business school has an assessment/portfolio-based partnership with the writing center that is not linked to any class, yet clearance is required by all students in the college, as chapter 5 explains in more detail. Table 1.1 shows the SRUWC's different partnership types, based on data from the 2014–2015 annual report. The table shows the wide variety of partnerships the SRUWC creates via collaboration with departments and colleges across campus, in addition to working with nearby high schools and other local colleges. These approaches take place in face-to-face and online environments, both one-on-one and in small groups. When faculty approach the SRUWC with a need not represented in what they already do, administrators work with the faculty to create something new. In its annual report, the SRUWC presents each partnership individually, rather than grouping them under broader categories like those in table 1.1. This decision reflects the SRUWC's emphasis on customization and their attempt to see each partnership as new, individual, and context specific.

Table 1.1. SRUWC partnerships

Approach	Mode	Disciplinary Partners
Discipline-Specific (includes course-embedded tutoring models) Consultants receive context-specific training to work within a particular discipline or course so that they can work with faculty on assignment design and help students with writing projects.	Face-to-face or online; individual or group	Architecture; Biology; Biotechnology; Business (undergraduate); College of Education; Digital Media; Economics; Marketing; ELET; History; Math; Nutrition; Women's Studies/GLBT
Writing Studio Consultants meet with students outside of class to work on writing assignments and facilitate group peer review.	Face-to-face or online; group	Art History; English; College of Technology; History; Honor's College (thesis writing groups)
Assessment- and/or Portfolio-Based[a] Upper administrator or project manager design student-writing assessment and work with faculty to create writing support based on the results.	Face-to-face or online; individual	Business (MBA and undergraduate); Graduate College of Social Work; College of Education Teacher Education Program, Law Center, College of Technology
Workshop-Based Project manager designs workshops to take place inside or outside of class to fit particular departmental writing needs.	Face-to-face or online; group or class-based	Business (undergraduate); Biology; History; College of Pharmacy; Political Science; Graduate Student Writers
Community Outreach Program/project managers and consultants work with students/clients outside SRU to improve their writing.	Face-to-face; individual, class, or group	Wheatley HS; Kashmere HS; Rice University Religious Studies; Texas Institute for Measurement, Evaluation, and Statistics (TIMES) Research Division
Staff Development, Mentoring, Training[b] Often facilitated by the associate director and experienced staff members, these workshops are most often single events focused on professional development.	Face-to-face or online; individual, class, or group	Bauer College of Business Staff Professional Development; Hybrid Instructor Orientation for English; Hybrid Facilitator Development for English
Curriculum Design/Support Work with individual instructors or departments on assessment, assignment design, development of rubrics, or scaffolding.	NA	Political Science; Engineering; Nutrition

[a] Here, the SRUWC seems to focus on pre-partnership assessment via an "assess and address" approach. In my research, I came across only one assessment of student writing post-partnership. While the SRUWC seems to emphasize assessment, and "action-based research" as Sam describes it, most of it tends to focus on student satisfaction and perceived usefulness of SRUWC services rather than on student writing. A further consideration of the SRUWC and assessment is given in the final section of this chapter.

[b] In addition, under "Faculty Services" on the SRUWC website, the center offers assistance with curriculum design, student writing support models, research and assessment, rubric development, and teaching-assistant training.

WRITING CENTERS AND AGENCY IN THE
TWENTY-FIRST-CENTURY UNIVERSITY

While there is no single way to establish or acquire agency, writing center administrators should consider to what extent their center has agency, and how certain elements contribute to that sense of agency. In the case of the SRUWC, agency is established at least initially by location (separate from English), funding (financial support from across the university), and risk-taking (willingness to act in ways that were perceived by some as controversial). Then, through the writing center's organizational structure, multiple roles enable layered relationships with faculty and students, again enhancing the writing center's sense of agency. In particular, the project manager role is critical in facilitating faculty-consultant-writer relationships outside upper-administrative concerns about assessment, resources, and funding. Finally, through this organizational structure—and perhaps because of it—consultants and writers alike are encouraged to establish and maintain agency: consultants, in both their individual development and collective growth through their paid participation in Reading Group, despite existing outside administrator-led professional development sessions, and students, referred to as writers, who own their papers and are capable of articulating what they mean, even if their writing suggests otherwise.

Even though they are not always able to change location, funding, or organizational structure, writing center administrators can recognize how these elements impact a sense of agency and find ways of creating agency either through or despite these factors. What does seem within grasp is language choice. How do the ways we talk about our writing centers, consultants, student writers, and work encourage or prevent agency? And for whom? How can we create layered relationships in the writing center that support various stakeholders (partners and students) in different yet necessary ways? Especially in writing centers without substantial financial support, establishing agency may depend primarily on how writing center work is approached, positioned, and described.

Furthermore, at least in the case of the SRUWC, the administrators and the disciplinary partners with whom they work tend to lack a sense of agency in regards to the teaching of writing, even though partners likely have a greater sense of agency in other university roles. If such is the case, how might this knowledge inform our work with partners who may not perceive themselves as capable of acting, making decisions, and making meaning around the teaching of writing? In ways similar to their work with student writers, the SRUWC encourages the development of agency with their partners through attention to local context and awareness of the need to build unique, discipline-specific partnerships across campus. The SRUWC administrative staff often discuss their partnership approach in terms of "uniqueness." Hannah (project manager) is perhaps most adamant about it, explaining that there is "not a prescribed model . . . instead, partnerships could take place in any way that they [faculty] wanted," even when faculty do not initially have the pedagogical know-how to create effective support for writing.

Given that the partnership approach is central to the SRUWC and strongly determined by individual partners, chapter 2 explores these relationships from the partners' perspectives more fully through analysis of the language—particularly the metaphors—that they use to talk about their work with the writing center.

APPENDIX 1.1. WRITING CENTER STAFF MATRIX

Melissa	Melissa has been the executive director of the writing center for fifteen years, has a PhD in British literature, and loves her work because "every day is different."
Sam	Sam has been the associated director of the writing center for twelve years, has an MAT in English and a PhD in creative writing, and wanted to work in the writing center to "contribute to student success."
Hannah	Hannah has a BS in communications and is an assistant director of Writing in the Disciplines and is the head of Consultant Management. She started in the writing center because of her interest in writing and helping students.
Jeremy	Jeremy is the STEM program coordinator and leads some consultant training initiatives, has a BA in history, and first began working in the writing center because he needed a job.
Lindsay	Lindsay is an assistant director of the writing center's General Services Programs, has a BA in creative writing and an MA in English, and began her work in the writing center because she "enjoyed the thought of being of service."
Dan	Dan is a program manager who works specifically with developmental English, has a BA in creative writing, and enjoys his writing center work because it allows him to "utilize [his] talents" while "genuinely help[ing] students."
Anne	Anne is the program coordinator for Writing Studios, has a BA in both English and political science, and enjoys the exploratory nature of the writing center.
Max	Max is an assistant director of Writing in the Disciplines and develops hybrid/online training, has an MA in English literature, and is currently working toward a PhD in British and American literature.
Warren	Warren is a program coordinator for Writing Programs and works specifically with the business school and online services. He has an undergraduate degree in creative writing and enjoys his writing center work because it allows him freedom.
Hao	Hao is the technology director at the writing center, has a BS in computer science, directs the web and mobile application development team, and appreciates the writing center's collaborative environment.
Sydney	Sydney graduated in 2014 with a BS in psychology and a minor in education. She enjoys social activism, swing dancing, playing the ukulele, and biking.

Tim	Tim graduated from SRU with a BA in history and a minor in Italian studies. Working at the writing center has allowed him to work with a variety of different academic disciplines. In his free time, he enjoys cooking Italian food, walking around the city, and listening to classic LPs.
Clint	Clint is a communications major and minors in history. He is currently working towards graduating with a degree in interpersonal communications with a minor in history. He intends to obtain an MA in public administration after he graduates.
Claire	Claire graduated with a BA in English and a minor in art history. While planning for graduate school, she is continuing her involvement in the arts with activities like curating, photographing, writing, and leading tours as a docent.
Tania	Tania double majored in English and anthropology and minored in education as an undergrad. She is now a graduate student working on her master's in anthropology.
Leah	Leah completed her undergraduate and graduate degree at SRU. In 2013 she earned her BS in communication sciences and disorders (ComD) with a minor in medicine and society, and in 2015 she earned her MA in ComD with a concentration in medical speech-language pathology.

2

COUNSELORS, TSUNAMIS, AND WELL-OILED MACHINES
Partners Defining Their Writing (Center) Partnerships

Scene @ 16:30 minutes

> CHRIS (biology): So, I'm presuming my students don't know how to write to save their lives, so if you've never written a paper, that's how you can start [prints and hands over copies of his writing guidelines and assignment]. And then this . . .
>
> REBECCA: And most of them haven't done a lot of writing in biology when they get to your class, right?
>
> CHRIS (biology): No. And, I mean, not to be offensive, but the English Department ruins them all so . . .
>
> REBECCA: So, what—in what ways do you see?
>
> CHRIS (biology): So, in the sciences, you know, what we're trying desperately to do is we're trying to teach them how to express ideas, and I mean you guys in English, they're doing the same thing, but the idea is to express their ideas in a succinct way. In other words, get to the point, give us your evidence, give us your hypothesis, give us your evidence, and let's move on. Whereas in the English Department, they're like, "express yourself," and so, the idea here is that we want to strip that "express yourself" out. You're not supposed to be part of the report. It's the material that you're reporting on that's the report. So, you know, part of that is breaking that bad habit. And it's not a bad habit, it's just not appropriate for the field.

During my forty-minute interview with Chris, a biology professor, I had to bite my tongue. While I was impressed with his candid descriptions and his lack of concern about how I, an English teacher, would respond to his criticisms, Chris's account of his students' writing was troubling. He built his entire pedagogy on the premise that "students don't know how to write to save their lives," and he blamed their "ruin" on the English Department. Here, successful writing is linked to survival. If students were in a life-or-death situation they would not, Chris suggests, be able to write their way out of it. *Survival* requires the ability to keep living "in spite of an accident, ordeal, or difficult circumstances"

https://doi.org/10.7330/9781646421770.c002

(*Oxford English Dictionary*, hereinafter *OED*), which, in this case, writing presents. As we continued our interview, Chris discussed his partnership with the SRUWC as one way to help students survive their writing, using additional clinical, mechanistic, and corporate metaphors to describe how he understood writing and his partnership with the SRUWC.

Analyzing metaphor in talk about writing, alongside more explicit statements, provides another layer of meaning that both reveals and masks writing experience. In *Metaphor and Writing: Figurative Thought in Written Communication*, Philip Eubanks argues that we can learn much about writing and writers by examining our use of figurative language and metaphor in storytelling and our everyday conversations. In particular, Eubanks says, metaphors "are enmeshed in a constellation of relationships that complicate what people mean by them and how they are likely to influence people's writing" (2011, 2). Thus, when four figurative language clusters emerged from interviews with partners from across the disciplines, I paid close attention, as they indicated prevalent underlying attitudes toward writing and writing centers.

In this chapter, I present four metaphor clusters that emerge from my data: clinical, survival, mechanistic, and corporate. Whereas the use of clinical metaphors forwards the idea that the SRUWC is a place for students in need of counseling and diagnostics (such as references to "the counselors in the writing center" who "are very good at knowing how to diagnose the program"), survival metaphors indicate that the SRUWC is also necessary for both student and teacher subsistence (e.g., the writing center helped with the "burden of paper grading" that can only go so far as the "human limit"). Mechanistic metaphors perpetuate the idea of writing center as "fix-it shop" and writing as primarily skill-based (e.g., referring to the writing center as a "tool" with partnerships that run like "well-oiled machines"), yet also recognize the degree of specialization involved in writing center work and the disciplinary identity of writing studies. Corporate metaphors provide the context for and language in which these cross-disciplinary "partnerships" were understood by the partners themselves, as well as a recognition of their transactional and customer-service elements. Overall, clinical, survival, mechanistic, and corporate metaphors reflect an awareness of the SRUWC's agency, as a unit that can effectively impact writing instruction, curriculum, and student writing.

To understand this agency, we must look past our assumptions about what these metaphors seem to mean and instead see the implied professionalism and care in clinical metaphors; the crucial support needed and provided in the context of survival metaphors; the recognized expertise evident in the use of mechanistic metaphors; and the willingness to be collaborative, innovative, and supportive of writing in the use of corporate metaphors. Even though the four major clusters—clinical, survival, mechanistic, and corporate—use language that tends to be associated with remediation, marginalization, and business-model approaches to education, the talk that surrounds these metaphors suggests otherwise. First, these clusters imply a recognition of the writing center's agency, expertise, and necessity in the university as well as a strong sense of respect for writing center work. Second, partners do not always act in ways that reflect the assumptions embedded in their language use. Finally, despite some initial misperceptions about the writing center and/or their initial beliefs about writing, partners are willing to change their understanding of and approach to writing through partnership.

These findings also suggest that our potential writing center partners may not be who we assume them to be. For instance, Chris's assumptions about English teachers represent much of what the field of writing studies has been working against for the past couple of decades, making him seem like the kind of person who would not make for a good partner for the writing center. Although Chris's assumptions do not necessarily represent reality, they are significant because he seemed to draw directly on his students' writing experiences and abilities—perhaps both perceived and real—to formulate his beliefs. Besides, he is a dedicated writing teacher. This became clear as he described his multilevel peer-review process for his Biology 3324: Human Physiology course and proudly shared his complex writing assignment: six pages of guidelines, six pages of instructions, four pages of possible topics/prompts, and six pages of rubric and writing evaluation information. Chris is also a supporter of the SRUWC, despite claiming that he was "kind of forced" into the relationship. To receive a grant that would pay for a piece of lab software, Chris and the Biology Department had to "prove to the university that we were doing something special." Since science majors often struggle with writing, Chris's department created a writing assignment to go with the lab that would use the new software, thus justifying the department's use of the grant.

Although Chris admits that the Biology Department incorporates writing into its assignment and initially works with the writing center to get the new software, he also notes the partnership's impact on writing: "Students who went [to the writing center], their grades went up." In this case, the SRUWC offers something that the first-year writing program cannot: a context-specific approach to writing support within a curriculum created by faculty in the disciplines. The SRUWC itself is not tied to its own programmatic objectives the same way an office of first-year writing is, nor is it tied to a staff primarily made up of English faculty and graduate students. In the case of supporting Chris and his students, undergraduate peer writing consultants with backgrounds in the sciences are likely better suited to work with his students than consultants or instructors with backgrounds in English. Or maybe, the degree of discipline-specific familiarity is not all that important here, but the SRUWC's willingness and ability to work within his specific curricular structure matters most. In a sense, Chris's experience seems to justify why it makes sense for the SRUWC to be housed outside the English Department; Chris's writing center partnership helps him teach students how to write in biology, something the English Department did not, and perhaps could not, do.

Since it is willing to work with nearly all faculty on discipline-specific writing support, the SRUWC develops a steady reputation as an approachable program. This is likely due to its willingness to engage in what Tiffany Rousculp calls a "rhetoric of respect," which requires active engagement from partners whose contributions help shape programmatic structures. Rather than insisting on their own expertise and "essentialness" to the development of a writing partnership, the SRUWC focuses on conversation and building relationships (Rousculp 2014, 100). This approach also "draws attention to how we use language in relation with others; how we name and classify, how we collaborate, how we problem-solve" (25). If we work from this assumption, then we have to be interested in understanding language use that differs from our own and even be willing to change our language in pursuit of creating common ground and understanding.

Attention to figurative language and metaphor is part of this process, and writing studies as a discipline has long been interested in what figurative language suggests about writing. Most recently, scholars have focused on metaphor in writing program administration that indicates both similarities and differences across experiences (Naydan 2018; Phillips, Shovlin, and Titus 2018; Adams Wooten, Babb, and Ray 2018). For instance, Nikki Caswell, Jackie Grutsch McKinney, and Rebecca Jackson (2016) acknowledge the cultural function of metaphor and its connection to rhetorical action for new writing center directors, which reveal similarities across institutional contexts, thus giving us a sense of trends in the larger field. Alternatively, Jennifer Riley Campbell and Richard Colby's use of metaphor show how two people can experience their work in the same position through different metaphorical lenses. These scholars intentionally use metaphor and narrative to make sense of their administrative work, a move that many before them have made (George 1999; Baker et al. 2005; Brown and Enos 2002; Brueggemann 1992).

Yet, few studies have explored metaphor use by teachers of writing outside the field of writing studies, with the exception of Neil Baird and Bradley Dilger's 2017 article, "Metaphors for Writing Transfer in the Writing Lives and Teaching Practices of Faculty in the Disciplines." These scholars found that instructors across the disciplines used simple (i.e., encompassing only small change, often through application), rather than adaptive (i.e., involving active repurposing or transformation of writing knowledge), metaphors in their teaching, but mapped these metaphor types onto existing categories established by WPA scholars rather than enabling interviewees to create their own.

However, there is great value in considering metaphor use among disciplinary faculty's experiences with writing and SRUWC partnerships on their own terms. This work requires engaging with the implications of metaphor that both align and conflict with the SRUWC's perceptions in particular and writing studies' values in general. Rather than dismissing, tolerating, or overlooking differences due to the writing center's (or writing studies') perceived expertise in writing instruction, working from a rhetoric of respect means attempting to understand and value "multiple views, approaches" (Rousculp 2014, 25), even when they are different from our own. This can be a challenge for writing center administrators who are used to taking on the role of expert, one that some partners expect from them. In the interviews conducted for this book, disciplinary faculty and administrators use metaphor extensively in their descriptions of writing center/departmental partnerships. By identifying both larger patterns across talk and attempting to understand the implications of specific word choices, writing centers can learn more about how partners perceive their work.

The most prevalent metaphor cluster, which appears in every single interview, is corporate, or business-like, language in reference to both the value of writing and SRUWC partnerships as a commodity (such as the writing center being a "rare amenity" with "customers"). These clusters have specific implications for how writing centers can work with departments across campus via strategic partnerships and reveal perceptions of collaborative work with a twenty-first-century university writing center. In particular, they offer more nuanced ways of viewing our work together, through metaphors that suggest that writing center work is both remedial and meaningful as well as necessary for survival. They also put forth the mechanistic concept of writing as a tool/skill for the workplace, while using corporate language to describe writing program "partnerships," both of which can be used to inform writing program collaborations across disciplines. In particular, many of these partners embrace Tiffany Rousculp's concept of "writing partner" through a rhetoric of respect that acknowledges the SRUWC's strengths and values as well as their own. The relational elements of these partnerships that create and sustain a rhetoric of respect differentiate the SRUWC not only from other writing programs on campus, but also from potential replacement when disruptive innovations emerge. As discussed in chapter 1, relationships rooted in partnership help build social capital (Hall 2010) that enables trust across partners, as resources are shared in a mutually beneficial scenario. When the writing center has social capital, both existing and potential partners are more likely to turn to the writing center for support, rather than searching for external, third-party options.

CORPORATE METAPHORS: BUILDING
WRITING (CENTER) PARTNERSHIPS

While metaphor types across administrators and faculty varied, corporate metaphors were used by *all*. These metaphors surfaced both explicitly and implicitly. For instance, the most explicit use of business language was in direct reference to the monetary exchanges that occurred between the SRUWC and some departments. Although this topic is taboo throughout this research, five interviewees noted that their own departments or colleges were at least partially funding the partnerships—Charley (hotel and restaurant management), Kyle (business), Tara (law), Linda (math), and Carol (marketing). This literal business-model practice of exchanging goods or services for money was discussed as "the cost estimate process," which took place most explicitly in the larger programmatic partnerships at the college level with deans (Business, Hotel and Restaurant Management, and Law). When asked about how the writing center partnership approach could be improved, Charley suggests a menu of options with cost estimates:

> [The writing center should] have a menu of services versus cost, and talk about outcomes for each one. Because I think that's important to know upfront. Too often we think about building partnerships, and then at the end of the day, we say here's your price tag. Well, it's impossible. So, I think a menu of services versus costs associated with outcomes is really critical.

The corporate language implies that the writing center should operate like a restaurant, something not surprising given Charley's disciplinary background, where faculty and deans become the customers and the writing center the salespeople of writing instruction. Unsurprisingly, though, these participants also describe their relationships using heavily corporate and business-related metaphors. For example, as Charley discusses what made his partnership with the writing center work, he says this:

> One was realistic expectations. They already had this model working with [the business school], so it wasn't something we were creating from scratch, so they had a model we could use. The second piece is, I think, they were upfront on the deliverables. And I think . . . they never over-promise, and what they said is, a couple times, and I love Sam [writing center director] for this, he goes, "If you want this, absolutely. Here's the money associated with this." And then I said, "Phew! Can we do this for somewhat less?" . . . Let's build them into teams and put a graduate assistant there and not a full-time staff member. So, you know, my expectations were modified by their perceptions of what they could do.

For Charley, "realistic expectations" are linked to "upfront deliverables," which are worked out via conversations about cost. Mapping out how the partnership will work logistically in terms of resources and costs seems to communicate to Charley the labor involved in supporting writing on a large-scale, programmatic level. Alongside this economic discussion of how the writing center would work, Charley also notes that the success of the partnership is linked to its relationality, collaborative nature, and honesty. He describes his partnership with the writing center as all about building a strong relationship through trust, and he explicitly states that they are "not sales jobs . . . not a service," despite his suggestion about offering a menu of options.

While the five interviewees who pay for their writing center partnerships have very explicit business-model relationships with the writing center, the other six also use corporate metaphors to describe their relationships, meaning that these qualities were present regardless of whether or not there was an exchange of money. For instance, Amir (architecture) describes the writing center as a "rare amenity" and one that he, as a new tenure-track faculty member, found "invaluable to the instructors, the professors, and the students too." Perhaps the most enthusiastic writing center supporter, Amir describes the advantage of having students work with both writing center consultants and professors because it provided them with multiple perspectives on their writing. Near the end of our interview, Amir returns to the idea of the writing center as an amenity with success evident in its products:

> I know there are other institutions that don't have this amenity. Since I joined, I've been thrilled to have this amenity available. The writing center

is a model, in some ways, that other institutions could emulate. I really do feel like the proof is in the product, and they already have a very strong contribution that they're making.

As Amir discusses writing center as amenity, he highlights the positive connotations of the word; he suggests that writing centers are desirable and luxurious places, that partnerships are pleasant and special, and that this kind of resource was rare, something that other institutions don't have. But he also links the amenity and its value to the extent to which it provides "proof in the product," although he doesn't mention what exactly that product is or how it is measured.

The most prominent corporate metaphor used by administrators and faculty is more implicit. They use the concept of "partnership" to describe the relationship between their program and the writing center. These two parties act as "partners," who are at times "engaged in the same activity" of providing adequate writing support for students and at other times, or sometimes instead, are the kind of "partners" who have "interests and investments in a business or enterprise, among whom expense, profits, and losses are shared" (*OED*). In other words, some partnerships keep students and student writing at the center of the relationship while others seem equally focused on outcomes, product, assessment, and the monetary exchange that should guarantee their satisfaction as customers. Even in those partnerships that function via a more corporate model, student writing was still a concern, even if overshadowed by the business model. Thus, these different kinds of partnerships are not mutually exclusive. Faculty and administrators discuss their partnership work with the writing center in such detail that certain qualities emerge across interviews, including relationality, collaboration, logistics, honesty, and flexibility, as table 2.1 shows. As table 2.1 also shows, most interviewees emphasize how their partnerships with the writing center were relational, collaborative, and honest. In particular, interviewees discuss "collaboration," although their definitions for this word varied. Therefore, this concept should be thought of as both a teamwork/healthy relationship kind of term and a business-oriented, unequal relationship kind of term.

The presence of corporate metaphor across all administrators and faculty in their talk about working with the SRUWC suggests that, at least to some extent, they all view their relationship in business terms. This is not necessarily a bad thing, especially in conversations with deans who help financially support the partnership. Further, this professional, corporate approach is perhaps what some writing centers want, as the notable shift in terminology from tutor/student to consultant/client language further works toward a professional, businesslike writing

Table 2.1. Administrator and faculty perceptions of writing center partnerships

Quality of Partnership	Definition	Who Recognized It
Relational	Partnerships are about building "relation-ships" that "work because [they] trust each other." They are "not sales jobs" and are "not a service."	72% (n=8)
Collaborative	Partners "work together to create something" via "listening" and "talking through the process."	100% (n=11)
Logistical	Partnerships involve determining a "cost estimate" before any work begins and could work best from a "menu of services versus cost" and "outcomes for each one."	55% (n=6)
Honest	Partnerships are "built on trust" and, thus, partners must try to be "transparent," have "honest discussions," work from "good faith effort," and set "realistic expectations."	91% (n=10)
Flexible and Adaptive	Partners meet regularly to discuss "how the project went" and to "provide feedback" to one another that is then used to "improve for next time."	64% (n=7)

center persona (Hallman 2016). The concept of "partnership" as a particular kind of relationship between disciplinary programs and SRUWC collaborations seemed to speak across disciplines and thus offers writing programs a useful language from which to collaborate. To provide a better sense of how particular partners perceive "partnership," two stories—one from a long-term partner, one from a new partner—are shared below.

Charley's Hotel and Restaurant Management Ten-Year SRUWC Partnership

The Hotel and Restaurant Management (HRM) program's partnership with the writing center began over ten years ago and is attached to two courses: a sophomore-level law course and a junior/senior-level leadership course. Students spend one day "at lecture" in the hotel and restaurant management building and one day a week working on their writing assignments in groups at the writing center. This "hybrid model" became the structure when Charley received too much pushback from students about meeting in the writing center "above their classroom experience," so instead, the writing center group meetings became literally half of the class time itself.

Since Charley never taught these courses but rather worked from the position of associate dean to set the partnership up, most of our conversation focused on that process and what made it work. Charley explains that the partnership is built through three initiatives: (1) the writing center's help with design; (2) the university's writing across the curriculum (WAC) requirement; and (3) the fact that the department itself had identified writing to be a "major critical problem" among its students. The work with the writing center began simultaneously with the WAC curriculum initiative, and thus the SRUWC worked with Charley to incorporate writing into already existing courses. Charley explains:

> We never claim to be the experts. The writing lab really did the best job of working with us to lay that out. So, we didn't tell the writing lab, "These are the three things." What we said is, "We want them to improve their writing," and they came to us with a good plan. And, they work one-on-one with the instructors . . . the writing lab was more customized depending on the instructor's needs. Which I think made it—and that's the reason we've had a relationship now for almost ten years.

Here, Charley suggests that the writing center partners are the writing experts, and part of their job is to "plan" how student writing could be improved. The one-on-one instructor-based customization helps make the partnership sustainable. Charley further explains that the writing center developed the rubrics to go along with the hotel and restaurant management assignments, and the center also gave instructors "some broad guidelines . . . to fit assignments into, like 'Students need to edit their work at least once or twice.'" From there, Charley says that they tried to make the writing assignments "the responsibility of the instructor," but that did not work; so instead they moved to a "new format where it's peer evaluation, which tends to be better in terms of resources." After about three years, the department's partnership with the writing center began to fall into a rhythm. Charley says that they did have to work through some changes, one of which included making the students' work in the writing center a part of the class itself. The second change relates to faculty involvement, and a moving away from attempts to train faculty to evaluate their own students and toward a "peer evaluation" model, where students in the course are trained by a writing center consultant to evaluate one another.

Amir's Architecture Two-Year Partnership with the SRUWC

Providing the perspective of a relatively new SRUWC partner, Amir (architecture) speaks at length when I ask him what makes the partnership work well for him:

It's collaborative, first and foremost. I think that's a key part of it—we're working together to achieve the same goal, which is to facilitate and enable students to improve their writing. So, there's a shared goal structure. I think it's also really important that from the beginning we clarify our own independent roles, too. So, I know from experience that the consultants generally will not be able to address and are not intended to address issues of content. They're not there to give the students additional resources and references relative to the discipline. They're not really there to offer a critique of the philosophies—that's really my domain, that's really what I offer as the professor. So, there's a clarification of some specificity to what each participant offers to the collaboration, and I think it's really great that we set that up really early. And the students know that. They don't go to the writing center with the expectation that they're going to find someone who can give them hyper-specific knowledge on architecture and design. They know that, and they understand that, and they almost in some ways take advantage of it. They tweak their language and their discourse to ensure that it's accessible.

Other positive parts of it—I think the ongoing, continuing connectivity over the course of the semester is great too. The writing center, and all the others that are there are very communicative, they're always keeping me in the loop and vice versa, and I try to be as responsive as I can be, as well. If things come up or when anomalies emerge, we are able to respond to it very quickly and very efficiently because of the communication that's very strong. Other issues that are very helpful—I think that the feedback that I receive from the writing center has been invaluable too. So, they're very willing to offer feedback to help make the experience even better. And I'm willing to do that as well. It's a two-way street where we work with each other and we are willing to discuss with each other how to make the relationship even better.

While some of his language does carry corporate terminology (e.g., *consultants, shared goal structure*), Amir's description of his partnership with the SRUWC is not focused on faculty satisfaction or a concept of writing as instrumental. In addition, Amir's enthusiasm and commitment to teaching writing suggest that his satisfaction is linked to improved student writing. And while the assumption that disciplinary knowledge is primarily content based and thus separate from writing is problematic, it also acknowledges the complex labor involved in the teaching of writing and how people unversed in composition pedagogy might especially struggle to navigate curricular decisions like scaffolding assignments, using rubrics, encouraging drafting and peer reviews, and working with new disciplinary writers.

MECHANISTIC METAPHORS: THE WRITING
CENTER AS A TOOL FOR WRITING

Working from a similar assumption about writing as separate from disciplinary content, 73 percent of administrators and faculty (n=8) use mechanistic metaphors, yet in a variety of ways. For instance, they refer to their SRUWC partnerships as both like and unlike a machine, to writing as a kind of "skilling" or mechanics that is both simple and complex, to writing studies as a field of study with specialized disciplinary content. Some of the same mechanistic metaphor types also conflicted in terms of how they are used. For instance, Charley (hotel and restaurant management), Kyle (business), and Chris (biology) all describe their writing center partnerships as functional machines or tools. Chris (biology) uses this kind of mechanistic metaphor below:

> When I say collaboration, I mean you guys [at the writing center] have the skills and the know-how to have it done, but ultimately, it would be me saying, "this is the skill that I want done, right, that I can't accomplish in the context of my classroom," so you become that extra tool in my belt, and that's not a great way to think of yourself. . . . [T]hat's a horrible way to think about it [laughs]—I'm the tool in the belt of the faculty, but the fact of the matter is that, even though you're an entity unto yourselves, really you are a tool for all of the other departments to come and say, "fix these problems." But at the same time, I don't mean to diminish the role. . . . [I]t's an important role.

In Chris's description above, the writing center has little agency. While he does acknowledge the writing center as a place staffed by people who have "skills" and "know-how" as well as the "important role" the writing center serves, he also says it functions simply as a tool that attempts to teach the desired skills of the instructor. The role of the student is also absent from this depiction of "collaboration." As he speaks, Chris recognizes that reducing the writing center to a tool of the faculty was problematic, yet he proceeds with the metaphor anyway and reinforces the idea a second time: "really you are a tool for all of the other departments."

Working from the same idea of writing center as tool, Kyle (business) argues that after several years, his partnership with the writing center was "running like a well-oiled machine." Likewise, Charley (hotel and restaurant management) suggests that "at some point, [writing instruction] has to be put on cruise control. And what I mean by that is, it needs to be like IT—once you build it, it goes on the back shelf and operates. And I know that sounds horrible, but there's too many activities going on." Both Kyle and Charley seem to believe that writing instruction, once figured out, can operate on its own, seemingly without the need for further updates or maintenance. Both Kyle and Charley are also deans, meaning that they are not involved in the day-to-day operations of the partnership and in many ways had a low level of stakeholder engagement. Thus, they are likely not aware of the particularities of the partnerships in practice and the small changes that are made over time. Further, Kyle's experience, even as a dean, with the business school's SRUWC partnerships shows how even well-established relationships change over time, as described in chapter 4. Thus, despite their suggestion that partnerships can run automatically as machines without error, both Charley and Kyle also describe important moments of change, indicating that in practice, neither ran like a machine.

Still working from this idea of writing center as a machine, Rick (art history) uses mechanistic metaphor to describe what his writing center partnership is *not*:

> For me, it's not providing a service; it's more like forging a team around the practice of writing and feedback. And I feel like I'm just part of that team. I don't feel like the writing center is giving me some of the "fuel-me service," like I'm getting my car filled up, while I'm here teaching. . . . I think that it started kind of like that, but that did not create the transformational sort of events that I think led to the successful collaboration.

Here, Rick acknowledges that the writing center can function as a kind of "fuel-me service" in the way that Chris (biology), Kyle (business), and Charley (hotel and restaurant management) suggest it does—as a tool or service paid to accomplish certain goals. Yet, he also argues that the partnership can become "transformational," when all parties "forge a team around the practice of writing and feedback." Rick's explanation suggests that his partnership with the writing center became collaborative over time, which indicates that perceptions about teaching writing and writing centers can shift. He acknowledges that his teaching is not an activity separate from the writing instruction students receive in their work with the writing center, but rather sees them as integrated.

Even more common than the use of mechanistic metaphor to describe writing partnerships as a machine is the idea of writing as a mechanistic, skill-based process. While skill is associated with expertise and the ability to do something well, the concept of "skilling" is linked to training a worker to do a particular task (*OED*). The worker who is "skilled" or "skilling" often uses tools to assist in carrying out a particular function connected to physical labor. A tool is a "device . . . especially one held in the hand" (*OED*). Just as the pencil or computer can be considered a tool for writing, so too is the skill of writing itself a kind of tool, at least in the etymological sense. As well as being considered a thing, a tool can also be a person who is used or exploited by another. Thus, writing centers and consultants can also be considered tools used in the process of "skilling" or helping others acquire a particular skill, as Chris suggested. When university administrators and disciplinary faculty consider writing to be a skill, they evoke the idea of writing as a tool, which negates any mental labor. This way of thinking implies that writing is not about thinking but about reproducing a physical labor.

Building from the idea of "skilling" as a way of training a worker for a particular task, administrators and faculty regularly suggest a writing-as-skill approach that seems to work from the premise that writing is a necessary skill or tool for getting a job, and that writing instruction should work from this awareness. These ideas conflict with major theories in writing studies, especially the idea that writing is developmental and that all writers have more to learn (Adler-Kassner and Wardle 2015). Further, since genres and audiences are always changing, even within specific disciplines, writing studies scholars tend to believe that there is no generalized definition of "good writing." Yet, the SRUWC partners seemed to believe in such a concept.

Making a direct association between writing and skill, Amir discusses the "mechanics" of writing as concepts that are best taught by those in writing centers, all the while recognizing that there are some architecture-specific approaches to writing.[1] Amir explains that the writing center partnership allows him to focus on content, rather than on mechanics and other writing-specific issues. He says:

> A key thing that [writing center partnerships] offer that I should clarify is that it lets me as the professor really just focus on the content. I don't have to spend as much time . . . on the mechanics, the structure, the articulation, the formulation of the arguments, the rhetoric of writing. So, the writing center really liberates me to really focus on my own expertise as an architect. And that's thrilling.

Amir suggests that his "expertise as an architect" is different from the writing center's expertise in writing. Although he uses *mechanics*, he further qualifies what he means by listing four other elements of writing that are higher-order writing concerns.

Carol (marketing) explains that her partnership with the writing center means, "I don't have to get down to the sentence level. . . . I hate to use the word *mechanics*, but I guess you're handling the mechanics of improving a draft." Although she refers to writing simply as "mechanics" here, Carol offers more nuanced writing and communication advice to students during her class, where she emphasizes the importance of clear communication over any other grammatical or writing-based issues, asks her students to imagine their audience as they write, and spends a large amount of class time having students talk through their research projects for both experts and nonexperts. Much of Carol's feedback attempts to reiterate to students their projects, as she understands them, and to help them talk in concrete, rather than abstract, terms.

Although not explicitly, both Amir and Carol follow their descriptions of writing support as mechanics with descriptions that extend that work. This indicates that "mechanics" may simply be the first thing that comes to mind when university administrators and disciplinary faculty think about teaching writing; they are not necessarily reducing all writing instruction to a single idea of writing "mechanics." Simplified ways of talking about writing and writing center work as focused on mechanics, sometimes as grammar, may actually suggest a lack of writing studies knowledge and language more than a narrow understanding of writing and teaching writing. Given these responses, a focus on "writing mechanics" may also include attention to audience, organization, source integration, clarity, analysis, and argument.

While the mechanistic metaphor types discussed so far have been somewhat problematic in their view of writing (and writing centers) first as a kind of machine or tool, and second as a kind of skill-based, mechanical process, there is also a third way interviewees used mechanistic metaphors, and it works against the idea of "skill" as remedial. Although it stems from the idea that disciplinary content is separate from writing knowledge, several administrators and faculty make this distinction to indicate an understanding of writing as a professional field with content and best practices of its own. For instance, Morgan (computer science) explains that she began her partnership out of frustration: "I didn't have the skills. I don't know how to teach people how to write, so I needed that help from the writing center. And that's what makes it a good partnership." Through her work with the writing center, she learns that her assumptions about them and about writing in general are wrong:

> I thought [the writing center] would do copy editing on students' work . . . so clearly, my impression was wrong, but I learned that they actually do something deeper, something more important, which is helping students to effectively express their thoughts in the written form. And so, I think that helps me better understand—I learned that I shouldn't be copyediting students' work. I should be saying, "This is clear, you did a good job here. This is not clear, this is why it's not clear, we need to talk about it." I also learned that the writing process doesn't start when pen meets paper—you open your file and you start typing. There's a whole thought process that goes into it. And that you can actually clarify some of your ideas by talking about them and then it's easier to commit them to paper.

Here, Morgan acknowledges that the SRUWC goes beyond copy-editing and does complex work that involves helping students "express their thoughts in written form." Her example comment suggests a working knowledge of effective teacher feedback that includes praise, explanations for suggestions, and the invitation for a conversation about writing. Further, Morgan recognizes a "process" involved in writing and that students often benefit from talking about writing and ideas alongside the activity of writing itself.

Like Morgan, Rick (art history) recognizes writing studies as a field with scholarly content. He explains that one valuable aspect of his partnership, perhaps what helps create a partnership that was "transformational" rather than a "fuel-me service," with the writing center has to do with learning about writing pedagogy as it relates to art history. Rick explains:

> I did not control any literature in rhetoric, writing pedagogy, you know, just even data, like, the idea of thinking about how students react to comments and when you give them. That was just completely foreign to me. . . . I do not have the time, nor do I really have the inclination to, like, master the literature myself—but it's really important to have people you trust telling you things that are coming from that . . . and I think that's when I started thinking about writing in the disciplines more seriously and the idea of students not mastering the discourse but sort of getting into a particular conversation/discourse like art history.

In the above comment, a few important things are happening. Rick suggests that basic writing studies–based practices are "completely foreign" to those teaching writing in the disciplines. Rick even admits that in his work with the writing center, he began to realize that "if you scribble red all over something at the end of the semester and then leave it out in front of your door, it just does not do very much good. And I believed that immediately because I'd seen it for fifteen years." Then, he recognizes the value of learning about rhetoric and writing from people in the field and using that knowledge to inform his own approach to writing instruction. Finally, he explains that learning about rhetoric and writing helped him think about writing in art history as *introducing* students to a conversation, not *mastering* the discourse. For him, the partnership with the writing center was valuable because the writing center "respect[ed] the passion of the discipline . . . [and the writing center partners were] really interested in the art historical discourse. Not that they were going to, like, master it and then tell me about it, but that they really respected the passion that we had here, for turning out really seriously trained people." Rick suggests that discipline-specific knowledge was not necessary for effective writing tutoring; writing studies knowledge and a respect for, and interest in, art history were sufficient.

Administrator and faculty use of mechanistic metaphors put forth several ideas about writing. First, they suggest that writing center collaborations can be both machine-like and not machine-like, yet in practice, even the "machine-like" partnerships change and adapt. Second, they imply that writing instruction is skill-based, and that writing mechanics, although seemingly reductive, involve attention to organization, source integration, clarity, analysis, sentence-level issues, and argument, along with audience awareness. Third, their understanding of disciplinary content and writing mechanics as separate in part indicates a recognition of writing studies as a professional field with content and knowledge expertise different from other academic disciplines.

Use of mechanistic metaphor in administrator and faculty talk complicates what are often assumed to be simplistic approaches to writing as skill-based; writing as skill, according to some, does not necessarily imply a lack of expertise, but rather constitutes some recognition of writing studies as a discipline. These approaches position writing center administrators as expert in writing instruction, yet do not quite acknowledge the valuable role that disciplinary faculty can and should play in writing instruction. In other words, administrators and faculty seem to work under the premise that disciplinary content and writing instruction are separate, rather than recognizing that content and form are complexly intertwined.

CLINICAL AND SURVIVAL METAPHORS: WRITING (CENTER) AS REMEDIAL LIFELINE?

Despite their assumptions about writing as a skill separate from content, partners also recognize the relational and necessary role of the writing consultant in their work with student writers. For example, 64 percent of interviewees (n=7) use clinical metaphors, which include the words *counselors* and *counseling*, much more frequently than *tutor/tutoring* or *consultant/consulting*. While writing center studies have continuously debated what writing center practitioners should be called (Hallman 2014; McCall 1994; Runciman 1990; Russell 1999), the idea of writing centers as staffed by counselors is not a label that has been embraced. For instance, Peter Carino (1992) notes the field's earliest conceptions as writing clinics or writing labs and acknowledges this history as problematically contributing to writing centers' continued remedial identity. Meanwhile, Leigh Ryan and Lisa Zimmerelli acknowledge "counselor" as one of the "many hats" a tutor wears (2015, 31), even though this hat appears last in a list with seven others.

One typical example of how interviewees used *counselor* in their talk about writing comes from Chris (biology), as he explains,

> And so, where I think the writing center really benefits the students . . . when you have well-trained counselors, they can break that habit and say, "This is what the assignment says. Where in your paper have you done x?" And that forces the student to kind of confront their own writing to say, "Aha, it's not there."

Here, Chris connects the role of "counselors" to those who could break student habits so that they better follow Chris's expectations as professor. The particular habit being broken is not clear, and the work being done in the scenario Chris describes actually seems more focused on teaching students how to interpret discipline-specific assignment prompts than on habit breaking.

The persistence of clinical language among those who collaborate with the writing center is telling. Although writing centers may be inclined to resist identification with clinical language because of its association with the remedial, there may be elements worth embracing. Traditionally, *counseling* involves "guidance on personal, social or psychological problems," as well as "guidance in resolving" these kinds of problems or difficulties (*OED*). A counselor is someone who both "advises" and is an "advisor," as well as someone who "specializes in the counseling of clients," and "one who consults." Given that writing itself is a personal, social, and psychological activity (Adler-Kassner and Wardle 2015), writing consultants may indeed be called on to work through problems related to these areas.

Further, if *counselor* carries with it the concept of a specialized advisor, then perhaps there is something to be gained from this term and its use by writing center partners. While the idea of a medical clinic staffed with doctors evokes illness, short visits, diagnoses, and medication, counseling often involves regular meetings over a longer period of time, where the goal is to "empower" individuals by equipping them with "strategies to overcome obstacles and personal challenges" through a collaborative process of talking, listening, goal setting, improving self-esteem, and encouraging healthier behavior patterns (American Counseling Association). In counseling, the end goal is client autonomy and agency. Given that the SRUWC attempts to recognize student writers' agency, the idea of writing consulting as counseling is not necessarily so far off the mark.

Similarly, the concept of diagnosis within the writing center context has some drawbacks, while simultaneously communicating something both significant and potentially beneficial. For example, Walt (English Department chair) explains that the writing center director and her staff were "very good at knowing how to diagnose the kind of programs that would be good for those units, those departments." Rather than associating diagnosis with an individual, Walt suggests that diagnoses are made programmatically, perhaps indicating an underlying pedagogical issue, and that the writing center is "very good" at uncovering.

The idea of the writing center performing this kind of diagnostics is indicative of the partners' respect for the SRUWC's work and an acknowledgment of its expertise. To *diagnose* means to "distinguish and determine [a disease's] nature from its symptoms; to recognize and identify by careful observation" (*OED*). While the act of diagnosing student writers goes against writing center pedagogy that recognizes writing as developmental, making programmatic assessments has different implications. Walt's example above positions writing center administrators as the experts who make the diagnosis, or the match between the department and the kind of partnership that will support student writing. When read with Chris's use of "well-trained counselors" who can help students "break" (and perhaps learn new) habits, the writing center becomes not only a place with agency and expertise, but also a place where students can develop agency as writers.

The idea of the writing center as a place of counseling and diagnostics positions it as a support center for instructors and students who are struggling. This struggle is also visible among the 73 percent of interviewees (n=8) who used survival metaphors to talk about how SRUWC partnerships help alleviate the amount of work involved in responding to papers and grading them. These interviewees seem aware of the labor involved in teaching writing and were often able to differentiate between their role as writing teachers and that of the writing center in supporting student writers. Yet, they also express a concern about the well-being of instructors. For instance, Kyle (dean of business) describes the managing of student writing itself as a threat to survival. In his description of staff limitations and the "burden" of evaluating student writing, he explains, "what was happening was, think of it like this tsunami of papers to grade all at once." Although he does not connect this threat to its impact on individuals, Kyle seems to think about the workload of paper grading as something that could be survived with support from the writing center.

Speaking to his own individual experience, Rick (art history) notes that the writing-intensive course he taught was the only one in the college and was far too big. Rick explained, "forty-nine students in there. . . . It's killer. If it were not for the writing [center] experiences and a good TA, it would be impossible." Similarly, Linda (math) describes her initial approach to feedback on student writing as a two-week process that involved reading, annotating, commenting, and grading. She explains, "It is really intense, and I do it three times during the semester and one time during finals. Phew, what a job. What a chore." Linda admits that conferencing with each student as they drafted these essays, a needed activity, was beyond her, since there is a "human limit on what you can do." Hence, she begins working with the writing center to help her manage the labor of teaching writing.

These depictions of student writing as labor-intensive, chore-like, and taken to the human limit are likely familiar. Yet, the awareness that administrators and faculty have of this work is encouraging, as is their understanding of writing center partnerships as necessary to their own survival. While *limit* suggests a boundary "beyond which something ceases to be possible or allowable," it also may indicate "the worse imaginable or endurable . . . the last straw" (*OED*). When coupled with the concept of "burden," the need for a sense of shared responsibility and collaborative work becomes even more necessary, since *burden* indicates a "load of labor" that evokes both "duty [and] responsibility" as well as "blame, sin, [and] sorrow" (*OED*).

Alongside metaphors about instructor survival, interviewees also use metaphors that imply that the writing center aids in student-writer survival. For instance, Carol (marketing) describes the role of the writing center consultant as a kind of guide.[2] When I first asked her to describe her understanding of my role as a course-embedded consultant in her graduate course, she says:

> It's like you're handholding . . . you know, confidence building. Academic writing is confusing for students because they don't know which way to go. They might know when and why they need to make changes, but they don't really know how to do it. It's like you're literally guiding them through the maze, and dropping breadcrumbs along the way.

Here, Carol describes the role of the writing center as a guide for students who "don't know which way to go." The maze/breadcrumb metaphor suggests that consultants can lead students through the wilderness of academic writing by helping them stay on the right trail so they do not get lost, serving as guides who "direct the course of" as well as "keep *from* by guidance" (*OED*). Although the idea of "handholding" is somewhat patronizing for both consultants and students, the actual task that Carol describes—helping students learn *how* to make changes in their writing—is not.[3] Thus, working in partnership with the writing center becomes an act of survival both for faculty who teach writing and for the student writers. These metaphors around survival and writing suggest that not everyone makes it through; there are some fatalities in both writing and the teaching of writing. Perhaps the interviewees who used these metaphors recognized that without the ability to write well, students were less likely to "survive" in the academy, and thus their writing could be the reason they do not make it.

The presence of clinical and survival metaphors in administrator and faculty talk suggests a deep discomfort—and possibly some degree of fear—about the teaching of writing. The urge to label students as problematic writers and to then send them to "counselors" in the writing center reinforces a kind of detachment between student writer and instructor. In these scenarios, writing may become the student's problem (and, in a sense, the writing center's problem), rather than the instructor's. Yet, associating tutoring with counseling and SRUWC administrators with diagnostics, both of which are linked to surviving academic writing, suggests an awareness of both relationality and expertise. These metaphors were most prevalent in stories about how and why the partners began working with the SRUWC and indicate why working through partnership was so necessary and valuable for them. Thus, writing centers are simultaneously positioned to alleviate the instructor's burden and help "save" at-risk students, making them potentially remedial yet necessary.

WHAT WE CAN LEARN ABOUT ADMINISTRATOR AND FACULTY TALK ABOUT WRITING PARTNERSHIPS

Although every partnership develops differently in practice, the initial reason behind starting the partnership approach in the first place was to help both writers and teachers of writing survive. The first SRUWC partnership was created as a more ethical, pedagogical solution to large class sizes with underprepared students. John, a creative writing program administrator with a background in rhetoric, shares the story of the first SRUWC partnership, which is not linked to the business school, as many interviewees assumed, but rather to the English Department and the teaching of basic writing. When the state took away adjunct funding to support these courses and English faculty did not want to teach them, John selected the strongest graduate teaching assistants to teach the courses. After assigning himself two sections of the course to teach, John realized that the basic writing course "could not go forward as a regular composition course" and that instead it "needed to be broken into small groups . . . and to work in a situation that was non-threatening but that gave [students] fairly specific and practical guidance." Students would then work through a series of assignments on a final portfolio that they could revise as many times as they wanted with help from an experienced writing tutor. Once completed, the portfolios would be submitted to TAs who were hired to read and score the portfolios on a pass/fail basis.

This shift in pedagogical model for teaching basic writing increased the passing rate for these students from 30–35 percent to 80 percent. John attributed this success to the experienced undergraduates who worked with the writers in small groups and "could speak practically about writing and were not so large of an authority figure that the students were intimidated by them or embarrassed about their writing." The program was going so well that John and Melissa (the executive director of the SRUWC) asked one of the vice presidents for $100,000 and they gave it to them, an idea John then realized was a "goldmine." Over time, John's position shifted away from first-year writing and he lost touch with how the courses ran and how the writing center operated. Yet, he explained in very corporate terms how he perceived what happened next:

> And, it seemed from the outside what happened is there became a shift in the model. . . . And what happened is kind of a franchise model. What it began to do was to seek partners in various units and to figure out how the writing center could assist those units, I guess, in teaching the kind of writing that they wanted taught.

In particular, John identified two other issues with the writing center partnership model: first, that the focus became more on faculty satisfaction and "getting their students to do what these people want their students to do" than about student writing, and second, that writing becomes something solely instrumental, with "no intellectual integrity of interest in and of itself." Thus, John explains that the partnership approach has become "a kind of franchise model." This was disappointing for John, since in the beginning "what we were trying to really prevent ourselves from doing was creating another fixed institutional structure that wasn't responsive to people." In John's description, it seems as though partnership is counter to ethical pedagogy. Yet, this does not seem to be the case in interviews with disciplinary administrators and faculty outside of English.

While some of the partnerships that grew out of this model explicitly describe their work with the writing center as "outsourcing" a kind of writing instruction that university administrators and disciplinary faculty do not want to teach (like Chris in biology and even Charley in hotel and restaurant management), most have a high degree of faculty engagement and interest in teaching students to write better (including Chris, Charley, and many others, like Rick in art history, Morgan in computer science, and Amir in architecture). Rather than wanting less to do with student writing, some writing center partners instead recognize the value of the undergraduate, peer-to-peer writing environment, where some struggling students may feel more comfortable.

Even though these views of writing across the curriculum come from administrators and faculty at a single institution, they speak from extensive experience with writing center collaboration across departments and positions. The use of corporate metaphor in discussions of partnership work with the SRUWC suggests a productive strategy for working across disciplines and programs to support student writing. Given the use of clinical, survival, and mechanistic metaphor alongside business metaphors, writing center administrators need to recognize the complex, even if somewhat conflicting, ways in which disciplinary administrators and faculty view writing and their meaningful work with writing centers.

Overall, disciplinary administrators and faculty acknowledge that writing is both social and rhetorical, given their interest in collaborating with the SRUWC as well as in their use of clinical metaphors, which Adler-Kassner and Wardle have noted as one of the foundational concepts of writing in *Naming What We Know: Threshold Concepts of Writing Studies* (2015). However, Adler-Kassner and Wardle also note as an important concept the awareness among writing instructors that all writers have more to learn. Unfortunately, this concept was not apparent in how most instructors talked about writing. For them, writing, once mastered, is a generalizable skill that can be transferred (as evidenced in the mechanistic metaphors). Part of this may be due to disciplinary faculty's tendency to view writing and content as separate, thus making the teaching of writing easier and more convenient to outsource to the writing center, for some.

Others, while committed to improving student writing and to collaborating with the writing center, also find great value in the way that such a partnership lightens their workload in terms of reading and commenting on student writing (as shown in the use of survival metaphors). Further, disciplinary administrators' and instructors' use of mechanistic metaphors suggests a view of writing that is more about reproducing a physical, automatic skill than about mental labor. This seems to work against Adler-Kassner and Wardle's fifth threshold concept, that writing is (also always) a cognitive activity, although the presence of clinical metaphors like consultants as counselors implies it. Yet, the variety of metaphor use across interviewees still suggests a complex understanding of writing and teaching writing worth careful consideration, as writing centers consider their positionality in and across the curriculum of twenty-first-century higher education.

While this broad understanding of how SRUWC partnerships work across disciplines and contexts provides an important background, the particularities of how partnerships work require careful attention to individual relationships across multiple stakeholders. In the case study chapters that follow, three different partnerships unfold across programmatic (first-year writing), college-level (business school), and departmental (electrical engineering) settings. In these cases, each partnership provides a potential response to disruptive innovation in higher education—online teaching, public-private partnerships, and the "Go Pro Early" movement. Glimpses of these metaphorical ideas about writing and the writing center present themselves both explicitly and implicitly in practice, contributing to partner perceptions of themselves and one another, as well as how the partnership functions overall.

APPENDIX 2.1. PARTNERS MATRIX

Name	Position/Discipline	Brief Bio
Charley	Former Associate Dean in Hospitality and Restaurant Management and Endowed Chair	He has worked with the SRUWC for ten years, ever since the university implemented a writing across curriculum (WAC) requirement and considers the SRUWC to be the "writing experts." His partnership is linked to HRM 4353: Leadership in the Hospitality Industry, a class that requires students to meet six times with a writing consultant on two different assignments.
Tara	Associate Dean for Student Affairs in Law Center	She began working with the SRUWC eleven years prior to our meeting, when the previous dean asked law firms for feedback on how their interns and recent graduates were doing and found out that interns and recent graduates "really need to improve their writing."
Kyle	Undergraduate Dean in Business School	He has worked at SRU since 1987 and in the Business School since 1992. His work with the SRUWC via the Business School began when Kyle felt that the school needed to have some kind of writing assessment to support students whose writing was below the school's standards. The Business School has six partnerships with the SRUWC that reach across the undergraduate, MBA, and doctoral programs.

continued on next page

Name	Position/Discipline	Brief Bio
Linda	Lecturer in Math Department	Linda teaches two writing-intensive courses meant to prepare students to teach math in public schools. She works closely with the SRUWC in two classes and her partnerships have a reputation among the SRUWC staff as being "the best." She has been teaching at SRU for the past thirty-nine years as a dedicated, enthusiastic teacher who provides her students with explicit writing instructions.
Carol	Endowed Chair and Marketing Professor in Business School	Carol has partnered closely with the SRUWC for the past eight years. She is deeply committed to teaching writing and is quick to criticize most published writing in the field of business. She teaches writing in the MBA and doctoral programs.
Amir	Assistant Professor of Architecture	Amir is in his first year as a tenure-track assistant professor in the Architecture Department, and his SRUWC partnership course focuses on the history of architecture and urbanism in the post-1945 world. Students work one-on-one with the same consultant three times, face to face, over the course of the semester, and they work on an evolving project meant to integrate visuals and text, in addition to presentation. He inherited the partnership when he began teaching the course and is enthusiastic about the relationship and its impact on student writing.
Chris	Instructional Associate Professor of Biology	Chris teaches a 250-person biology class that takes students through a multi-tiered, anonymous peer review process for the writing of a scientific report. Although his course is not classified as a writing-intensive course, Chris says that he teaches writing because he "thinks it's a skill they should have."
Morgan	Assistant Professor of Information and Logistics Technology	Morgan has worked extensively with the SRUWC via a partnership that incorporates online studios into hybrid writing courses. She collaborated with colleagues on an empirical research project that compared student writing in a SRUWC partnership course with student writing for a different section of the same course without the partnership. She found that writing significantly improved in the partnership course.
Rick	Professor of Art History and Department Chair	Rick has a longstanding, good relationship with the SRUWC and has partnered in courses at both the lower and upper level in face-to-face and online formats.
John	Associate Professor of English and Director of Creative Writing Program	John worked closely with Melissa (writing center director) to establish the first SRUWC partnership linked to the university's basic writing course, English 1300.
Walt	Professor of English and Department Chair	Walt worked closely with the SRUWC to develop a partnership linked to approximately twenty-four sections per semester of hybrid English 1303 and 1304, both first-year writing courses, in part to alleviate the labor of teaching writing for new graduate students.
Fernando	Assistant Professor of Political Science	Although he was not formally interviewed for this project, I sat in on an early project meeting with Fernando and a SRUWC administrator during which they discussed changes to his curriculum. I listened to him describe his course, his writing assignments, and his approach to teaching writing, which involved a strong recognition of writing in the profession (WIP), a concept more fully discussed in chapter 6.

3

REWORKING WITH THE ENGLISH DEPARTMENT
Partnering Online with a First-Year Writing Program

At the 2012 Conference on College Composition and Communication in St. Louis, I attended a panel titled "Thirdspace Portals: A Hybrid/Writing Studio Model for First-Year Composition." Building on the writing studio concept used by Rhonda Grego's and Nancy Thompson's (2008) Writing in Third Spaces *where the writing studio approach is used to create an interactive, small-group space within large writing classes, the presenters—a writing center administrator, a first-year writing (FYW) instructor, and an online studio facilitator—spoke about piloting the first hybrid writing courses with online studios. I sensed collaboration, but also complication, as this seemed new and strange. I remember having an uncomfortable, visceral reaction to what I considered to be a radical approach to teaching first-year writing. The idea of a "facilitator" reading and responding to students' drafts in online discussions outside the classroom space that were inaccessible to the instructor was foreign to me, as was the idea of the instructor seeing students only once a week. At the time, I was a prospective PhD student at the university from which these presenters came, and I would eventually be part of the first new graduate teaching fellows (GTFs) cohort who, instead of teaching FYW, would spend their first year in the writing center facilitating studio groups, mostly for hybrid FYW courses.*[1]

Although I did not realize it at the time, this hybrid first-year writing/online studio partnership was a direct response to the disruptive innovation of online education. For many academics—especially in the humanities—the rapid move toward online programs presents a kind of "crisis" that challenges the values that universities place on in-person, seminar-style, real-time learning. However, most universities are rapidly expanding online and hybrid courses in response to increasing demands for online learning environments in general (Best Colleges 2017; Babson Survey Research Group 2018) and hybrid courses in particular (Anderson, Boyles, and Rainie 2012; Alexander, Becker, and Cummins 2016). Although more research in online education is needed, one issue is clear: The online environment requires a reimagining of teaching and

https://doi.org/10.7330/9781646421770.c003

learning particular to the space (Kebritchi, Lipschuetz, and Satiague 2017; Hewett and DePew 2015). Simply moving face-to-face best practices online is not sufficient. At SRU, the hybrid course offered a more comfortable alternative, or entry point, into the development of online writing courses because it maintained some face-to-face teaching while also helping reduce the need for physical classroom space. The hybrid course was also a more accessible option for a student population made up primarily of commuter students who worked full-time, while simultaneously enabling the university to grow its distance education program to reach students outside of the city, state, and country.

In these ways, the hybrid/online studio partnership presents an internal, university response to what Horn and Staker identify as the primary reasons why leaders of K–12 institutions are turning to "blended" learning, which mixes in-person with online options. These scholars identify three desires that drive the move toward this particular online disruptive innovation: personalization (related to retention and acknowledging different learning styles and needs as well as the seeming lack of growth made over the course of the school year at the individual student level), access (especially to advanced and specialized courses that provide college credit even in rural areas), and cost (given budget cuts, schools are looking for ways to provide more one-on-one attention in a "tutor-like" scenario without the additional costs) (2015, 11–12). In the higher education context, leaders may make similar decisions when they consider moving to online learning environments. Potential students, who are ultimately the ones making the choice about where and how to attend college, likely consider some of the same factors in making those choices.

Working in response to somewhat similar desires, the SRUWC hybrid first-year writing/online studio partnership acts as an alternative to both outsourced online education (via options like massive open online courses, or MOOCs) while simultaneously disrupting traditional university approaches to online education, first-year writing, and writing center tutoring. First, it upsets the familiar teacher/student dynamic by creating a new, "outside but alongside" (Sutton and Chandler 2018) studio space facilitated by an experienced writing teacher who was not the classroom instructor or a peer tutor. This model drew directly on Grego and Thompson's conception of studios as spaces where individuals are engaged in regularly producing writing alongside peers (Grego and Thompson 2008). In this particular model, the writing instructor was not even allowed to "see" the online studio space, as it was created in a separate Blackboard shell outside the classroom shell. This created some initial tension, as instructors were resistant to giving up some of their authority (Miley 2018). Furthermore, the studio came with an additional writing teacher who provided more individualized support, thus increasing resources for students.

Second, the hybrid/online studio format radically expands the traditional peer review, a partner-based, face-to-face, FYW practice. Despite students' initial resistance, peer review is widely used and has been shown to improve students' writing performance as well as to motivate them to revise (Corbett et al. 2014; Corbett and LaFrance 2016; Huisman et al. 2018; Brammer and Rees 2007). By creating a stable, recurring peer review group in the online studio, students not only provide and receive feedback, but they see and engage with others' peer feedback as well. The online, asynchronous space also enables continuous, captured, and public exchanges; students can ask clarification questions in response to peer review and learn from other peers' and facilitators' responses. This more extensive process is just one example of how the studio approach slows down and expands the writing process, which can help alleviate the concerns some scholars have raised about the speed at which writing instruction has moved online (Allen and Seaman 2012; Monske and Blair 2017; Peterson 2001; Reinheimer 2005). Studios in online classes also help familiarize students with interacting in the online environment as a nonevaluative space.

Third, this kind of course-specific, online, group tutoring is different from the primarily one-on-one, asynchronous (not in real time, such as email exchange) or synchronous (in real time, such as live-chat) approach to online writing support that most writing centers offer (Coogan 2001; Harris and Pemberton 2001; Healy 1995; Hewett 2016; Kastman Breuch and Racine 2000; Van Horne 2012). Most writing centers have been especially resistant to asynchronous consultations, in part because of the one-off exchange and the lack of continued discussion beyond the submission of the text and the return of feedback (Bell 2011; Coogan 2001; Harris and Pemberton 2001). The writing center's online studio discussed here requires regular, asynchronous discussion about drafts in small groups in a two-part first-year writing sequence. Despite this shift in format, collaborations between writing centers and first-year writing programs have a long history, as research in this area has been extensive and most recently has focused on course-specific writing center support for FYW programs (DeLoach et al. 2014; Titus et al. 2014; Racia-Klotz et al. 2014; Bugdal and Holtz 2014; Gentile 2014; Pagnac et al. 2014; Wilson 2018). Yet, none of these studies consider the affordances of online, small group writing center support in FYW courses.

Expanding conceptions of what online writing tutoring might look like and how writing centers can create programmatic partnerships that include course-specific, online writing studios opens up new opportunities for growth and subversive responses to the disruptive innovation of online education. For instance, by integrating writing center pedagogy that values talk about writing process beyond the classroom, embedded online writing studios have the potential to support student writers in a space that continues to have significantly lower retention rates (Bawa 2016; Sewell 2016), especially for students who are low-income or from under-represented backgrounds (Protopsaltis and Baum 2019; Dynarski 2018). Since writing studios have been linked to retention (Chemishanova and Snead 2017) and high performance (Santana, Rose, and LaBarge 2018), adding them into online environments via writing center tutor-facilitators could provide much-needed, additional support to these students.

Writing center partnerships best respond to disruptive innovations when they react to the specific "DNA," or context, of a department, program, or teaching environment, as is the case in the online writing studio, specifically envisioned for hybrid first-year writing courses. Within this context, partnerships work best when partners explicitly acknowledge mutual benefits across participant groups and map stakeholder engagement over time, something practiced in this partnership to varying degrees. Strategic partnerships that incorporate online writing studios at the programmatic level are beneficial across a wide range of stakeholders (e.g., administrators, instructors, facilitators, and students) because they deeply integrate writing consultants into ethical, individualized, and group feedback spaces. Yet, without regular engagement from all major stakeholders, especially in partnerships with work that primarily takes place online, lack of communication leads to an uneven distribution of labor. By attending to both mutual benefit and stakeholder engagement, writing centers can make meaningful, curricular contributions that support teachers and students of writing, especially as they learn to teach and write in new environments.

CREATING AN ONLINE STUDIO/HYBRID FIRST-YEAR WRITING PARTNERSHIP

Since its split from English in 2002, the writing center had little connection to the English Department until 2010, when it piloted online writing studios in hybrid first-year writing courses. The pilot began when Megan, the assistant director of Writing in the Disciplines in the SRUWC and also a graduate student in the new Rhetoric, Composition, and Pedagogy program at SRU, was assigned ten English graduate teaching fellows (GTFs) in the writing center.[2] Drawing on a previously successful hybrid course/online writing studio model used to support a writing-intensive course in the College of Technology, Megan decided to write a proposal that would incorporate online writing studios into first-year writing courses. Simultaneously, an English Department writing fellow, Molly, was trying to figure out a unique program that would be valuable enough to keep her employed by the university.[3] Molly decided to propose a series of hybrid first-year writing courses, which would please the university's push toward online education while also maintaining some face-to-face class time, thus making the option appealing to the English Department. Since both hybrid courses and online writing studios were new and innovative approaches to writing instruction that took place in the online writing environment, the English Department and writing center linked the two proposals to create a pilot project.

The shared GTFs and Megan's past success in creating a similar hybrid/online studio course made linking especially helpful for Molly's proposal. In her assessment research with colleagues in technology, Megan was able to show that a writing-intensive course with a studio indicated a substantial improvement in student attitudes toward confidence, revision, and writing ability, and resulted in students scoring on average one rubric level higher on a four-point rubric scale on the final assignment, compared to students in that same course without the studio (Kovach, Miley, and Ramos 2012). After seeing the linked proposals with data-supported evidence for improvement, the provost approved a pilot project for five sections of hybrid first-year writing with online studios facilitated by GTFs assigned to the writing center.

In a book chapter that explains the start of this partnership, Molly notes the program's ability to both "retain essential outcomes of first-year writing and respond to institutional pressures for alternative course deliveries" (Gray 2018, 186). She mentions the program's ability to meet the needs across parties because of its flexibility for commuter students, training opportunities for graduate students, and ability to lessen the use of physical classroom space at the university level. In this way, the partnership was created with an awareness of mutual benefits across stakeholders, even if not formally referred to as such.

The course structure required students to meet face to face with their instructor once a week as a class and complete other coursework online, either through instructor-led activities in the university's learning management system, Blackboard, or through the online writing

Table 3.1. Structure of the hybrid/studio-supported writing class

Face to Face (one day per week)	Online Class Activity (conducted in Blackboard)	Online Writing Studio (conducted in Blackboard)
Traditional face-to-face instructor-led activities. For example: lectures, group activities, individual student presentations, in-class peer reviews.	Weekly instructor-directed online activities. For example: online blogs, journals, discussions, quizzes, instructor-created or outside videos, research activities.	Additional writing support in facilitator-guided online writing studios. Small groups of students (5–6) asynchronously post and respond to each other's works in progress during a weeklong studio session.

studios, facilitated by a GTF in the writing center. Logistically, the course involved the components shown in table 3.1. Table 3.1 shows the three-part structure that hybrid courses follow. Hybrid instructors create syllabi that present week-by-week schedules following the format above, thus suggesting to students that the course should be considered in three parts. For most courses, there are three studios (one for each major assignment), and students are asked to participate in each studio three times. For example, the first major writing assignment begins in Studio 1. Then, students might participate in a brainstorming studio (Studio 1-A), an introduction/thesis statement studio (Studio 1-B), and a final, full-rough draft studio (Studio 1-C). Then, Studios 2 and 3 follow this same kind of structure for major assignments two and three, respectively.

These online studios were intended to provide a space for informal conversations about writing and rhetoric that were not linked directly to the value or improvement of a product—namely, the major writing assignments. In her research and development of the studio program at SRUWC, Miley (2013) defines the studio as a space for students to work through the "messiness" of the writing process through "dialogue about the drafts" with a "more immediate audience" (235). In this model, studio facilitators are housed in the writing center and report to a writing center administrator, rather than working directly with the instructor. To ensure a writing center–like environment (i.e., a nonevaluative space driven by student need during the writing process), instructors are not allowed to engage with or check into the space. Instead, they receive a basic, monthly report from the studio facilitator of students' attendance and an occasional, descriptive note about what was discussed.

Along with supporting student writers, the online studio also provides facilitators, who are new GTFs, with a supportive, less labor-intensive teaching environment. Rather than becoming instructors of record in their first year in the program, GTFs become facilitators. They receive support and training in providing written feedback to students without the added burden of grading or extensive curriculum development. Facilitating studios online also gives GTFs valuable experience in an innovative teaching environment, and online teaching in particular, which will likely make them more appealing on the academic job market. This partnership also moved graduate students into the writing center in larger numbers, something that had not been done in the past, since the writing center was primarily staffed by undergraduate consultants and full-time administrative staff. Melissa (writing center director) was interested in expanding support to graduate students by employing graduate student consultants and had even talked about creating a separate graduate student writing center. This partnership was one step toward expanding her writing center staff to include more graduate students.

Given this valuable programmatic shift for both the English Department and the writing center, the English Department chair and the writing center director were prepared to make the case for the writing studio as a necessary support for hybrid writing courses, even though upper administration did need some convincing. As Walt, the English Department chair, explains, the development of the hybrid course "was always driven by an attempt to get the best in multimodal teaching in the department and it could only be done with the collaboration of the writing center. Absolutely essential." In particular, Walt notes the writing center's resources, space, budget, and environment as "kind of a third space . . . that allows for innovation to take place much more creatively than if you're working through the coordinating board." Walt also mentioned that he and Melissa (writing center director) approached the provost for funding together, and they received approximately $135,000 of support to expand the project beyond its pilot years.

At the time, this move was both controversial and unannounced, because Walt and Melissa secured the money to expand without consulting either of the other program administrators (Megan and Molly) or the English faculty, including the members of the Composition Committee. Yet, the university's support enabled the FYW hybrid/studio model to grow quickly: When it began in fall 2010 there were nine sections, and by fall 2015 there were twenty-four. Still, the online studio provided support for the hybrid instructors, the online facilitators who were often new teachers, and student writers by creating a heavily scaffolded, feedback-rich, student-driven environment.

This response to the disruptive innovation of online teaching provides additional support by centering the relationships across writing stakeholders—program administrators, instructors, facilitators, and students. Rather than creating online courses that expand caps or work primarily through programmatic modules with little teacher interaction, as external online education options often provide, the hybrid/online studio partnership at SRU adds a second writing teacher to the class environment through the creation of highly interactive, nonevaluative spaces. Thus, pedagogical and ethical approaches to the teaching of writing are not diminished by administrative constraints and preferences for online/hybrid teaching models.

DEVELOPING MORE EFFECTIVE TEACHERS: THE ONLINE STUDIO AND THE HYBRID INSTRUCTOR

Preparing GTFs to be instructors of record for first-year writing courses has a complicated history—fraught with labor issues, a lack of ongoing professional development beyond an initial pedagogy course, and a regular practice of student teachers relying on previous personal experience rather than on disciplinary knowledge to guide instruction (Wisniewski 2018; Hillocks 1999; Reid, Estrem, and Belcheir 2012), especially since composition studies scholarship is often new or unknown for GTFs (Restaino 2012; Brewer 2020). When new teachers move into the online environment, they have to think about teaching writing, teaching online, and teaching writing online, which are three distinct teaching contexts (Hewett 2016). Hybrid writing courses are unique because they require instructors to think about the course taking place in two different environments (face-to-face and online), rather than in one environment or the other. With the exception of one, none of the six hybrid writing instructors who participated in my focus group had prior experience with teaching writing online beyond that of the online studio facilitator in the SRUWC the semester prior. Thus, the transition to online teaching was a challenge, even at the halfway point in the semester, when the focus group took place. For instance, Mike admits that he was surprised to find that he could do more with the online space than he originally thought, even though getting used to having only one weekly face-to-face meeting has been a slow process. Mike explains:

> Last year I sat and watched Patrick [a fully online writing instructor] make all these video lessons, and it hadn't occurred to me that I could do the same thing, in this space. I was like, why did I not think of that? My mind, I guess, is still fixed on the brick-and-mortar structure and hasn't yet freed itself to say, how much more can I do with this? Now the light is sort of

coming on, and I need to make this work to my students' advantage and not feel like I'm at a disadvantage because I'm only in class half the time.

Mike's conscientious reflection indicates his commitment to figuring out how to make the online writing environment a fruitful one for his students. He admits that his mind is "still fixed on the brick-and-mortar structure," yet in the same breath he suggests that video lessons are a way out of that structure. Since "video lessons" tend to be recorded lectures, pedagogically they mimic a traditional face-to-face content delivery method that maintains, rather than breaks away from, the brick-and-mortar structure. Thus, although Mike senses that he can do more with the online space to support students, he seems unaware of how the online teaching environment provides a different kind of scenario for instruction. In other words, Mike is right that he can do more, but his sense of how he might push writing pedagogy beyond the traditional classroom seems limited.

In part, these hybrid instructors struggle to create a meaningful online writing component for their courses because they tend to perceive it as "extra" rather than "inter" curricular. As he puts it, Mike is "only in class half the time," yet his students are not technically in class less. They spend fewer hours onsite and likely do not interact directly with Mike as much as he was used to, but they are still in writing environments at least as often. Similarly, Elaine compares the online portion of the hybrid class to "homework," another traditional brick-and-mortar tactic that often carries lighter intellectual weight than instructional hours. She explains, "When I do person-to-person [face-to-face teaching] all week, I rarely give homework, and this [online portion] is basically just giving homework. Like, substantial, meaningful assignments." Elaine's need to qualify homework here raises questions about the value of assigning homework for both instructors and students. Why would Elaine assign "homework" in a hybrid course and not in a face-to-face course? What distinguishes the "substantial" and "meaningful" homework of the hybrid course from other kinds of homework?

Offering one possible explanation, Nick describes how student engagement in the online portion of his course increased when he more directly linked their work to larger writing assignments. At first, Nick used the online space as a place for students to practice what they learned in class so that they could then apply those same strategies when they started to write their essays: Students did the work, "but a lot of them seemed like they were just doing [the online writing activities] so they could check them off." When Nick tweaked his approach "to make it more geared towards their papers" by, for example, having students write about the same sources they would use for their larger writing assignment, "they got a little more involved with it then, because they were like, well, if I do a good job on it, then I can integrate it into my paper."

Although he may be unaware of it, Nick adapts what he learned as an online studio facilitator to the online component of his hybrid class: scaffolding writing assignments and providing feedback on smaller pieces of writing, rather than working with a full rough draft in one sweep. While practicing strategies for writing about sources with common course texts works well in the face-to-face classroom because students can work together in small groups, this activity does not work well online because students are not interacting with one another synchronously (or in real time). Thus, the need to work through common texts in conversation together is not something that translates well online. Given that face-to-face classroom time is limited, Nick and the other hybrid instructors have to make decisions, first, about what to do in class and what to do online, and, second, about how to adapt work imagined for the face-to-face environment to the online space.

Lucy also uses the online component of her course to provide additional scaffolding for major writing assignments. She explains:

> My goal is to make the online space directly connected to the class in some ways, so . . . we did introductions one day, we did a thesis day, we talked about multiple body paragraphs. I've liked watching their essays develop. And, I've been able to catch a few of them, like, "Hey, that's not a thesis, we should address that before you write the rest of the paper." That has been really lovely, and it's much harder to pull that off in a face-to-face, full-time class. That's been my biggest pleasant surprise with the class—how much I'm able to track their essays, which I wasn't able to do in the face-to-face as well.

Here, Lucy notes how the weekly online discussion board exercises provide a useful structure for breaking down larger assignments and getting students to work on them piece by piece. She talks about the online space as "directly connected to the class," although it is not spoken about as *part of* the class. Yet, Lucy pays close attention to each individual student's writing process, which enables her to intervene before they write entire drafts.

After Nick and Lucy describe these online teaching strategies, Elaine explicitly acknowledges what both examples show: Previous experience as online studio facilitators determines how hybrid instructors teach the online component of their courses. Elaine says:

> I think being a facilitator last year helped me do online, the online part this year, because sometimes . . . you have to respond to two people and

that's how you complete the assignment, because I was sort of training them on how to do studio. . . . Last year, I was like, I'm doing God's work for this teacher, and this year . . . I have no idea what they're doing!

While their previous experiences as online studio facilitators seem particularly valuable, nearly all hybrid instructors admit that they know very little, or as both Elaine and Mike admit, "have no idea" what the online studio facilitator is doing with their students. Initially, this was an intentional element of the studio setup. The studio space was supposed to be for honest conversations about writing between students and facilitators without the teacher present. Yet, this format led to discomfort among the hybrid instructors about what kind of work students were doing in the space and how they were to balance the studio workload with the online component of the course. While hybrid instructors' previous experiences as online studio facilitators did lead them to provide more individualized feedback to in-process student writers, the extent to which this exercise was additive or repetitive for the students alongside their studio work was of concern to instructors.

Although a continuously challenging process, figuring out how to best utilize the online environment encourages instructors to better organize their in-class time and overall class structure. Mike talks about a "deliberate time management" that requires him to "resist the urge to elaborate" and instead to follow a specific schedule for onsite instruction with time stamps next to each item. This means that when students have additional questions, Mike feels the need to move on and instead asks students to speak with him after class. This results in regular, additional one-on-one time outside of class with students. Mike explains, "Even yesterday, five students followed me out of the classroom, and another hour and a half goes by as I help them each with their perspective." Although Mike feels rushed during his onsite class instruction, additional in-class time for content elaboration may not provide the same kind of one-on-one support students seek after class. In this way, the hybrid course structure and less onsite class time may encourage more one-on-one conversations about writing between student and instructor.

Similarly, Lucy admits to feeling she has less time for chit-chat at the beginning of class, which was so important to building community in past classes. Instead, Lucy says she feels like she has to speed up and focus on the most important course material. Despite this perceived challenge to community building, all but one hybrid instructor said the sense of community in their hybrid courses is at least as strong as it normally is in more traditional face-to-face classes. Elaine argues that this is because students are far less likely to skip a class that only meets once a week, meaning that the whole class is in attendance more often in the hybrid setting. As a result, students are more comfortable participating in class.

Further, the multiple moving parts of the course (face-to-face, online, and studio), require careful attention and tracking of attendance and participation. For both Mike and Elaine, keeping the course cohesive for students requires that they use the learning management system to track student engagement as well as to accept, respond to, and grade student work online. This way, both instructors and students can see how students are progressing and where they do not show up, which leads to earlier interventions for struggling students. Keeping all of this material online allows Mike to "easily show students a snapshot of their performance" during conferences or after class when they ask. In addition, Mike notes that his students seem more capable of tracking their work when it's online. Thus, increased attention to course organization and online tracking of student progress supports retention because it makes student work more visible and helps instructors intervene earlier as needed. In five semesters' time, the percentage of withdraw and fail numbers (W and F) in SRUWC online studio/hybrid FYW courses improved from 12.33 percent (n=70) in fall 2013 to 9.8 percent (n=63) by fall 2015. These rates are lower than W and F rates at comparable institutions for first-year writing, which tend to be in the 14–15 percent range for face-to-face courses and even lower in online environments (McKinney et al. 2017; Spangler 2019). Thus, the hybrid structure, especially with additional support from the studio facilitator, may actually create a scenario where the W/F rates are lower than other first-year writing course formats.

Despite the potential drawback of repeated work in the online portion of the hybrid course and the studio, the online studio's presence in the hybrid first-year writing program makes significant pedagogical contributions to instructor development. Instructors' previous work as facilitators helps them utilize the online instructional space for scaffolding and individualized feedback on writing early in the process. Analysis of the focus group with hybrid instructors suggests that both conscious and unconscious transfer occurs, where "the mind, seeing similarities to what is already known, extends what is similar to another activity" (Devet 2015, 121). In this case, hybrid instructors engage in near, procedural-procedural transfer because instructors view teaching writing online as similar to online studio facilitation (near) and so use the same tools and processes for feedback (procedural-procedural). Instructors rely on the same "sequence of repeatable skills" (Devet 2015, 123) and seem engaged in lateral transfer, where learning is transferred to the same level of hierarchy, despite a significant change in their role from studio facilitator in the writing center to hybrid instructor of record in the classroom.

The lack of awareness that a change in position requires adapting pedagogical practice and curricular decisions suggests an ongoing need for professional development. Nationally, online writing instructors have voiced a lack of necessary support and training (Hewett and Hallman Martini 2018). In this case, the SRU FYW program may work under the assumption that experience as an online studio facilitator prepares GTFs to be hybrid instructors. Yet, research has shown that making similar transitions (from writing center to the classroom, for instance) does not necessarily mean better preparedness (Book 2018; Child 1991; Nichols 2015). Still, the presence of the online studio and the facilitator in their classes leads instructors to better organize their courses and pay closer attention to student performance and retention. Having multiple components forces instructors to prioritize material in onsite class and to carefully track student progress, both of which contribute to a more supportive learning environment for students.

REFINING THE WRITING PROCESS(ES): THE ONLINE STUDIO AND THE WRITING CENTER FACILITATOR

Nearly all hybrid instructors drew on their experiences as online studio facilitators to design the online component of their courses. Facilitator training consists of weekly meetings led by SRUWC administrator Max, during which facilitators analyze and discuss sample HostPosts (the start of the studio notes with the prompt), participate in technology demos, brainstorm potential strategies, problem-solve as a group when challenges arise, and develop their materials. Early in the semester, discussion centers around how to construct effective posts, with attention to basic document design strategies like use of white space, bullets and numbering, and paragraphing. They develop their ongoing list of best practices for studio facilitation, which includes commenting early, wrapping up studios with a summarizing comment, focusing on only one or two issues at a time, teaching students to rethink their concept of "draft," and explicitly explaining why and how certain studio activities are meant to be useful for students. As a cohort, they consider how to introduce students to talking about writing through a shared language, develop an appropriate tone online, and write concisely while also prioritizing certain kinds of writing activities over others. These meetings provide a space for regular conversation about studio facilitation and pedagogy through which facilitators work together on studio curriculum, which helps them develop skills that they will eventually need as instructors of record.

Megan and Molly designed the online studio component of FYW with an awareness that the hybrid classroom is "its own unique kind of course" that requires a balancing of different pedagogical strategies onsite and online (Snart 2015). The very structure of this particular hybrid class helps account for this distinctiveness; online studios place more emphasis on both the production and process of writing, as well as the frequency of response to writing in process (from instructor, studio facilitator, and peers), while also enabling students to drive the discussion. There are no traditional classroom hierarchies in the studio; the facilitator will not be evaluating and grading writing, but rather noting attendance and participation based on whether or not students contribute to the conversation. This tracking is reminiscent of Inoue's labor-based contracting.

Online studios also work against student procrastination, a common issue among early college students and one that negatively impacts their grades as well as their mental health and well-being (Appleby 2017). By requiring them to post smaller "chunks" or parts of their writing assignments at a time well before full-draft deadlines, facilitators encourage students to take smaller steps toward large writing projects. Studios attempt to show the writing process as cyclical and recursive, rather than stage- and product-based. For example, studio facilitator Casey created a series of three studios linked to students' second major assignment in a research-focused, first-year writing II course that aimed to scaffold the assignment. This three-part research assignment included an exploratory narrative, an annotated bibliography, and a reflection. Over the course of three weeks, students were asked to do the assignments described in table 3.2. This sequence asks students to write a research question, cite a source, and summarize/evaluate that source (Studio 2A); state a claim, find and identify an opposing viewpoint, and determine how to incorporate the opposing viewpoint into the paper (Studio 2B); and write a thesis, identify an area of writing that needs revision, and work through a confusing peer review critique. These are not typical writing process activities (e.g., brainstorm, plan, draft, polish), nor are they organized by the assignment's three major parts (e.g., narrative, bibliography, reflection). Instead, this studio series encourages students to work on critical reading skills with source material, which largely contributes to the drafting of their major research project.

Table 3.2. Sample Studio Series with scaffolded assignments

	Student writing required by Casey's HostPost
Studio 2A	1. Research question; 2. One source related to question with the proper citation format; 3. A summary of the source and a specific claim within the source that will be researched in greater detail to support the writer's own thesis: (a) How is the claim supported in the source? What impact does this have on your thinking? (b) Do you agree with the claim or are you resistant? Can you find counterevidence external to the source?
Studio 2B	1. State your claim and support it with a little research (can draw on work from last week); 2. Post a source in correct citation format that opposes or contradicts writer's view; 3. Summarize the main points and identify the counterclaim. How can your paper be in conversation with the opposing viewpoint?
Studio 2C	1. Post a tentative thesis and a part of your draft that needs improvement, and explain your concern; 2. Post a part of your draft that was critiqued during peer review that confuses you, that you disagree with, or that you understand and agree with but don't know how to address. Tell us about the critique, and we'll discuss it.

One of the studio's most striking features is its extensive attention to peer review and response. In the above example, Studio 2C actually invites students to discuss their in-class peer review, which is rare in traditional composition courses. The extra time spent navigating the peer review process is likely worthwhile, since research shows that students who give and receive written feedback improve their writing, especially when they receive explanatory comments that help them perceive and use their feedback (Huisman et al. 2018). Yet, well before the more formal, in-class peer review takes place, students have already engaged in multiple peer exchanges via writing about their major projects in studio groups. These experiences get them more familiar with sharing writing, discussing their writing processes, and talking about their ideas along the way, all of which make them better prepared for formal peer review. A writing class that provides rich opportunities for a range of peer review feedback and activities, like the online studio, alongside more traditional peer review, can significantly increase students' writing abilities and attitudes toward writing. Overall, 83.4 percent (n=195) of the students enrolled in these hybrid courses with the online studio component found "peer review activities" to be very helpful or somewhat helpful, and 75 percent (n=177) of students rated the online studios to be very helpful or somewhat helpful.

Students as well as hybrid instructors note this valuable element of the studio. Instructors Mike and Nick encourage their students to carefully consider the range of perspectives. Mike admits to not wanting to "undermine the facilitator." Instead, he sees this as a teaching opportunity to tell the student that "there are multiple ways to approach the problem," and that when there's conflicting feedback between the instructor and the facilitator, "the facilitator isn't wrong; however, knowing how you're wanting to write this paper, this is the strategy I think you could see as more effective." Here, Mike gives the students some guidance based on his position as teacher and, ultimately, the one who will assign the grade. Nick, on the other hand, says that he doesn't give students an answer, but instead:

> I just keep telling them, there's lots of ways you could do it. . . . I don't want them to think that there's a formula. I don't want them doing the five-paragraph essay, so, the fact that they get so much response . . . it's like you have these two authority figures and then you have your peers. I mean, I'm sure some of them are wrong sometimes, but you get all the right answers.

This approach shows students the messiness of writing for a variety of audiences and also encourages them to work their way through the mess. Some students look to the facilitator for help in figuring out what to do with peer feedback. For instance, in end-of-semester student survey data, one student explains that they found the facilitator to be "helpful in establishing what I was going to do based off group member's [sic] thoughts." Another student notes how the facilitator "started the conversation" among group members by "directing" its focus. Thus, the facilitator plays a significant role in helping students navigate conflicting feedback.

Although it's not explicitly discussed during online studios, many students use the facilitators' feedback as a model for their own responses to peers' work and even use similar genre elements. Some students continue to focus on small-scale writing issues connected to grammar and to write short responses, but they also incorporate other techniques, such as starting comments with praise followed by suggestions, summarizing what they thought their peers' key arguments were, raising questions, and acknowledging that the writing was still in process. This format evokes Smith's (1997) recognition of "the end-comment genre," which she identifies in letter-like instructor feedback written at the end of student essays, and further suggests that the written peer review response works as its own genre. For example, facilitator Beth's early response to student writer Edward, which was posted in an online studio focused on writing about a meaningful place, provides an example of how to provide feedback that students can mimic. Annotations in bold brackets have been added to point out similarities across responses.

Beth's Feedback

> Hey Edward,
> I think this is an excellent start! **[praise]** Don't worry that you only have a couple paragraphs—this is a rough draft, and it's okay that it's not fully complete. **[acknowledging writing in process]** Posting it now and asking questions was a great move to make!
>
> I like the way you've started this piece! I especially like the way you start out with the "buzz words" about LA and some of the stereotypes that you disagree with. It seems like you are wanting to paint a different picture of LA than most people have . . . is that right? **[observational comment about what the writer seems to be doing]** What would you say your purpose is here? Why did you choose LA for your place? . . . **[raising questions to encourage further development]**

Beth uses a letter-like format and a positive, encouraging tone. She blends praise, questions, and recognition of the writing process to create a comfortable pace for setting up critique. Later in the same studio, students Luke and Edward both provide the following feedback for their peers using some of the same techniques and genre elements as Beth used:

Students' Peer Feedback

Luke

I don't know how you did but you managed to fill 5 pages without putting me to sleep, so good job on that part. **[praise]** In the last paragraph, there were a few sentences that did not start with capital letters. I know it is a draft, but you never want something so minute to prevent your paper from achieving perfection. **[acknowledging writing in process]** After the first few paragraphs, I was left wondering what is the purpose/question. I was looking for the obvious "?," but I had to continue reading to understand that catching the big one in a place you clearly despise was the purpose and the why. **[observational comment about what the writer seems to be saying]** When you start mentioning the battle with the willow tree, you can remove "the willow tree" after the first few occurrences and replace it with a pronoun because it became a little too repetitive, especially since ambiguity would not be a problem. I liked it. It was good, not great because I know that polishing is always in order with a first draft. **[acknowledging writing in process]**

Edward

Your essay to me, was well written out, **[praise]** but slightly choppy. your word choice is very black and white, everything compared is quite put to the extremes. **[observational comment about what the writer seems to be doing]** Your conflict is quite easy to empathize with, I just think you should try and bring it up earlier in ur essay. maybe an allusion is in order. **[raising questions to encourage further development]** but for some reason i love the intro. **[praise]**

Although there is much to be improved in this peer feedback, especially given the lack of specificity and reference to the writer's text (two techniques Beth used), Luke and Edward adopt a genre for feedback similar to Beth's. Given that students usually only see peer review feedback that they receive and rarely find such feedback helpful (Brammer and Rees 2007), the online studio environment exposes them to more peer responses and likely helps them develop better strategies for writing feedback to peers.

SPONTANEOUSLY STUDENT-DRIVEN: THE ONLINE STUDIO AND THE STUDENT WRITER

While attention to providing and incorporating effective writing feedback is a primary focus, online studios also offer an opportunity for student-driven conversations in a space geared toward supporting student agency. As Williams (2017) notes, writer agency "implies the possibility of action and decision" as well as the "perception" that such action is possible (9). This kind of agency can be hard to encourage in the traditional classroom space, where students are constantly under the eye of the instructor who assigns grades, especially according to participation. In the studio, however, students can drive conversations about writing process among their peers and a more experienced writer (the facilitator). The online writing studio, when housed in the university writing center, has the possibility to offer "not only a different approach to teaching, but also . . . the possibility of different emotional experiences of learning that counter the hierarchal and judgement-driven experiences in other university spaces" (Williams 2017, 132). Furthermore, given that the studio is online, students may feel more comfortable being open and honest with the privacy and anonymity of not being face to face. In this way, the online studio enables both spontaneity and agency as students discuss material concerns connected to writing (especially the amount of work required), build community, and encourage one another across a shared experience of writing labor. In particular, the space of the online studio and the role of the facilitator create an environment where students can (inter)act with one another about writing without the same level of judgment and evaluation, even though both are almost always present to some degree. Creating an environment rich for spontaneity and agency opens up a different kind of possibility for "trickster" moments than more traditional classroom spaces provide, as the next example shows.

Unsurprisingly, administrators often view moments of student spontaneity and agency as threatening, rather than as meaningful moments of working through productive resistance. During separate interviews, Anne and Max, both writing center project managers involved with the hybrid FYW/online studio partnership, mentioned one particular studio as an example of the "negative interactions" that can occur. During the first studio of the semester, one student responded in a way that Anne and

Max perceived as rude and indicative of a negative attitude toward studios. It caused anxiety, discomfort, and administrative intervention. Yet, it also offered a seemingly honest and authentic moment in which students voiced some of their real concerns and ideas about writing. Despite the initial (productive) resistance, students moved on to discuss their attitudes about writing and also seemed to play with the idea of attending a hypothetical picnic, using the question as a way to get to know one another, joke around, and build community. Writing center facilitator Casey wrote the opening studio HostPost. Her carefully constructed post suggests that she tried to use bold font and numbering to help prioritize important information. She also wrote a response post, or "model," the next day to give students an idea of how they might respond:

> Casey's HostPost for Studio #1A
> September 14, 2015 @ 1:29pm:
>
> Let's get started, shall we? This week, in addition to taking advantage of this space to discuss your assignment, I'd like to ask a few QUESTIONS to get to know each other as writers. In your **STUDIO 1A writer post**, due Wednesday, September 16 at 11:59 PM, answer the following:
>
> 1. Think about one of the tools you, as a writer, have at your disposal. (For example, you might consider vocabulary/word choice or varied syntax.) What is your theory about the use of that tool? How does it work and why is it effective? How does it play into your larger philosophy of writing? (This may seem like an obvious question, but I don't want an obvious answer. You are not allowed to use the word *communicate*.) [Word Count: 150–250]
>
> 2. What two food items would you bring to a picnic with people who have read your writing, but whom you've never met, and why? [Word Count: 100–150]
>
> 3. Tell me any concerns you have about your upcoming assignment or about this studio.
>
> I'm going to warn you here about something I'll ask you to do in **STUDIO 1B** next week so you can start thinking about it, but you don't need to address it until next week. I will bring it up again when I want your answer. For **ESSAY 1**, in which you consider how visual and verbal texts shape argument, try this exercise: look at your chosen text for five minutes, then forget about it and go do something else. After at least an hour, come back and look again for five minutes. What do you notice in each observation session? What strikes you differently, and how does this affect your thinking?
>
> Remember to write a short **response post** on each of your peers' **writer posts** by 11:59 PM on Monday, September 21!

In her post, Casey attempts to create a casual, friendly, encouraging atmosphere focused on getting to know one another and reflecting on past experiences with writing. Her organized and specific guidelines establish a careful ethos, positioning her as someone who takes the online studio space and the students' engagement in that space seriously. Yet, her pacing seems to be a bit quick, as she's already previewing the next week's studio at the start of their first week. Given that this experience is likely new for students (i.e., college, hybrid course, online studio, writing center), this move may come across as overwhelming, as Peter, the first student to respond, a day and a half later, suggests.

> Peter's Response for Studio 1A
> September 15, 2015 @ 8:56pm:
> First off I would like to say that unlike you, I am not an MFA candidate. I am an engineering major, and I hope that you realize when you ask me to write 400 words on my writing tools and what kind of food I would bring to a hypothetical picnic, that I also have university physics, computing, calculus and other "fun" classes that assign insane amounts of homework. I could ask you to solve a third dimensional relative force question or calculate the volume of a solid through integrals, showing you that I know how to do it wouldn't make you feel any better about having to do it. I guess you could label this as one of my concerns.
>   That being said . . .
>
> 1. I would definitely say that vocabulary and logic are my favorite writing tools, and I also enjoying [*sic*] taking an unexpected approach, or starting off with an approach only to instantaneously reverse and throw it all back in the readers [*sic*] face, so I guess you could say surprise. As far as vocabulary goes, I have no idea why, but when I start writing essays and important assignments it's almost as if my brain opens up some word bank kept under lock and key deep in the pits of my skull. I thoroughly enjoy making a good point while using some upper vocabulary, but I have learned to restrain myself, because if I don't it sometimes seems as if I'm just dumping a pile of fancy words onto my paper. It's also, in my experience, harder to disagree with someone who has great wording. As for logic, well it's hard to argue against logic, I mean it's possible, but you look silly doing it.
>
> 2. What two food items I would bring to this picnic. Well to be honest I probably wouldn't go to the picnic. Least efficient way to consume food, even with others, and still have a good time. You got ants, mosquitoes, weather conditions etc. For the sake of answering the question I will humor you. I guess I'd bring pizza and Buffalo wings, because who doesn't love pizza? And I love Buffalo wings, so if no one else likes them they won't go to waste. If I really wanted people to have a good time I would probably just bring brownies. Special brownies.

When I think back to my time as a college student in required courses seemingly unrelated to my major, Peter's initial post feels familiar. His style of writing is "listy" and exhausting, in some ways mimicking his own

frustration with the overwhelming feeling that results from the competing demands of being an undergraduate (and most likely a first-year)
student. The tone he uses seems representative of how students (and
instructors) respond when they feel overworked by trying to balance
multiple responsibilities within a finite amount of time. Despite his tone,
Peter does complete all of the assignment with some degree of detail,
answers all three questions, and meets the word requirement. In this way,
his post is somewhat subversive; Peter asserts his agency and positionality,
confronting his readers with the reality of his workload and challenging assumptions about seemingly fun, community-building activities
positioned as lighthearted (the hypothetical picnic scenario). Still, he's
careful to write a response that meets all of the assignment guidelines,
despite his obvious annoyance with the assignment. Peter seems to write
what many students likely feel or think but rarely say to their instructors.

Peter's post caused some distress in the writing center. Administrators
reprimanded him and told him he owed Casey an apology. After being
contacted by Casey (facilitator), Max (project manager) emailed the student to let him know that his tone was inappropriate. Casey responded
quickly to Peter's initial post, two hours later, in the studio, where she
acknowledges his frustration and assures him that studio will not be too
much work: "Fair enough, Peter. I think I can promise you that this studio
will be fairly manageable and that you will still have time for your other
classes." She also points out that he "seemed to have finished this [studio]
without any trouble" and proceeds to respond to Peter's point about word
choice and restraint. Peter immediately follows up the next day with an
apology post, explaining that he has "been informed that [his] response
may be seen as disrespectful and/or confrontational," but that was not his
intention. He admits, "Those were the words of a very tired student feeling overwhelmed in a trying time," yet he also reiterates, "my responses to
the questions asked were sincere though." Peter accepts that his post may
have come across in ways he did not intend it to, but he still reiterates the
sincerity of his concerns. Unlike English graduate students, undergraduates like Peter are rarely excited to write and often see their assignments
as just one of many competing demands on their time. Asking Peter to
imagine what he would take to a picnic may seem like a waste of time, and
given his material realities, it may be. Peter identifies this as one of his
concerns, which responds directly to Casey's HostPost prompt.

Peter's peers respond in ways that recognize his agency, or ability to
act and be heard. The studio participants seemed to understand and
appreciate Peter's honesty, and his experience seems to resonate with
them. This connection is explicitly acknowledged in most responses

and followed with thoughtful commentary on Peter's writing style and other strengths. Further, all students approach the question about what one would bring to a picnic with a playful tone, using their response as an opportunity to share something about themselves, as they jokingly comment about whether or not they would be interested in joining one another's picnics. This entire studio seems to be about community building and bonding over shared negative attitudes toward writing, a proven technique for creating community, even if challenging to do under the eye of an evaluative instructor (Bosson et al. 2006). Here, Peter's peers comment on his response and apology.

Students' Responses to Peter's "Rude" Response

Jia explains to Peter that his writing is good because it follows the prompt with a detailed response:

> Don't fret about coming off as rude. I don't think your post is rude. The discussion post directly asked you about one of your concerns, and you gave it, simple as that.
>
> The elaboration and description in the first paragraph of your post only made me understand you, the writer, and the intensity of this concern. . . . I'm sure if you had written "Yeah, one of my concerns is that I have a lot of work in my classes and it adds up and it makes me stressed," no one would REALLY understand how you felt. However, BECAUSE of the way you wrote the first paragraph, I can see how this concern is a legitimate problem for you. I can see how stressful it is, and I can feel the intense environment for you.

Grant encourages and sympathizes with Peter:

> I as well am an engineering major and understand your stress, so don't worry, we can get through this together. . . . Just from these few paragraphs above I can tell that your writing is very interesting to read and I look forward to reading more of it.

Andri responds with interest and points out "an engineer's mindset":

> I really enjoyed this post! As an engineering major, I can relate to your sentiment. That logic reasoning with the picnic question sounds exactly like an engineer's mindset.

The exchange shows how Peter's peers respond to his seemingly rude response with praise, sympathy, encouragement, and interest.

As the students in this studio continue to discuss their strengths and limitations as writers, they work through conversations about vocabulary, logic, elaboration, description, figurative language, fact-based and concrete writing, audience awareness, staying on topic, anxiety related to rambling about writing, and how image and sound can influence writing. For example, in another exchange, one student (Justin) voices anxiety over rambling in writing at the beginning of his primary post: "When thinking about the tools I use as a writer I am going to be honest I have no idea what I am doing. I like to just ramble on a page and then shape it into something that is worth a read." In response, his classmates write the following:

Responses to Justin on "Rambling"[4]

> *Jia sympathizes and offers another way of understanding how rambling works:*
>> Justin, your style of writing and thought process is kind of similar to mine. However, for me, instead of not having an idea of what I'm doing, I do have an idea of what I want to express and write. The part that makes us similar is that, with the idea of what I want to write in mind, I freely let myself express the idea . . .

> *Grant sympathizes and offers a strategy:*
>> I also am a bit of a rambler in my writing. I often find myself with a lot of run on sentences and getting off topic, but a few thorough proof readings helps me counter act this tendency.

> *Peter points out the benefits of rambling:*
>> Rambling is often a great way to start writing, Justin. You get to clear your head and get all your ideas and topic possibilities on paper, after which it is much easier to pick and choose what would work.

> *Andri offers a compliment:*
>> Rambling on a page sounds like the best way to jot down your ideas in opinion. I think as a writer you've got a pretty admirable approach.

This exchange shows Justin's peers' responses to what he identified as a limitation in his own writing style. Two of his peers admit that they also ramble, yet they reframe it as a writing strategy that leads to topic development. The other two praise Justin for rambling and redefine it as an effective strategy. According to Casey's HostPost, the purpose of this first online studio was for the students to discuss their writing strategies and to get to know one another, both of which occur. The students do not post drafts or discuss the course assignments. However, they are able to talk about writing techniques they use and their anxieties around writing.[5]

Since someone other than the course instructor facilitates the studio, students seem more comfortable asserting authority and determining how the conversation unfolds. The asynchronicity of the space also provides extended time and opportunity for students to respond to one another, rather than Casey dictating how long conversations go on or how many times students respond. Further, Casey appropriately steps back, allowing the students to interact with one another. Although she does respond throughout the studio, students rarely, if ever, respond to her. In this scenario, Casey seems to be closer to a scapegoat than the shared (writing) enemy, given that she directs and organizes the space. In a more traditional classroom, students are less likely to have the opportunity to respond directly to one another without instructor intervention. Yet here, the student writers seem more interested in what each other has to say, which subverts the assumed power dynamic between instructor (or graduate student facilitator, in this case) and student.

REFLECTING FORWARD: ANALYSIS OF THE ONLINE STUDIO/HYBRID FIRST-YEAR WRITING PARTNERSHIP

The SRUWC online studio/hybrid FYW partnership provides an opportunity for the writing center to respond to the disruptive innovation of online education in a way that both slows down the writing process and ultimately supports teachers and students of writing. In this way, the SRUWC undermines common administrative tactics like cost cutting by increasing the instructor-to-student ratio. Although not directly applicable across university contexts, this approach can be adapted for a range of writing center partnerships with disciplinary units or programs, especially those that are integrating hybrid or online courses into their curriculum, involving instructors who are new to online teaching environments, working with inexperienced graduate teaching assistants, or piloting course-embedded tutoring programs. Part of what makes this partnership successful is the awareness of mutual benefits across various stakeholders. This contributed not only to the partnership's strong pilot, but also to its quick growth propelled by strong institutional support at the programmatic level. Yet, there are some drawbacks—namely the lack of continuous engagement by the English Department, which leads to the writing center being the primary actor. Instead, the SRUWC and the main partner(s) need to carefully consider mutual benefits and stakeholder engagement at the start of a partnership and throughout to ensure sustainability and the likelihood of success.

What Worked? Noting Mutual Benefits Across Stakeholders

Part of why this strategic partnership succeeded administratively was because stakeholders paid careful attention to mutual benefits from the beginning. Not only was it important that each partner be aware of their own needs as well as one another's, it was equally critical to place those needs within the larger context of student and university needs, all of which were weighted differently. In "Mutual Benefit in a Globalizing World: A New Calculus for Assessing Institutional Gain Through International Academic Partnerships," Susan Buck Sutton argues for the importance of understanding mutual benefit as a matter of equity, or "fairness and justice," rather than equality, or "sameness" (2016, 182). Given that power is rarely distributed evenly across units, Sutton proposes mutual benefit as a situation where all partners gain value, even though that gain may sometimes be differential rather than equivalent. This distinction between equity and equality has important implications for writing center partnerships with a range of different departments and colleges, some of which likely have a lot of power and others of which likely do not. Although partnership benefits cannot necessarily be planned, the SRUWC and its partners should consider early on how each stakeholder might benefit and how and where those benefits overlap. Further, mapping out benefits early on creates an awareness of who the partnership is serving and how. Yet, as Sutton suggests, benefits should also be assessed throughout to determine whether perceived benefits become realities.

From the beginning, part of what made this SRUWC and English Department–FYW program hybrid/online studio partnership desirable were perceived benefits across stakeholder groups and participants: university administrators interested in growing online instruction, administrators in the SRUWC and English Department who wanted to create innovative writing curricula, hybrid instructors in the English Department who received additional support in teaching writing, online studio facilitators in the writing center who had a less burdensome first year of teaching, and student writers who were given far more feedback on writing than in traditional classroom environments. These perceived benefits also contributed to the partnership's success in terms of growth, student satisfaction, and increased participation. In particular, the partnership allowed for more flexible scheduling, provided graduate students with opportunities for online and hybrid writing instruction that would make them more marketable, and required less physical classroom space, which made scheduling easier for the university at large. Furthermore, administrators in the English Department and the writing center benefited in that the online studio supported hybrid (and eventually online) course development, both of which were being pushed on the English Department by upper administration. With little interest in or resources for supporting these first-year writing course formats, the English Department was eager to partner with the writing center, whose staff were also looking to build additional resources for graduate student writers, beginning with bringing graduate students

Table 3.3. Mutual benefits across stakeholders: mapping out the SRUWC and English Department partnership

Benefits	Type	Dimension
Strong programmatic connection between FYW program and SRUWC	Indirect, nonmaterial, long-term	D2 (shared benefit)
GTFs assigned to the SRUWC during first year in graduate program in English	Direct, material, immediate	D2 (shared benefit)
Curricular development of the hybrid program, especially among hybrid instructors	Indirect, material, long-term	D1 (benefit for English Department) D3 (potential broader development for university-wide hybrid pedagogy)
Writing center staff expanded to include graduate students	Indirect, material, long-term	D1 (benefit for writing center) D3 (potential broader benefit for developing specialized support for graduate student writers from peer graduate student consultants)
Additional support for student writers	Direct, nonmaterial, long-term	D2 (shared benefit among teachers of writing) D3 (benefit for students and higher education in general)

into the writing center staff—something that was not common practice prior to this partnership.

When approaching partnerships strategically, mapping how and where particular benefits overlap can lead to stronger commitments from stakeholders, thus creating greater sustainability. Sutton notes three different benefit types for which we should account: (1) direct/indirect; (2) material/nonmaterial; and (3) immediate/long-term. Alongside these benefits, Sutton argues, partners should try to anticipate potential negative consequences across all three dimensions. The first dimension considers the benefits that each partner receives individually, primarily as a result of the exchange. These often drive partnerships and require little elaboration. The second dimension acknowledges benefits that both partners share, as a result of collaboratively producing something new, something that did not exist before and could not exist without collaboration. These exist when individual and partnership gain are the same. The third dimension recognizes benefits to the broader environment of the university or to higher education in general and requires an acknowledgment of the potential contributions to the broader landscape.

In the case of the SRUWC online studio/hybrid first-year writing partnership, the benefit types and dimensions in play are shown in table 3.3. Table 3.3 anticipates, or in this case reflects, more shared benefits (D2) and broad benefits (D3) than individual benefits (D1). In addition, there are the same number of individual benefits for each key stakeholder. This suggests the likelihood for equitable mutual benefit.

What Didn't Work? Continued Engagement across Stakeholders

Despite the wide-ranging benefits of this partnership, there were some problems. For instance, although the partnership started out as highly collaborative and innovative, over time it became more or less fossilized. Simultaneously, as the level of engagement decreased, the hybrid first-year writing program slowly moved closer to being fully housed in the writing center, resembling a kind of outsourcing of the hybrid FYW courses. Reducing the English Department's involvement was especially problematic because it meant that the partnership was primarily facilitated by contingent administrators/faculty whose job security depended on the program's visible success (Miley 2018). Rather than assuming that what begins as a collaborative structure will continue to be so, effective strategic partnerships require explicit identification of each participant's responsibilities and strengths so that ownership and decision-making can be shared, rather than either assumed or outsourced to one partner or the other. This work creates a more sustainable partnership that stabilizes individual roles that do not depend on the particular people who hold those roles at the time of the partnership's creation.

This requires thinking about what Douglas Proctor has called stakeholder engagement, an "integrated approach" to project management that involves identifying and involving stakeholders from beginning to end (2016, 96). Rather than solely working together during the early developmental stages, stakeholder engagement requires ongoing input. In "Stakeholder Engagement for Successful International Partnerships: Faculty and Staff Roles," Proctor adapts an approach used by the International Association for Public Participation to determine the public's role in community engagement projects for international higher education. His model is useful because it requires a broad consideration of who should be involved and how. This helps partners think through and understand the roles of various stakeholders involved in a partnership while also recognizing that not all stakeholders require the same level of engagement or participation across various stages. Proctor's spectrum is useful for thinking about strategic partnerships in the writing center because they often require a range of participants, some of whom could be easily overlooked or eventually may fade out without

Table 3.4. Stakeholder engagement spectrum for strategic writing center partnerships

Increasing impact of engagement					
Who needs to be . . .	consulted?	informed?	involved?	collabo-rated with?	empowered to make the final decisions?
Typical stakeholders	Depart-ment chairs, colleges, faculty, TAs, instruc-tors, IT, centers for teaching, offices of technology	Depart-ment chairs, colleges, faculty, TAs, instructors, consultants	Support staff in writing center and partnering department, participants (consul-tants, instructors, TAs, stu-dents, etc.)	Support staff in the writing center and partnering department	Writing center administrators, part-nering department, and sponsors (may include deans, pro-vosts, etc.)

explicit attention. Proctor's model is applied to the SRUWC's strategic partnership approach in table 3.4.

Once partners determine stakeholder groups, an important step in and of itself, they should also consider both the anticipated and necessary level of engagement and the specific roles within each group. Although these will shift depending on stakeholder interest, and commitment will likely change over time, determining the groups and the roles of those within the groups deserves attention. Proctor suggests three primary roles within each stakeholder group: sponsor (who will pay or contribute resources?), lead (who will organize the partnership and make final decisions?), and support (who will actively participate in the work of the partnership?).

Although some stakeholder groups may only play one role, others will want to think carefully about how internal stakeholder organization works. Stakeholder groups should be considered in terms of individuals, roles, and level of engagement. Again, drawing on Proctor's framework, this mapping serves two important purposes: it supports project management by identifying who is responsible for what, and reducing the likelihood that duplicate work is happening within the partnership; and it makes these roles and responsibilities explicit, thus fostering what Proctor calls "efficient communication loops internally and externally (who talks to whom? how should issues/concerns be escalated?)" (2016, 102). The biggest challenge, according to Proctor, is identifying all relevant stakeholders.

Yet, in the case of this SRUWC/English Department partnership, it was actually the English Department that was under-engaged. This was likely in part because Walt (English Department chair) did not discuss the decision to grow the hybrid program with the Rhetoric, Composition, and Pedagogy faculty, who could have acted as major stakeholders and provided the much-needed ongoing pedagogical support to the hybrid instructors. In particular, hybrid instructors needed more resources to help them transition from facilitators to instructors, and especially with developing teacher personas that included greater authority. For example, in terms of supporting GTFs and ongoing professional development, the English Department could have applied Wisniewski's "detect-elect-connect" model for transfer, which "usefully highlights the different bridges that need to be crossed" in order to make transfer happen (2018, 52). This would help instructors anticipate challenges across new roles and teaching environments, as well as give them an opportunity to try out different strategies for adapting their knowledge across contexts. Since the writing center was primarily concerned with preparing the online facilitators, professional development for hybrid instructors from more experienced classroom teachers of writing was lacking. When writing centers work directly with graduate teaching assistants, they must find ways to keep other departments engaged so that new teachers also receive support from those with similar disciplinary backgrounds and experiences. Still, writing centers can potentially play a significant role in introducing GTAs outside of English to writing studies pedagogy.

This kind of issue is more likely to be alleviated when the most involved stakeholders also participate in high-impact decisions. In this partnership, the primary administrators—Melissa (SRUWC) and Walt (English Department)—were the ones who made the final decisions, yet they were not really engaged or involved with collaboration at the project level like Molly, Megan, and eventually Max and Anne. Furthermore, additional stakeholder groups should have been informed and consulted with, including the Office of Online Learning, the Center for Teaching and Learning, and the Rhetoric and Composition faculty members. Had these stakeholders been included, the ongoing level of engagement from the English Department might have increased more significantly. Adding the previous writing center partner who worked with Megan in the first hybrid/studio partnership, Morgan (computer science), might have provided some additional consultation as well.

Finally, the issue of potential overlap across online teaching activities points to the need for continuous stakeholder engagement across partner roles and activities, especially as they relate to logistics and curriculum. Opening up communication across spaces would help prevent unintentional overlap. Even better would be finding a way to integrate student perspectives and feedback into the partnership process.

As Alison Cooke-Sather, Catherine Bovill, and Peter Felten argue in *Engaging Students as Partners in Learning and Teaching: A Guide for Faculty*, bringing students and faculty together in partnership deepens engagement in the learning process by creating relationships rooted in respect, reciprocity, and shared responsibility.

Given that students are expected to be especially interactive in the studio space, including them on the curriculum design decisions in some capacity aligns well with writing center philosophies that position students at the center of their work. This consideration also matches up with the twenty-first-century university's attention to the student as customer. If we can engage students in ways that help us improve our pedagogies by making them more useful, then we continue to ensure our necessity to their college experience and we become better teachers of writing. The customer satisfaction–like surveys prevalent in writing center studies shortchange both us and our students.

Writing centers can respond to the disruptive innovation of online education by creating strategic writing center partnerships that incorporate online writing studios. While they primarily work to support both student writers and writing teachers, online studios also provide meaningful experiences for facilitators who are often new and developing GTFs. This partnership and others made the need for ongoing professional development for teachers of writing visible, especially for those outside the English Department. Thus, although not the central aim of the writing center nor the major work of partnerships, providing ongoing training for GTFs is another way the writing center can support writing at curricular and programmatic levels.

Strategic writing center partnerships are built on constant, participatory relationships that are mutually beneficial for administrators, instructors, facilitators, and students in ways that standard learning management system (LMS) software and third-party online support services normally incorporated into online courses—like Turnitin and SmartThinking—are not. While these disruptive innovations are often added into online courses, they also turn up in more traditional face-to-face classes, especially when local support for writing is deemed both necessary and expensive. I explore the disruptive innovation of third parties in writing instruction further in chapter 4 by examining how a writing in the discipline (WID) partnership between the business school and the SRUWC shifts as an external evaluator becomes an additional partner-stakeholder.

4

ENGAGING CHALLENGES
Partnering as a P3 with the College of Business

When I sat down with Kyle, the associate dean of undergraduate business programs, I wondered whether or not he would bring up the 2010 controversy that involved the outsourcing of business writing assessment to a third party, Rich Feedback, which worked through a program called "Virtual TA." This service provides writing feedback through both real people and computer-automated responses.[1] Sure enough, in the tenth minute, Kyle brought up Rich Feedback for the first of fifteen times in our over two-hour-long interview:

> At the time, one of the faculty teaching Business, Law and Ethics—now she's gone to another university—but somehow, somebody at the *Chronicle* found out we were experimenting with Rich Feedback and they wanted to write an article about it, but, as sometimes happens in the media to try to sensationalize it a little bit, I think the headline said something like "University of X Business School has now turned their grading over to a third party they kind of didn't want to bother with grading." Well, that got a lot of negative feedback and kind of tarnished our reputation. And so, we wrote a rebuttal to that, which I can share with you, you might be kind of interested. Because actually, in reality, from an accreditation point of view, having an objective third-party evaluation makes more sense because if you're evaluating your own students' writing, you have a vested interest in them doing well, and if a third party is evaluating, they're just giving you a third-party perspective. And so, from our point of view, as long as we're only using it as bookend measures, it makes sense, and that was our argument.

In this first story about Rich Feedback, Kyle describes the business school's work with the third-party company as an "experiment" that was eventually "sensationaliz[ed]" by the media. He notes the negative reactions to this act, but references the school's rebuttal, which explains why and how a third-party evaluator was a valid resource for assessing writing. Kyle is careful to qualify specifically how Rich Feedback was used, as "bookend measures," not for *all* writing instruction and support.

The article to which Kyle refers that made the business school's use of Rich Feedback public and controversial was "Some Papers are Uploaded to Bangalore to Be Graded," written by Audrey Williams June (2010) and

https://doi.org/10.7330/9781646421770.c004

published in *The Chronicle of Higher Education*. In it, she claims that the high numbers of business majors and the amount of writing feedback required caused the professor of a business law and ethics (BLE) course to "outsource assignment grading to a company whose employees are mostly in Asia." The professor explains that in her required, upper-level, writing-intensive course of around 1,000 juniors and seniors, each student writes 5,000 words per semester. From the business school's perspective, the previous "graders," who were graduate teaching assistants across multiple disciplines, "were great . . . but they were not experts in providing feedback" (June).[2] Thus, the professor turned to a third-party evaluator, Edumetry (now Rich Feedback) for support.[3] Rich Feedback uses her rubric, along with several sample papers evaluated according to that rubric, as tools for providing feedback on three assignments over the course of the semester. Before she sends students comments, the professor reviews them and assigns grades. At one point, she noticed that the comments from Rich Feedback were "way too formal. . . . We wanted our feedback to be conversational and more direct. So, we sent them examples of how we wanted it done, and they did it."

While this scenario is not all that surprising, the content on the article's last page is. The SRUWC, June writes, "helped give Virtual-TA its entree when the center decided to stop grading writing samples from nearly 1,000 students each year planning to major in business." Here, the focus shifts away from the use of Rich Feedback in the BLE course to its use as a large-scale writing evaluation tool as part of the Business School's Business Writing Evaluation (BWE) and SRUWC partnership. During my interview with Sam, he also mentions this controversy and explains that the use of Virtual TAs as first-round evaluators enables the tutors to "concentrate on working one-on-one with students," which, according to him, is "just a much better use of their time." Thus, the idea to outsource writing evaluation came from someone in the SRUWC, not the business school.

The relationship between the writing center and the College of Business has a long, complex history and a wide range of course- and program-specific partnerships. Although neither Sam nor Kyle saw the integration of a third party into the BWE and its accompanying business writing tutorial (BWT) partnership as problematic, it did lead to the use of Rich Feedback in the BLE partnership and eventually to the end of the writing center's involvement with that particular course. The use of Rich Feedback is different in each context, yet this example shows how the use of a third party can lead to unanticipated and unintended consequences.

The use of a third party is also representative of a relatively new disruptive innovation in higher education, referred to formally in recent research as a public-private partnership (P3). In *The Chronicle of Higher Education*'s report "The Outsourced University: How Public-Private Partnerships Can Benefit Your Campus," staff writer Scott Carlson (2019) describes the emergence of P3s as "a kind of marriage between an institution and a private company, where a company often finances, designs, builds, and operates a college 'asset.'" P3s primarily occur in the planning and construction of residence halls, sports complexes, and recreation centers; the argument is that, given university budget cuts, more institutions want to focus on the academic core—teaching and research—and reallocate other university activities to companies with expertise in those areas. Although Carlson's report focuses on four P3 case studies comfortably outside the teaching and research activities of academia, some projected data about the future of P3s is concerning for writing centers. For instance, 25 percent of the 250 presidents, provosts, and chief financial officers surveyed identified "coaching/mentoring/tutoring" as an area of particular interest for further creation of P3s, with almost 30 percent interest in skills training and 42 percent interest in online-program extension.

Like online education, P3s are a kind of disruptive innovation because they present a new approach that is seemingly cheaper and more user-friendly than what already exists. In addition, P3s are considered potential money makers for both the partner and the university, which challenges the traditional educational paradigm of universities creating their own resources and structures in house. Writing centers are especially well positioned to respond to the use of P3s for tutoring and coaching, because these are activities that they perform from a context-specific, intellectually engaged position. Although this case study of a P3 partnership with the SRUWC and the business school is an odd case, it provides a valuable opportunity to look at how and why a P3 is used to support writing. As upper administrators become more interested in outsourceable, P3 possibilities, writing centers need to understand how and why they may be considered. We especially need to think about how writing centers might respond to requests for the kinds of writing support that might encourage potential partners and upper administrators to turn to P3s: large-scale writing assessment and large-scale writing support.

Working through strategic partnerships with disciplines and colleges, writing centers can participate in these conversations and brainstorm approaches to these scenarios, which are far from the best case, yet still exist and likely will continue to exist across universities. As we keep the material realities of universities and the possibility of P3s in mind, writing center administrators need to think about how our work is different from and more effective than "outsourcing" to P3 evaluators, especially in terms of the kinds of relationships we create. This case study provides insight about how an upper administrator in a business school thinks about partnership with the writing center and a P3 and shows how two partnerships unfold differently: One continues to work across the writing center, business school, and P3, and the other continues between the business school and P3 only. Although the partners seem content with these outcomes, I find them problematic both pedagogically and ethically, in part because the initial decision to turn to a P3 was made in haste, to meet a quick turnaround deadline for a large set of writing exams. As a potential alternative, I adapt the concept of "negotiated space" (Helms 2016) as a way to prevent the likelihood that a partnership will need unexpected support from a third party. If partnerships begin from a negotiated space, then they can anticipate possible shortcomings early on and establish ethical and realistic boundaries around the work in which the writing center and partner are willing to participate.

UNINTENTIONAL OUTSOURCING OR BOOKEND MEASURES? USING P3S FOR WRITING ASSESSMENT, FEEDBACK, AND EVALUATION

P3s are often large-scale and profit-producing, yet smaller companies like Rich Feedback still raise concerns, even in short-term pilot-based projects. According to the website, Virtual TA is designed to support faculty and students by employing master's- and PhD-qualified experts across disciplines who provide "rich, timely feedback" that "can free faculty up for more mission-critical duties" (Rich Feedback, "Virtual TA"). This idea of giving faculty members time to focus on other, more "mission-critical" work aligns directly with the argument that P3s enable universities to focus on the "true" activities of the university, the assumption being that providing feedback on writing is not an important element of teaching or research. By way of anticipating concerns about overpricing, Rich Feedback implicitly identifies two ways its service can potentially raise money for the university. In response to the question, "Your service sounds expensive; can we afford it?" the site suggests on its FAQ page that, in addition to Virtual TA being cheaper than an on-campus TA, universities can "defray the cost" in two ways. First, the university can increase class size, since the use of a Virtual TA alleviates "rich-feedback grading." Second, professors can be assigned to teach more classes, again because they would not be expected to provide feedback. These two suggestions would likely more than cover costs for the use of Virtual TA, thus making the university some extra cash, truly in the spirit of the P3 model.

Although it is not mentioned directly on the website, Virtual TA provides a combination of human and machine scoring, both of which are problematic. Still, writing centers interested in creating strategic partnerships, especially through writing across the curriculum (WAC) and writing in the disciplines (WID) initiatives, must still consider how and why they appeal to upper administration.[4] First, global outsourcing of writing support raises questions both pedagogically and ethically in terms of labor conditions. In "Disposable Drudgery: Outsourcing Goes to College," Dingo, Riedner, and Wingard (2015) investigate the SRU Business School/Rich Feedback controversy as explained in the *CHE* article and argue through a transnational feminist lens that this particular kind of outsourcing is the result of a faulty WAC/WID initiative that resulted in questionable labor practices both globally and locally. Dingo et al. point out that the professor simply moved her outsourcing from the local (through use of cross-disciplinary TAs and SRUWC consultants) to the global, where workers were likely even more exploited than the graduate student TAs. This global outsourcing is also more pedagogically concerning because students "are not given the opportunity to engage with their writing or writing instructor in any meaningful way," which then turns writing into a "process of regurgitation that is easily disposed or commodified" (278). Yet, these scholars recognize that outsourcing work, especially that which is undervalued or undesirable, is likely perceived by administrators to be an effective solution to budget crises.

Second, and equally troubling even if differently so, machine scoring offers another possibility for managing the labor of writing instruction. Writing studies has long identified machine scoring as *problematic*. In 2009, the Conference on College Composition and Communication (CCCC) released a position statement on Writing Assessment, which was then reaffirmed in 2014. The second guiding principle states that "Writing is by definition social. Learning to write entails learning to accomplish a range of purposes for a range of audiences in a range of settings." Following this are three statements about best practices for assessment, one of which explicitly states a preference for assessment by human readers. The use of machine scoring "distort[s] the very nature of writing as a complex and context-rich interaction between people," while also simplifying how writing works.

Despite this resistance, research in artificial intelligence and computer science continues to push the boundaries of how computer-mediated resources can be used for what have primarily been thought of as human teaching practices. Automated Writing Evaluation (AWE) and similar evaluation and feedback tools are not P3s per se, but they are external products owned by other companies, thus fitting the broader definition of disruptive innovation and suggesting that they could eventually function as P3s. Research about how AWE can help support writers, particularly second-language writers, is booming (Hegelheimer, Dursun, and Li 2016; Shermis and Hamner 2013; Cotos 2011; Warschauer and Ware 2006). In general learning contexts, research suggests that students are overall satisfied with some elements of AWE, even though they still prefer a combination of machine and teacher feedback (Wang 2015). Research in this area has even gone so far as to explore a range of intelligent tutoring systems (VanLehn 2011), discipline-specific writing feedback (Chapelle, Cotos, and Lee 2015), and the creation of autonomous, virtual teaching assistants anonymously embedded in online courses alongside human teaching assistants (Goel and Polepeddi 2016). While some of these studies argue that AWE is at least as effective as human feedback and, in some cases, may be more effective (VanLehn 2011), others have pointed out some of the limitations of AWE. For instance, artificial intelligence that relies primarily on episodic memory may fail to account for non-normative student populations and identities, thus raising concerns about AWE for different demographic groups as well as the emotional impact of having a system that responds more attentively to the majority than the minority (Eicher, Polepeddi, and Goel 2018, 91). This particular kind of Virtual TA seems about as far away from the intended best practices for writing assessment established by CCCC as you can get, especially if we accept writing as social, complex, context-rich, and interactive.

Given these outsourcing possibilities made available by P3s like Rich Feedback, writing centers need to think about how to position internal, context-specific, human-to-human strategic partnerships as more effective and ethical alternatives. This requires consideration of how to support large-scale writing assessment and feedback. Even though it's preferable not to outsource, there may be some value in distinguishing when it may be relatively appropriate. In the case of the SRUWC and the business school, Rich Feedback became an integral part of two different but related partnerships under Kyle's oversight. In the first case, Rich Feedback became an assessment tool for an extracurricular partnership. In the second case, Rich Feedback replaced human teaching assistants and was used as a feedback resource for an upper-level, writing-intensive class. Eventually, Rich Feedback's Virtual TAs became seemingly just as effective as the in-person peer tutor follow-up, leading the writing center to fade out from that particular partnership altogether. Given that writing center practices and P3s function differently, this scenario raises questions about how and why, in a good, relationship-based partnership, outsourcing can happen. It also calls attention to the writing center's potential role in writing assessment and the responsibility we may have in helping it occur ethically, as well as the possibility of taking part in conversations about outsourcing to P3s.

Establishing a Large-Scale Assessment/Support Partnership with Business

When I asked him about his experience with partnerships, Sam's (associate director of the writing center) first example was the business school. He explains that the partnership began primarily because of two things. First, the college "had some challenges with student writing that had a lot to do with who their students were. . . . [They had] a high percentage of international students and second language students." Second, the business school had "an administrator with a very open mind." Sam further describes Kyle as someone who has experience teaching freshmen composition and someone who "understood how writing instruction is best done."

Working primarily as a "program development resource," the writing center—and Sam in particular—worked with Kyle in what was "an early case where we really said, 'we're going to be expansive in terms of what we're going to do.'" Given that the university's two required writing courses focused on general expository writing skills and research-based writing, students who were admitted to the business school rarely had any experience with business-specific writing conventions or genres. Thus, Sam and Kyle knew that they would likely need to develop some kind of business-specific writing curriculum.

To get a better sense of what kind of writing support to provide, they began with what Sam calls a "systematic needs assessment," which consisted of an exploratory but methodical collection of writing samples from a large number of students in a junior-level business class. During our interview, Sam tells me that their overall finding was that "anywhere from one fifth to one third of students probably couldn't meet expectations for basic competency in business writing." This did not come as a surprise, but it did raise questions about what they were going to do about it. Several weeks after my interview with

Sam, I came across a written report of the assessment, along with a cost-estimate proposal for the business school/writing center partnership in the writing center's archives. The eleven-page document written by Sam indicates that the assessment was an institutional review board–approved study that asked students enrolled in an upper-level marketing course to complete a writing assignment for extra credit. The assignment asks students to "write a brief and clear recommendation for or against city X" as a location for the South-Central Marching Band Booster Association convention. The prompt includes details about the association's needs and notes that the audience was the organization's steering committee, whose members "range broadly in age, ethnicity, education level, and economic status." Specifically, the steering committee was looking for a "clear, concise presentation [of] strong evidence" to help them make their choice. The assessment rubric indicates that samples were evaluated for audience effect, structure, sentence crafting, and style/mechanics.

The assessment considers 335 useable writing samples that are rated by "five experienced writing consultants under direct supervision of, and assisted by the Postdoctoral Fellow [Sam], using standard norming and preparation practices to ensure the validity of ratings." The norming sample ratings are also completed by business college faculty and used to assist the consultants in getting on par with writing expectations in business. Results indicate that there is a strong correlation between "audience effect" and "structure," with about 20 percent of samples rated as ineffective or unacceptable in "higher-order composition values" and 10 percent rated as ineffective or unacceptable in "basic writing skills." Overall, 26 percent of students "failed" the assessment. Demographic data suggests that around 50 percent of those who scored "ineffective" were Asian/Pacific Islanders and 47.7 percent transferred to SRU from "junior" or community colleges.

The full report includes nine additional pages of graphs that visually represent the findings along with several recommendations. There is an in-depth analysis with specific examples from writing samples that display "basic writing problems" (problems considered "ineffective or unacceptable") and "effective writing problems" (problems that have to do with "accomplishing the task and fulfilling audience need"). While both problem types need "some kind of instructional program to develop into effective professional writers," the first group is identified as below the "competent basic writer" category. The report concludes with four recommendations for programmatic, curricular change: (1) the creation of a "Writing Skills Support Program to Produce Competent Basic

Writers," which would involve identifying and then tutoring the "at-risk" writers; (2) a new "Discipline-Specific Writing Instruction Curriculum to Produce Effective Professional Writers," which would include both integrating writing into existing courses, even those that are large, by incorporating at least one assignment with "more extensive, project-based realistic writing requirements with instruction that includes process, feedback, consultant[ion], and revision"; (3) developing additional, business-specific writing support for instruction and consultation by having "a tutor available on a walk-in basis during hours convenient to students"; and (4) adding a specific writing-intensive course and creating a "writing-intensive culture," which would involve developing "shared goals and expectations for writing" within the business major by offering writing awards, hosting workshops or colloquia, and providing incentives to encourage and recognize excellence in the teaching of writing among faculty.

As a result, Kyle and Sam decided to make two changes to the business school curriculum, the first being the integration of a writing-intensive project in a junior-level course (which would eventually become BLE). The second change was adding a Business Writing Exam (BWE) and Business Writing Tutorial (BWT) graduation requirement, where students would complete a BWE upon entry to the college to determine their writing ability. Then, if students did not reach target competency, they would be required to complete the BWT, an extracurricular, portfolio-based, pass/fail project that they worked on for as long as they wanted with a writing center tutor. The BWE, created by Sam and orchestrated by the SRUWC, is a one-hour, proctored business memo writing assignment. Although considered a graduation requirement, the BWE is integrated into the business school's curriculum as a requisite for a sophomore-level business class. However, the scoring of that exam has no impact on the students' grade for the course. Referred to as a "hurdle test" by the business school, the BWE is scored according to a four-point rubric. The business faculty initially worked with Sam and Kyle to determine that a cutoff score of 2.0 on a 4.0 scale would "require a follow up business writing tutorial." All exams are graded by two readers in the SRUWC, who are often undergraduate writing consultants, and averaged together for a composite score.

In part because nearly 50 percent of its students transfer in credit for first-year writing, the college considers the BWE to be "an evaluation of writing skills at the point of entry, not a follow up to remediation" (Kyle). When students take the BWE, they are placed into three different groups:

- **Scores of 3, 3.5, or 4**: the BWE requirement is met (no further requirements)
- **Scores of 2 or 2.5**: the BWE requirement is met (no further requirements, but follow-up with the SRUWC is recommended to improve writing skills)
- **Scores of 1 or 1.5**: referral to the BWT (student is required to begin the BWT the following semester)

Approximately 18–20 percent of students who take the BWE each semester fall into the "BWT required" category. Each of these students is then paired with a writing consultant in the SRUWC who helps them through the BWT, which requires them to complete "a career-related assignment (a resume and cover letter) and a business academic assignment (solicited proposal)." Students can spend as much time as they want on the BWT, and most of them meet with their writing consultant at least eight times. Clearance of the BWT for students who fall into the "required" category is a mandatory graduation requirement, and Kyle, with Sam's help, monitors these students' progress, placing holds on their accounts when necessary.

Before deciding to create the BWE/BWT and after conversation with business faculty, Kyle and Sam realized that if they were to require a class, students who are already struggling writers would be put at yet another disadvantage in that they would have to sign up for and pay for an additional class that they then might struggle with and fail. Instead, Sam and Kyle wanted to provide something more individualized to students who needed the extra support. The portfolio structure of the BWT enables students to revise as many times as they want and to meet with their assigned peer tutor as often as they need. The portfolio itself needs to be passed, or, as Kyle puts it, "cleared," in order for business school students to graduate, yet it is "open-ended in terms of how long it [would] take" students to pass. This enables them to "keep drafting and revising until they meet the basic standard" and does not delay their progress toward their degrees.

Although this approach does require additional extracurricular work on the part of the student, Sam and Kyle seemed to create this exam with portfolio project very much with the student in mind. This particular partnership is a good example of a disruptive innovation itself, because it works within a reasonable budget to support student writers in a way that enables them to take an individualized approach to completing the BWT. As it stands, students are allowed to meet with their assigned writing consultant as often as they like, and the business school pays for those tutoring hours. The decision not to put a hard deadline

Table 4.1. 2004 cost estimate for BWE and BWT

Estimated Cost for Writing Program Exam (to become BWE)		
Start-up/one-time costs	Includes web content development (exam publicity), piloting costs for exam	$10,300
Yearly operational costs for assessment	Includes administration, rating, analysis, reporting, and overhead	$11,700

We've estimated that the cost of the Writing Proficiency Exam, if managed completely by the Writing Center, would be $11,700 per year, with a one-time start-up cost of at least $10,300 (thus first-year total of $22,000).

Estimated Cost for Tutorial Support (to become BWT)		
Start-up/one-time costs	Includes development of dossier assignments and assessment materials, piloting costs for tutorial plans	$9,800
Yearly operational costs for tutorials	Includes tutors (writing consultants, teaching assistants), readers (writing consultants, teaching assistants, faculty), expert raters (teaching assistants, faculty) and administrative support	$31,750

We've estimated that the cost of the Writing Proficiency Tutorial, if managed completely by the Writing Center, would be $31,750 per year, with a one-time start-up cost of at least $9,800.

or limit on students' time with their writing consultant accounts for the range of writing needs among students with diverse backgrounds and empowers them to be the ones who make their own decisions about how their relationship with the writing consultant works. This seems to be a pedagogically ethical way of supporting writers who need more one-on-one attention.

Before piloting the BWE/BWT in practice, the SRUWC determined a cost estimate for the partnership. Archival writing center data includes several memos and email exchanges initiated by the SRUWC in 2004, just one year following the junior-level writing assessment described previously. These "cost estimates" would eventually be approved and used in some version over the next five years until the switch to Rich Feedback for the BWE component in 2009. The cost estimate for this partnership included the information in table 4.1.

This brings the total cost estimate for the BWE and BWT to $43,450 for each operating year. The document dated earlier in the year breaks down these categories more specifically and offers a slightly lower estimate. The details assume that the BWE would be taken by approximately 1,900 students per year and that the BWT would require the work of approximately 28 writing consultants, "at least 190 man-hours service by administrative readers," and "at least 38 man-hours service by expert raters." If around 20 percent of those who take the BWE must take the BWT, then 380 business school students would need regular tutoring sessions (approximately eight each). This totals a tutorial cost for around 3,040 consultations.

During my interviews with the SRUWC staff, I was told that the costs for partnerships are based solely on the pay required for the student consultants. However, the detailed budget breakdown from 2004 suggests pay for additional staff, including the "Pedagogy Specialist" (Sam) who is budgeted to make $75 per hour, a "Statistical Analyst" who is budgeted to make $50 per hour, a "Development Coordinator" who is budgeted to make $25 per hour, an "Administrative Assistant" who is budgeted to make $18 per hour, and "Writing Consultants," who are budgeted to make $12 per hour. These writing consultants, who are undergraduate peer tutors, would be doing the bulk of the work in terms of both assessment and the tutorials, not to mention being trained for each, resulting in 18,204 hours of labor, far more than all of the other staff positions combined.

This estimate represents what large-scale writing assessment and support resources at the local level look like. Yet, Kyle's and the business school's willingness to invest both their material resources and their time into writing assessment and writing support is commendable. The decision to support writing programming also suggests a recognition that, just like the teaching of writing should be everyone's responsibility, the support and funding of writing should be shared across campus. The potential for writing centers and business schools to work together through partnerships is immense, as is the undeniable recognition that, as shown above, business schools tend to have substantial funding. Although little has been explicitly written about the conflicts between business schools and writing centers, the fact that many business schools have their own writing centers is indicative of the philosophical differences that are sometimes perceived as non-workable. The uniqueness of the business school writing center has received some attention (Griffin 2001), yet the best way for university writing centers to work with business schools is understudied. In the case of SRU, the writing center plays an integral role in the business school's writing curriculum. This has implications for why non-business-specific writing centers and business schools should maintain a relationship to some degree.

BRINGING IN A P3: OUTSOURCING WRITING
ASSESSMENT TO RICH FEEDBACK

After five years of the BWE/BWT partnership, Sam eventually decided that the workload was too much for the writing center to handle.

He explains the decision to outsource the BWE, specifically to Rich Feedback, in the following way:

> Ultimately, we worked with the business college to outsource that rating [of the BWE] because we considered that the best use of our writing consultants' time is working with students and not . . . scoring writing evaluations. And I'm sure as part of your research you've looked up the *Chronicle of Higher Education* article about a related issue with outsourcing [laughs], outsourcing writing evaluation that's connected to the business [law and ethics] class. And, a decision to have the grading outsourced . . . to Rich Feedback.

Although he does not provide any additional details about the BLE course, Sam does say that Rich Feedback now evaluates and scores the BWE according to the same rubric used by the SRUWC in previous years. Then, the SRUWC groups students into the three major categories based on Rich Feedback's scores, and students are contacted for participation in the BWT.

Similarly, Kyle explains that at the beginning of the BWE partnership, the SRUWC was providing writing assessment and feedback in addition to working with students one-on-one. There are two main reasons Rich Feedback became a viable option. First, Kyle explains, the business school's decision to use Rich Feedback was not to determine grades for students. Instead, they turned to Rich Feedback because it was a more cost- and time-effective option than training in-house instructors to grade and/or provide feedback for hundreds of students. Second, Rich Feedback was a resource to help the business school meet accreditation standards in a way that increased the consistency and calibration among readers and scorers who are objective. When they attempted to create an in-house BWE, Kyle explains, it did not work; so, they decided to consider a third party:

> [Hiring graduate students] was a revolving door in terms of training and it was still costing us a lot of money because they were in salary. So, we thought, "What if we identified a third party and offloaded the training and that revolving door to them?" [Then] they would be required to maintain consistency in terms of calibrating what was the 1, 2, 3, or 4 on the business writing evaluation and providing the written comments that students would get back on their papers so that then the students could go to the writing center for one-on-one consultations, but offloading the evaluation.

In a sense, then, in Kyle's mind the third party "removes the burden" of evaluating student writing so that the writing center consultants can focus on conversations about the writing itself. This suggests that assessing along with supporting writing was beyond the scope of what the writing center or the business school could do. Approximately fifty to one hundred students from each cohort begin the BWT, and some of them continue to meet with consultants well beyond one semester's time. More than 1,000 incoming students take the BWE every year, resulting in a huge amount of writing that needs assessment. Kyle explains later that:

> it really got to be too much for them [the SRUWC]. They didn't have the staff to do it, because what was happening was, think of it like this tsunami of papers to grade all at once. Well, they just weren't equipped to ramp up staff. They had staff for all year round, but they couldn't get it back to us in a timely fashion, and so they recommended that we look for a third party, and they suggested Rich Feedback.

Both Sam's and Kyle's stories indicate that the business school's use of Rich Feedback began as a large-scale assessment tool for incoming business majors, not as a means of evaluating and grading student writing as part of a course. Yet, it set precedent for outsourcing writing feedback, and it eventually presented itself as an easier option for the course.

The use of Rich Feedback went on for several years before the *CHE* article targeting the BLE course was published. Soon after, the business school released an explanation of its use of Rich Feedback on its website, which includes a short history of the college's commitment to writing, including the beginning of its partnership with the SRUWC in 2003; the connection between its accreditation program, Association to Advance Collegiate Schools of Business, and the goal of improving written communication skills; and its decision to assess students with the BWE during their sophomore year. The statement says that "about 18 percent of our students are required to participate in the BWT." Following the BWE/BWT, there is another attempt to improve writing via a required upper-level course, BLE, which is described as a SRUWC partnership that began in 2007 and changed to incorporate Rich Feedback in 2009. The document includes the following statement about funding and evaluation:

> Currently, we are using funds from a private foundation for Rich Feedback's services in order to improve the quality of our writing program. This project receives ongoing evaluation from both the college faculty and the SRUWC to ensure quality control and meaningful results for our students.

Further, the business school argues that the evaluation provided by Rich Feedback was "identical" to the evaluation by the course instructor and the associate director of the SRUWC, in addition to providing "effective and appropriate" feedback that aligns with the goals of the course.

Yet, there is no specific evidence of what "meaningful results for our students" means. There is no data that presents student feedback included anywhere in this document, the program assessment reports, or the SRUWC archive.

The statement continues in a Q&A format that explains the company's background and addresses issues related to the Family Educational Rights and Privacy Act of 1974 (FERPA), claiming that there are none, since SRU's general counsel approved the contract and determined that Rich Feedback was "compliant with the requirements set forth under FERPA." The statement also provides the exact language shared with students in the BLE syllabus that clearly states the course's use of Rich Feedback to "assess," "score," and provide "feedback," leaving questions and concerns related to the grades and feedback to the "course administrator or TA . . . who will provide a second review."

The business school also provides a context for BLE and the decision to move from onsite TAs to Virtual TAs in the report, describing the training program involved and noting that "over time we discovered that more time was spent managing this process than spending time with the BLE students." Finally, the statement concludes with three benefits of using Rich Feedback: (1) the college's ability to maintain the intensity of the writing program; (2) the improved efficiencies in the feedback and initial scoring process; and (3) the quality of the evaluators, who are "experts at providing feedback on written work."

After sharing this statement with me, which was once publicly shared on the business school's website, Kyle tells me about the context surrounding the report and its reception. He explains that the report was:

> an explanation to administrators in the provost's office who had read the [*Chronicle of Higher Education*] article and were asking the question, "What are you guys doing over there? This is bad press." And we wrote a response, and they read it, and they said, "Oh, okay, we get it now." And really, that's all there was to it.

Since the article's publication, the business school has continued to use Rich Feedback for both the BWE and in the BLE course.

Perhaps in his most convincing defense, Kyle explains that the decision to make writing a priority was a choice, and not such an easy one, as he acknowledges that focusing on something other than writing would have been easier. In this moment, Kyle also links the choice to use Rich Feedback to the business school's accreditation:

> We didn't do it lightly. And, we really felt like it provided a quality improvement over the way we were doing it where we had a teacher hire

and train TAs that were a revolving door. . . . I mean, we wouldn't have to make writing our learning outcome for accreditation, it could be something else that could be measured with Scantron. But, the reason we picked writing was because we cared about that as a skill and that's what employers cared about. There was nobody in the higher education hiring board that forced us to do it, nobody in the admin at SRU made us do it, we chose that. We chose to assess writing, and we called upon what we thought was a reputable third party to help us in the assessment process, and to give our students meaningful feedback.

Here, Kyle acknowledges the workload involved in training new TAs who change from year to year (sometimes even semester to semester), the ways in which TAs sometimes act as graders within a course (another way of "outsourcing" grading in that the professor doesn't do it), the challenge of teaching writing in large classes, the "alternative" as not doing any writing (this is not a replacement model but rather the addition of writing support that otherwise would not be there), and the college's (and potential employers') commitment to writing.

While Kyle does admit that they have found the use of Rich Feedback to be appropriate for their accreditation requirements and assessment, not for grade-based or curricular purposes, he also recognizes that using Rich Feedback is not the most pedagogically effective option. Here, Kyle seems to anticipate the limitations of working from a deficit model of writing instruction, despite the programmatic decisions he's made:

> If somebody said we're not going to do a third party, that's fine. Provide us with funding, to fully staff the kind of in-house staff [needed] and we'll do it. Or . . . instead of hiring another accounting professor, hire a PhD in rhetoric and composition to teach business writing and do that in house. It's all a matter of funding. If you've got the funds, it probably would be better to do it all in house. And, it'd be better to have sections of only 30 students and embed writing in every single [business] course. That'd be great. That'd be ideal.

Kyle admits that using Rich Feedback is not the best-case scenario. This suggests his preference to work internally with the university's writing experts. Still, in this less-than-ideal case, he says that Rich Feedback does a pretty good job: "We wouldn't keep doing it and pay money if we didn't feel like it added value and our accrediting agency would look at that askance too, and say, 'well, you shouldn't be doing that,' but we really haven't gotten pushback," other than after the *CHE* article was published.

When Kyle spoke about the ongoing assessment of the BWE/BWT program, he also shared a report that contains the most recent longitudinal assessment data from 2014. In collaboration with the SRUWC,

Kyle assessed the impact of the BWT on student success by following student GPAs one year after the BWE. He looked at three groups of twenty students each: (1) those who were referred to the BWT but did not complete it; (2) those who were referred to the BWT and completed it; and (3) those who were cleared by the assessment score. The key finding states:

> Students who were referred for tutorial due to low BWE assessment scores and completed the BWT tutorial performed academically (as measured by GPA) *nearly on par with* their 1,300-student cohort as a whole, and *considerably better than* students who were referred for tutorial due to low BWE assessment scores but did not complete the BWT tutorial.

Thus, the BWT works and the BWE does a good enough job of scoring student writing accurately. In addition to considering how those who completed the BWT did in comparison to the rest of their cohort, the difference in terms of program retention between those who completed the BWT and those who were referred but did not complete it is significant. The above sample also indicates that 25 percent of those who are cleared by the assessment were no longer enrolled in the program after a year, a fairly significant withdrawal rate from the major itself. In contrast, nearly all the students who completed the BWT graduated from the program. This is not surprising, given that the BWT was a graduation requirement. Still, the connection between the BWT and retention is significant in a major with such a high withdrawal rate among students after they initially commit to the major.

Despite the substantial assessment data collected by the business school and the writing center to assess the impact of the BWE/BWT on writing performance and student success in the major, there was and still is no inclusion of student perspective or voice about how they experience the partnership. In fact, near the completion of this book, I reached out directly to both the current SRUWC director and to Kyle to see if there has been any assessment data collected around student experience with the BWE/BWT to date. Both told me there was nothing. No doubt student voices are crucial, not only in understanding the success of this partnership, but also in thinking about how it should move forward in years to come.

Despite his acceptance of the assessment results as indicative of the BWE/BWT program's success, Kyle still acknowledges the limits of using a Virtual TA service and computer-generated feedback in relation to human feedback. This suggests that Kyle too has limits in terms of what kind of outsourcing is acceptable. He explains that when papers are submitted to Rich Feedback, they are "read by at least one human," adding that he thinks "there may be an initial analysis by a machine grade, and then the two scores are compared." He also claims that there was a break in Rich Feedback's leadership, during which some wanted to "go with machine grading" and others "felt like that was not going to provide the quality feedback that [they] believed in and that the clients had believed in." Kyle went with the latter group that became Rich Feedback. Still, Kyle suggests that Rich Feedback's Virtual TA is a useful tool that provides something different, but still useful, from human feedback:

> [T]here's an evolutionary component in terms of the robustness of the technology. What might not have been appropriate 5–10 years ago, in 5 years, the way that computers can do some analysis of somebody's writing will be a lot more sophisticated, and it might also just be different levels of analysis, whether it's grammatical, or organizational, looking at transition words, things like that versus what a human would really do a much better job at in terms of analyzing tone or awareness of audience or something like that. I don't know, but it's just another tool.

While I had trouble finding a central website for Rich Feedback, I did find one for Virtual TA. On their homepage, they proudly display a link to the *CHE* article. Their recruitment materials suggest that they are looking for people with MAs or PhDs in academic fields. They also feature SRU under their "Success Stories" link, along with two other colleges. Almost as if the company read Dingo et al.'s chapter, the company seems to celebrate its ability to alleviate the labor of writing instruction. "Turn to the specialists; leave it to them to do the drudgery," they urge.

CREATING AND MAINTAINING A NEGOTIATED SPACE: AN ALTERNATIVE METHOD FOR SUPPORTING LARGE-SCALE WRITING ASSESSMENT AND SUPPORT

One important element of both Sam's and Kyle's stories that was mentioned but not fully explored in the *CHE* article was how the business school's use of Rich Feedback began as a large-scale assessment tool for incoming business majors, as Sam's story suggests. In addition, the idea of *rating*, or scoring student writing for assessment purposes to determine whether they would be required to take the BWT, is conflated with *grading*, a process of evaluating writing and assigning a grade within a course for credit. These two terms also seem somewhat removed from the concepts of *feedback* and *evaluation* of writing, both of which should provide students with a written response to their writing that gives them a sense of how to improve and revise. Further, despite the article and its controversy, the business school continues to outsource writing assessment for both the BWE and the BLE course. However, the writing center requirement has dropped completely. Kyle explains:

> [It has] evolved over time—he [the current professor for BLE] used to have his students go to the writing center [to discuss the feedback and use it for revision], but Rich Feedback was providing such meaningful comments that when the students would take their papers over as required by his syllabus, the writing center consultants would basically say, "well, yeah, they made some really good comments, we agree," and the students were not sensing that they were getting much more. When [the professor] told me this, he wasn't criticizing the writing center, he was just praising Rich Feedback for doing such a good job. So, he no longer requires them to go to the writing center.

What began as a move to outsource the scoring of writing so that peer tutors could focus on conferencing with students was eventually eliminated. In this case, a tool that was first used for an extracurricular, large-scale assessment replaced both the role of TAs and the role of peer tutors in the classroom. This example suggests that, once we start outsourcing, even if only for a particular task in a single context, the practice may be continued elsewhere in ways that were initially unintended.

Part of what makes discussion of this specific partnership tricky is that neither the SRUWC nor the business school minded when the BLE partnership ended its connection to the writing center. And the partners continued to work together through several other partnerships, in addition to the BWE/BWT, where writing assessment was still outsourced to Rich Feedback. Yet, from my position as an outside writing center director looking in, this scenario raises concern both about ethics and about sustainability. For instance, what happens if one of the partners retires and someone new comes in? Will they understand the decision to use Rich Feedback for some writing support and the writing center for others? How is such a decision made? What if there are additional budget cuts that require the use of P3s even more? Will the track record and working relationship with Rich Feedback be grounds for additional outsourcing in the business school, and even in other colleges across the university?

The potential implications that could result from outsourcing reach beyond a single program or department. For this reason, planning for how to respond to ethical questions before they arise may help partners anticipate and best respond in ways that do not lead to the partnership's end. For instance, in "Emerging Priorities: Strategic Planning and Dealing with Ethical Dilemmas," Robin Matross Helms argues that consideration of how partners might respond to ethical dilemmas that arise is one of the most important concerns for partnership management, based on a 2015 report written by the American Council of Education (ACE). Helms argues that each partner must determine "where they need to draw the line on controversial issues and what compromises they are willing (and unwilling) to make to move a relationship forward" (2016, 212). Further, Helms describes the space through which partners can address conflict as "negotiated space," a term that appears in the ACE's original report. "Negotiated space" recognizes that the terms of any partnership exist in a shared space that requires openness and honesty, as well as collaboratively developed ethical frameworks. This concept has also been used to acknowledge different worldviews and cultures, including differences in knowledge systems (Mila-Schaaf and Hudson 2009; Smith et al. 2008). Partners who work across academic disciplines especially must consider different worldviews as part of establishing "negotiated space," since such perspectives often contribute to ethical (mis)understandings.

In the case of the SRUWC and the business school, an unanticipated conflict that arose in the BWE/BWT partnership was the writing center's inability to handle the writing assessment workload. At that point and under a time crunch, the writing center determined a possible solution to the problem, and the business school simply agreed. Not much here was negotiated. Instead, the writing center—and Sam in particular—determined that it preferred to work directly with student writers, rather than on scoring/assessing writing. Such was likely the case early on in the partnership as well, but there never seemed to be a conversation specifically focused on laying out each partner's strengths, preferences, and abilities to deliver over time. Nor was there an explicit discussion of anticipated challenges.

This scenario raises the question: Who should handle large-scale writing assessment on college campuses? While best practices suggest that individual departments and programs should do it (Conference on College Composition and Communication), this approach does not adequately account for the number of people in departments outside of writing and the humanities who have little if any experience with writing or writing assessment. Thus, turning to the writing center is a reasonable approach.

However, whether or not the writing center could continuously participate in annual assessment deserved closer attention earlier on. Had Kyle and Sam considered other local avenues for supporting annual writing assessment, such as the Center for Teaching and Learning or the Office of Assessment, they might have prevented the use of Rich

Feedback at all. And, in doing so, the possibility of unintentionally using Rich Feedback in a writing-intensive class as the sole means of generating writing feedback would have likely been avoided. Assessment also could have been a concern to discuss with the business faculty, especially with instructional faculty who taught many students across the major. Given that there was clear involvement from them early on in establishing the partnership through their willingness to help develop the assessment rubric and identify strong samples of student writing, some business faculty members could have become stakeholders with a higher level of engagement.[5]

While the above suggests this writing center and business school partnership likely would have benefited from early conversations about determining and sustaining stakeholder engagement (chapter 4 of this book), they also would benefit from working through some of these hard questions from the start. For instance, in "A Positive Breakup: Managing a Soft Landing with Strategic International Partnership Termination," Anthony J. Shull gives advice about how to end things so that partners remain on good terms. Yet, his advice is equally helpful when thinking about sustainability and anticipating challenges. Shull emphasizes the importance of identifying a "common thread" that ensures partners can learn and grow together because of an identifiable alignment across programmatic missions and visions. This connection can help create committed dialogue in the "negotiated space" because it includes "mutual recognition that weaker areas need to be addressed with support, resources, and experience" (2016, 69). Shull's questions are useful for creating strategic writing center partnerships because they require consideration of both hypothetical questions about the means of each partner and tangible actions to take as a result, per table 4.2.

Working through the questions above and creating a more involved group of stakeholders from early on may have helped support the design of the BLE course in such a way that the use of Rich Feedback would have been not only unnecessary but also deemed ethically unacceptable. Maintaining a group of stakeholders also would have made determining appropriate writing assessment and support more people's problems and responsibility, rather than just Kyle's, Sam's, and those of whoever happened to be teaching BLE. During my interview with Kyle, I talked to him about the SRUWC's partnership with a graduate-level marketing course, MARK 8397: Communication of Academic Research, which works as a kind of writing fellows/course-embedded tutoring program in which a writing consultant is assigned to a specific class, attends that class, and works with student writers specifically within the context

Table 4.2. Identifying common threads in the negotiated space

Before the partnership begins, ask:	Once the partnership has been established, discuss and negotiate:
Would there be mutual benefits for each party? If so, what are they?	What are the key terms used within each partner's mission/vision? How might a shared language for writing be created?
Would the partnership align well with the mission/vision of both parties?	What are the areas of strength and resources that could be provided and sustained by each partner? What are the weaker areas outside the resources/expertise of the partners?
What are the motivations of each party in establishing a partnership? How are they similar and different?	Map out anticipated growth in the areas of each partner's operations that would be positively affected by the partnership. Note any areas that may be stunted due to anticipated growth.
Would each partner be able to make good on their commitments to programmatic, academic, assessment, and support services?	What are the non-negotiables in terms of what each partner will not or cannot do? Are there any potential outcomes of the partnership that may cause harm and thus should be avoided?

of the course. While Kyle appreciates the model, he brings up the following concern:

> [C]ourse-embedded programs require a tutor that really has a dual expertise, because you've got your writing skill but you know the context within which they're having to write. I think the challenge there with that model is scalability at the undergraduate level. It works with PhD, and even maybe MA, and possibly with some senior-level small sections, but it gets a little expensive and unwieldy if you're trying to scale it out at a university our size. And so maybe that's where technology will have a greater role in outsourcing to companies that can do it efficiently. Maybe part of the comments come from a third-party vendor, along with that tutorial model . . . which is what we have, we've got the tutorial as well as the Rich Feedback.

Yet, what Kyle seems to miss here is that course-embedded tutoring works because it is context- and course-specific and thus cannot be outsourced to other companies. The scenario he ends with is what actually happened with the BLE course, except the tutorial element disappeared, even though it has been maintained in the case of the BWE/BWT partnership. Although Kyle and I did not spend much time trying to think through the ways a course-embedded tutoring model might work on a large scale, such questions are worth exploration by a group of stakeholders who bring different levels of expertise to the conversation. Perhaps the marketing professor who was also in the College of Business would have had some ideas to bring to the table, in addition to some of the writing center's other partners who worked through adapted course-embedded tutoring models with class sizes of fifty to seventy-five students. But, when the problem of writing assessment and support becomes that of just a few people, the likelihood of such conversations is small. The much easier solution is to think about outsourcing.

While the end of the writing center's partnership with the BLE course seems undesirable, what appears less clear is how to resolve the BWE/BWT partnership in a way that still maintains a close connection to the writing center. Further, the question of what role writing centers might play, and are willing to play, in large-scale writing assessment deserves closer exploration. Clearly, their ability and willingness to play some role is crucial. Conducting preliminary assessment before establishing a partnership, especially a programmatic one, seems like a useful early step. Yet, alongside conversations about what such an assessment might look like, there needs to be conversation in a "negotiated space" that helps set parameters based on what the results may reveal. Both writing centers and disciplinary partners need to determine what their non-negotiables are in terms of their participation in the partnership, even when some compromising is needed. If writing centers are willing to participate in larger conversations about assessment and large-scale writing support, then they may also be able to help departments think through the benefits and drawbacks of working with P3s. If local resources are unavailable, writing centers may be able to help partners decide how P3s are used and to what extent. Even if writing centers would prefer not to have such conversations, our participation in strategic partnerships via disruptive innovations means that we will likely encounter them. If we choose not to respond at all, or choose not to participate in widescale writing assessment or feedback, then we risk the possibility of P3s that may start as situated disruptive innovations but have the potential to take over our tutoring work in other areas, courses, and partnerships.

5
NAVIGATING WORKPLACE REALITIES
Partnering with STEM in the College of Engineering

In the first couple weeks of the semester, Fernando, a Latino assistant professor of political science in his second year at SRU, began working with the writing center to "completely change" his writing curriculum, as he started asking himself if there was a way to "teach his students writing in a way more useful beyond college." He scrapped his syllabus for an upper-level, writing-intensive Politics of Mexico class that emphasizes research-based, academic-style essays in favor of having students practice the writing genres that they would likely encounter in the workplace as researchers and consultants. Fernando's new assignments include a series of op-ed pieces to be posted publicly on a class blog, in hopes that students will "be creative" rather than "writing in a dry academic style," and two policy memos. The series of op-ed blog posts require students to focus on a contemporary problem or contingent event in Mexico for a newspaper or magazine-like venue. These assignments attempt to engage students in public writing for a wide range of potential readers. Students are also evaluated on how they respond to one another's blog posts.

In one of the policy memos, Fernando envisions a job in the "market research division" of an oil and gas company and asks students to write for this imagined company, addressing concerns raised by the directive board. He requires students to incorporate information from their reading and research and to make a recommendation. The "rubric," which displays a breakdown of how students will be evaluated, seems to work from generalist writing concepts with little attention to the particularities of the disciplinary genre, although other details from the assignment suggest that Fernando is indeed looking for students to think and write like political scientists, especially given the imagined audience he created. These assignments, which all still require researching and writing like political scientists, seem quite removed from the traditional, academic research essay. These blog post assignments, like the policy memos, ask students to write in a non-academic genre for an imagined workplace audience.

Fernando's rationale and genre choices show that he anticipates the likely writing forms and audiences for whom his students might write in the real world. This attempt to create a workplace scenario within the

https://doi.org/10.7330/9781646421770.c005

classroom is an example of a writing in the profession (WIP) focused curriculum; it does not give students actual, workplace writing experiences, but it asks them to imagine and write as if they were in them. Although conversations about writing pedagogy in political science are not often connected to those in engineering, WIP was present at SRU across eleven diverse disciplines that shared the purpose of making curricular changes that motivate students to understand the connection between writing and their lives as working professionals.

While WIP runs complementary to the field of professional writing in terms of its focus on workplace contexts and, primarily, business and technical writing genres, it is different in that this pedagogy emerged directly in conversation with faculty across the disciplines who teach writing and is thus highly contextualized within particular fields. So, for instance, as Fernando's policy memo assignment shows, students need to know both the genre of a policy memo as well as disciplinary content knowledge about relocating a business internationally and how to balance the economic and social concerns of a directive board with market expansion.

As was the case for Fernando, many of the SRUWC's partners worked with the writing center to change their curriculum with a particular interest in having their students work with writing consultants who could provide an outsider perspective on their writing. For example, Linda (math) teaches writing-intensive courses for math education students who need to be able to explain complex math concepts in simple, understandable language for middle and high school students. Linda considers the writing consultants' role in helping her students become better writers as absolutely necessary and as different from what she could offer as someone with an advanced degree in math. In addition to valuing an outsider perspective, faculty also emphasize basic writing concepts that they believe are universal, such as clarity and analysis, as well as somewhat new assignment components like requiring students to compose across modes and write in teams.

Thus, WIP works from four primary concepts. First, students must learn to compose visually and orally, in addition to alphabetically. Second, students must learn to write in team-based/collaborative environments that require effective project management. Third, students must learn to develop clarity in their writing. And fourth, students must learn to write in ways that are accessible to nonexpert audiences. Although attempting to understand the writing center's exact role in supporting and developing this curriculum is not the focus of this chapter, it is worth noting that the common factor across a wide range of disciplines that operate from a WIP curriculum is their writing center partnerships. This is not surprising, given that the writing center is well positioned to work with writers and faculty who are composing with a nonexpert audience in mind that requires attention to clarity. Yet, case study data suggests that current writing center practitioners primarily tend to assume that they will work with students on traditional, alphabetic-text writing.

This kind of attention to the demands of post-college writing reflects a cultural shift across the disciplines, likely resulting from higher education's increasing attention to career readiness and how colleges are (or are not) preparing students for jobs after graduation. This concern has impacted how universities and students view the value of different majors as well as how young adults and parents discuss whether college is even worth it. One relatively new career-focused disruptive innovation with great potential to significantly impact higher education is the "Go Pro Early" approach, in which students work full-time jobs, and while doing so, their employer pays their tuition (Busteed 2019; Fain 2020). In "This Will Be the Biggest Disruption in Higher Education," published in *Forbes*, the president of Kaplan University Partners, Brandon Busteed, argues that in this "new world" students will be "going to a job to get a college degree" instead of going to college to get a job. Not only is this approach popular among parents (74 percent of K–12 parents surveyed for Busteed's report said they would consider this option for their children), but many employers are also already offering these programs, such as PricewaterhouseCoopers, Walmart, Amazon, Discover, Starbucks, Disney, UPS, Publix, Wells Fargo, Comcast, and Papa John's Pizza.

While these approaches may be well suited to some students, the emphasis on job and employer satisfaction over college education seems inevitable, since the employer is the one footing the tuition bill. Yet, few in higher education have responded to this move, with the exception of Stanford University Dean of Education Geoffrey Cox's "Can Starbucks Save the Middle Class? No. But It Might Ruin Higher Education," published in the *Chronicle of Higher Education* in August 2019. In the article, Cox acknowledges how company-university partnerships may impact tuition costs for other students, as well as withhold access from those who are already excluded from higher education. Further, he worries that linking employment to college could cause problems similar to those resulting from healthcare's link to employment, especially in terms of how state and federal government support for higher education may shift. Yet another cause for concern is how such programs could impact curriculum. For instance, there has been a trend across some universities to make deals with local businesses that plan to hire students in exchange for curricular influence and financial support. Similarly, companies that pay tuition for large numbers of students may eventually request similar curricular weight.

In contrast, a WIP curriculum pays more attention to workplace and community writing, and even connects with some employers, but maintains its focus on student-driven projects—which are experimental in nature—but that ultimately give students the opportunity to apply their writing and research abilities to their own project designs. In this way, students, not businesses, impact curriculum and oftentimes eventually the businesses and potential investors themselves. Further, a WIP curriculum can effectively prepare students for post-graduation writing, lessening the concern over unemployment and the pressure some may feel to join "Go Pro Early" programs.

In this scenario, the writing center becomes an important site for curricular development by helping faculty think through assignment design and genre choice as part of their conversations about how collaborative partnerships can best work to support student writers. Further, tutors are well positioned to play the role of external audience members, oftentimes outside both the classroom and the discipline. This helps prepare students to interact with stakeholder audiences outside the university, rather than just writing for the professor as imagined audience. While creating imagined audiences is a well-intentioned move, part of the limitation is that such a context does not really activate genre knowledge because, as Christine Tardy has pointed out in *Building Genre Knowledge* (2009), the activity is likely not real for students. She argues that for students to fully gain and activate genre knowledge, the motives and texts must become real for their users. In her longitudinal research that traces the experiences of four multilingual graduate students in engineering and computer sciences, Tardy acknowledges that performance of genre knowledge is also deeply connected to identity, and that to use genre knowledge, even when mastered, students also must feel authorized to do so. Thus, not only is a WIP curriculum valuable, but the WIP classroom—where students have the opportunity to discuss their experiences with writing in workplace genres with peers, writing center tutors, and their professor—can also significantly contribute to helping them develop the authority and confidence to write outside the university.

WIP also acknowledges the complex communities in which students will need to learn and communicate over the course of their lives post-graduation, in particular the kinds of heterogeneous, literate practices that will develop over the span of their lives, as part of what Paul Prior has called their "trajectories of semiotic becoming." In his 2018 Watson Conference Keynote, Prior used this phrase to describe a story about his daughter's embodied, mediated, dialogic learning that happened across many moments of life and within messy discourses, rather than in settled domains. Writing that takes place both within and outside the classroom, across academic, community, and workplace audiences, and in response to shifting genres, helps students move across discourses in a dialogic process that may better represent their post-graduation writing and learning lives.

Rather than focusing on concepts generated from a single partnership as in the earlier case studies presented in chapters 3 and 4, this case study chapter draws on interview data from faculty partners across the disciplines to develop WIP and then shows specific examples of WIP in practice via the SRUWC's partnership in the College of Engineering with Electrical-Electronics Technology (ELET). In addition to being an example of WIP pedagogy, the ELET partnership is also an example of a transformational partnership (Sutton 2016; Enos and Morton 2003), where change occurs at the individual, the institutional, and the community levels. In contrast to a transactional partnership, where resources are exchanged in an instrumental, product-oriented way through a simple relationship, a transformational partnership involves a deeper connection through which resources are combined, curricula are developed collaboratively, and the partnership dynamically changes and grows over time.

A WIP writing curriculum that moves students to write for audiences beyond the university in real-world genres creates a rich environment for a transformational partnership because more is at stake than that which occurs within in a single classroom or writing center session. The writing center's ability to encourage, support, and co-create WIP curricula via transformational partnerships provides one important way to respond to higher education's emphasis on career readiness by supporting students' experiential learning through writing. Although the monetary benefits of the Go Pro Early movement cannot (and perhaps should not) be resisted, greater attention to and support for WIP curricula provide universities with another way to connect with employers in the workplace while continuing to emphasize university learning over workplace activity, and while simultaneously highlighting the connection between the two. In this way, creating a WIP curriculum through strategic partnership with the writing center is a local, ethical kind of disruptive innovation because it responds to corporate university pressures to acknowledge career readiness and life beyond the university while still centering the students' experience in the classroom.

SETTING THE CONTEXT FOR A TRANSFORMATIONAL, WIP
PARTNERSHIP: SRUWC AND ELET'S PRE-PARTNERSHIP MEETING

One of the most significant aspects of a transformational partnership like ELET is the pre-partnership meeting, where discussions about stakeholder engagement, mutual benefits, and roles/responsibilities take place. In a sense, this is where negotiated space is critically created. While the first pre-semester meeting of a new partnership is especially important (like the one with Fernando), ongoing early semester meetings are also important even with established partners so that the changing student populations and disciplinary genre expectations are taken into account as part of the partnership's setup each year. Early in the fall 2015 semester before any formal interviews had taken place, Hannah (SRUWC middle administrator) explained to me some of the frustration surrounding the ELET partnership. ELET is housed in the College of Technology and requires students to create viable technology applications to improve current electronic practices. ELET works closely with the writing center across four required courses. The SRUWC administrators all voiced frustration with this partnership. For example, in chapter 2 when I referenced Hannah's description of the partnership as familial—"it's like we're [the SRUWC] the mom, the partners are the dad, and the students are the kid. They need us to organize everything and don't usually listen"—she was referring to ELET.

While I found this to be a surprising metaphor, Hannah explained it with a story about the first time ELET tried to work with the SRUWC. Without any warning and with no scheduling, the teaching assistant (TA) in charge at the time brought a group of nearly fifty students to the writing center to work with consultants.[1] The department head had scheduled a time for the ELET students to meet with consultants in the SRUWC, but because of other class scheduling conflicts, the TA decided to bring the students over a day early. When the SRUWC could not meet with any of the students since they were "completely booked" and "no longer worked with walk-ins," the TA was frustrated and they had to sit down and have another meeting, along with the department chair, to explain why impromptu consultations with fifty students would not work. "They can't really come in anytime they want to," Hannah explains, and that was what the ELET partners seemed to expect.

While this story stands as perhaps the largest mishap of communication between the SRUWC and the ELET partners, it is one of many miscommunications. The ELET administrative partners, although seemingly responsible for the assignments and the large course lectures, do not grade or read student writing. Instead, TAs work on writing assignments. Between ELET administrators, TAs, students, and SRUWC administrators and consultants, there are many opportunities for miscommunication. Given the amount of confusion students had about their TA's expectations and because they seemed to be an important stakeholder absent from the pre-partnership meeting, I sought out a meeting with one of the ELET TAs, Abhi.

It quickly became clear that there is a disconnect between Abhi's ideas about writing and those of Mehdi and Darid (the ELET administrative partners). First, when I asked him about the kind of writing ELET students would likely do after graduation, Abhi explained that only some companies and some departments write, and that the primary purpose of having students write in ELET courses was to prepare them for MA/PhD programs, which would require them to publish in Institute of Electrical and Electronics Engineers journals. This explanation of why writing was part of the ELET curriculum reflects Abhi's career path, but it strongly conflicts with Mehdi's and Darid's perspectives, as well as with the implications of hosting an annual Undergraduate Research Symposium for a wide range of audience members and the overall writing curriculum in general.

When I asked Abhi if he had noticed student progress over the course of the semester, he said no, since he does not read or grade any writing until the end. The major writing issue he notices is report formatting and "copy/pasting," which seemed to mean putting things in the wrong places without realizing it, although I had trouble understanding what Abhi meant by this. He also explained that when students participate in group writing, they each write separate sections. Abhi did not acknowledge the challenge of four or five different writers trying to construct a coherent and consistent document or discuss how students should approach this task. When I asked him about "writing" he answered me by discussing "research," thus suggesting that Abhi understands writing as the display of knowledge from research, rather than an additional task. This aligns with the ELET 3405 students' experience of receiving some guidelines about research in class, but not about writing.

In addition to the many players in this partnership, the SRUWC has nearly 1,000 student interactions with ELET each year, making it one of the largest. Thus, the ELET partnership has a reputation for being challenging among the SRUWC staff, not only because of the communication difficulties and the lack of involvement from TAs, but also because students are often as frustrated. The experimental nature, the project-driven curriculum, and the confusion over how to balance the expectations of the professor with those of the TA who grades the writing all cause anxiety too.

The SRUWC/ELET partnership began in 2008 with support from a Quality Enhancement Program. The SRUWC first documented these projects beginning in its 2011 annual reports, at which time there were partnerships linked to three ELET courses, including ELET 2103 and 4308, both of which still exist today. In 2012, the ELET partnerships changed to include all four courses that are currently in working partnerships. In 2014, STEM partnerships including ELET grew with the addition of a new STEM manager (Jeremy) to the SRUWC's full-time staff. During that same year, the SRUWC staff "interacted with 3,704 STEM majors and collaborated with 23 STEM faculty." In particular, the report points to the ELET partnership as an "example of a successful Writing Center/STEM course interaction." Per ELET's website, the goal of the program is "to provide students with a high-quality applications-oriented undergraduate education based on state-of-the-art technological equipment associated with electrical technology." ELET students participate in hands-on group writing and research projects that culminate in a proposal for and the eventual building of a prototype in their senior course sequence, along with a formal report and an oral presentation at the department's annual symposium.

Each ELET course enrolls between forty and fifty students, and there are at least two sections of each, every semester. The department's partnership with the writing center involves three to four required meetings for each writing team with the same writing consultant over the semester. The ELET course sequence consists of the four parts, as shown in table 5.1.

Although I did not have the opportunity to interview the ELET administrative partners,[2] I attended the beginning-of-the-semester meeting in August before the partnerships themselves began. Jeremy (STEM project manager) mentioned the meeting to me casually, and I asked both him and Hannah, who oversees Jeremy, if I could attend. According to Hannah, the meeting would be "just about scheduling," but Jeremy added in his conversation with me before we met that he thought they would also discuss whether to bring back the junior-level ELET 3405 partnership, since it has not worked all that well in the past. Jeremy admits to being a bit nervous about the meeting, since he had not met either of the ELET administrative partners (Mehdi and Darid) before. A few minutes before the meeting began, I introduced myself to Mehdi and Darid, explained my interest in understanding how the SRUWC and the ELET department worked together to support student

Table 5.1. Fall 2015 SRUWC/ELET partnership courses

	Course description	Major assignments	Required meetings
ELET 2103: Digital Systems (sophomore level)	Experiments in digital systems, including basic gates, combinational and sequential systems, binary arithmetic circuits, MSRU/DEMSRU, decoder and encoder devices. Use of modern software simulation tools is emphasized.	Students work in groups to write a proposal, progress report, presentation, and final report.	(1) proposal; (2) progress report submission; and (3) final report, presentation, and demonstration.
ELET 3405: Microprocessor Architecture (junior level)	Architecture and operation of microprocessor-based systems including basic hardware, software, and interfaces.	Students work in groups to write a project proposal with literature review, progress report, presentation, and final report.	(1) proposal; (2) progress report; (3) presentation and demonstration; and (4) final report with literature review.
ELET 4308: Senior Project (senior semester 1)	Senior projects in computer engineering technology including proposals, project management, integrated hardware, and software design.	Students write individual project proposals. From the forty, the ELET faculty choose the strongest five ideas. Then, students get into teams and work on creating a plan for building one of the five selected projects.	Meetings 1–3 focused on writing the proposal and a mid-term progress report.
ELET 4208: Senior Project Laboratory (senior semester 2)	Senior project laboratory in computer engineering technology including progress reports, prototypes construction and testing, final project reports, and presentations.	Students build their protypes with a small departmental stipend and formally compose an interim presentation, project presentation, project report, and large poster.	Post-proposal approval, meetings 1–4 focus on preparation for their final report and presentation.

writing, and asked if I could listen to the meeting. As we informally chatted, we talked about how challenging it was for students to learn how to communicate as engineers, given that they are often writing for a wide range of readers at any given time. Mehdi admits that this was part of why the SRUWC/ELET partnership is so valuable: It requires students to clearly explain their work to writing consultants who are often not engineers.

At the start of the project meeting, conversation focused on "just scheduling," yet such scheduling was integral to the work of the partnership because it required the deadlines for projects to be set and all parties to decide on when it would be most beneficial to have students meet with consultants. Although stakeholder engagement and mutual benefits were not directly discussed, the meeting space did function as a negotiated space, as the partners talked about possible changes to the curriculum. The plan had always been, and still was, for students to meet in their project groups with a consultant during part of their lab time, three or four times over the course of the semester. In addition to setting the schedule, the SRUWC and ELET administrators spent some time discussing what would be done during these group meetings. For example, Mehdi mentioned that proposals written during the first semester of senior-level ELET were often a bit easier because these students had "more energy," but that the final report written by the second-semester senior-level ELET was more challenging. He explains that it is most important for them to learn from the project itself, even if the prototype does not work as the group intended.

At one point, Hannah suggests that one of the partnership courses move to an online model using the Blackboard course shell—the sophomore-level ELET course. However, the ELET administrators overlook this idea by quickly moving on to a conversation about how to use Blackboard to get necessary materials to the TAs and to send email reminders to students about their group meetings in the SRUWC. Continuing the meetings in face-to-face, in-class form seems non-negotiable for the ELET administrators, although they do not explicitly state it as such. Then, conversation moves to the junior-level ELET group, which Jeremy thought might not make a reappearance. Darid points out that the teacher of the course is a part-time faculty member and told us, "I don't want to add extra work having them manage [the partnership]." Thus, Darid offers to be the "point of contact" for this ELET course and any other ones that are deemed "vulnerable." Hannah also asks what kind of writing the students do in the junior-level ELET course and admits that, in the past, the SRUWC had trouble communicating with the TAs in the course. Again, the partners did not explicitly discuss stakeholder engagement, but their awareness of it as an issue and an important consideration was present throughout the meeting.

Since Darid mentions that students will work on a report and a literature review, everyone agrees to develop a partnership plan for ELET 3405. Darid says that the department has developed new rubrics for ELET 3405 that should help with clarity and communication for students working on the written report and literature review. Instead of having students "doing just a summary," the department now requires a literature review section. Hannah suggests adding the literature review to the current rubric so that students see that they will receive credit for that part of the writing project. This way, the consultants can use

Table 5.2. ELET/Writing Center meetings for ELET 3405

Meeting Date/Time at CBB Room 238	What you will need to bring
October 20 @ 1–2 pm	Students will **bring in their articles** intended for their literature review. Students should also **bring a two-sentence summary** of their articles.
October 27 @ 1–2 pm	Students will bring a **draft of their literature reviews** to work with consultants on. Students will also bring **outlines of their progress reports**.
November 3 @ 1–2 pm	Students will bring copies of their **progress reports** to discuss with consultants.
November 17 @ 1–2 pm	Students will begin to prepare drafts of their **final report and presentation**. Students will also have the opportunity to have mock presentations.

the rubric with the description and points associated with the literature review to help explain to students why it is important for them to move beyond summary. Again, Mehdi chimes in by saying that the literature review "doesn't need to be advanced writing or very good, but some kind of story," instead of reading like three separate papers that are not connected. Hannah suggests that, in addition to having students bring drafts of the full proposal, they incorporate a visit with a librarian into one of their meetings to talk with students about finding sources. Then, students can bring in the articles/summaries before the proposal draft so that they can focus one session on organizing the sources.

Darid explains that having students work with sources in the way that Hannah describes "was always the intent" and that the literature review is a major project that should "be like a spiral, adding more each time," since the students will be writing additional literature reviews later in classes. After deciding that three to five sources would be appropriate for the literature review for ELET 3405 students, they set a time for Jeremy to visit the classes during their lab times to present the partnership and talk about the SRUWC. They also decide on four meetings and set agendas for all four, which Jeremy finalizes in the creation of table 5.2. This table and collaborative semester plan for how each team meeting with the writing consultant will unfold is typical across courses.

Conversations about the three remaining ELET course partnerships go fairly quickly, as they had been running smoothly for a while. Darid and Mehdi request the times for ELET 2103 be set later, since they are still working on setting that schedule. Despite the hesitancy of both Hannah and Jeremy, who seem to fear that not pinning down dates and times now could result in a long delay and the need to make last-minute plans, they agree to move on to discussion of the senior courses, which

Darid and Mehdi request "get started immediately." Hannah asks for Darid and Mehdi to attend the first meeting with herself, Jeremy, and the consultants assigned to the project, making a case for the value of such a meeting. Both agree they will try to attend. Before leaving, Darid and Mehdi mention the end-of-semester symposium and ask if someone from the SRUWC would be interested in delivering one of the two keynotes at the event. Hannah happily agrees and mentions that Sam (SRUWC upper administrator) might be a good candidate for a keynote.

Hannah's description of the meeting as "just scheduling" speaks to the tendency among writing center administrators to underestimate or simplify their work (Grutsch McKinney 2013). Not only is this kind of scheduling integral to the successful functioning of a partnership, but it also often leads to deeper conversations. For instance, in the ELET meeting, partners also discussed genre, assignment design and evaluation clarification via rubric, scaffolding, students' previous writing difficulties, and the material realities of the ELET instructors as part of the scheduling conversation. Yet, Hannah does seem to have some awareness of the work and initiative that the SRUWC takes in working with these students.

Further, this conversation involves big curricular decisions, and the writing center plays a major role in determining which changes are made and how, as is the case in transformational partnerships. In fact, it was because of ELET's partnership with the writing center that Darid and Medhi decided to create a ninety-two-page document called *The Senior Project ELET 4308/4208 Guidelines and Policies Manual,* which outlines the two-semester project. After the meeting ends, Hannah, Jeremy, and I continue to talk about the ELET partnership. Hannah gives us additional historical content about the project itself, explaining that the students have created lots of interesting projects in the senior design courses, including drones, robots that can disarm bombs, and electronic glucose measurers. Companies from outside the university give the department support for student projects, and when one of those projects works out, the university receives the funds and the student gets recognition. While this does not seem all that fair, according to Hannah and Jeremy, the program did recently start the symposium, which now enables the students to report projects themselves, thus giving them a greater sense of ownership and recognition.

In the sections that follow, I draw on interviews with faculty across the disciplines to explain each concept of WIP. Then, I use observations, interviews, and consultant notes from ELET partnership meetings to highlight how a WIP curriculum works in practice. The final section uses an example of one ELET student project to show how a transformational partnership can unfold within a strategic partnership–supported WIP curriculum. In this way, the SRUWC/ELET partnership offers a valuable way of responding to the disruptive innovation of career readiness programming in a manner that maintains the university's central role in the students' college experience. This approach privileges the learning and writing that can happen for students across university and industry/community audiences outside a full-time work requirement.

ESTABLISHING A WIP FRAMEWORK

The ELET partnership provides the most comprehensive example of WIP. Yet, WIP was also present in some form across all interviews with faculty and administrators from architecture, law, art history, business, biology, math, computer science, marketing, hotel and restaurant management, political science, business, and English. The components below provide both descriptions of pedagogical approaches and specific curricular displays of WIP.

WIP Concept 1: Students must learn to compose visually and orally, in addition to alphabetically.

One particular faculty member, Amir, an assistant professor of architecture, speaks with great enthusiasm and appreciation for his writing center partnership, which began the year before, when he was a part-time faculty member teaching a writing-intensive course. This year, his first in a tenure-track line, Amir continues his commitment to teaching writing, which he intentionally discusses as a project, not a paper. Amir emphasizes the need for visual communication (models and drawings) and written communication to work together simultaneously. Amir explains:

> Take a look at the structure of the assignment. You'll note that there is a writing component, which is the sort of bolded item at the top of the page, and then you'll notice at the bottom, there are presentations they offer as well. So, the structure of the assignment involved both writing as communication and visual communication as well. Really a part of the goal that I've set up in the assignment is that they're working hand-in-hand to achieve the objectives. So, in their submissions, they would be inclusive of visual communication. . . . Whether it's photography as a capturing of visual reality, whether it's collage, whether it's a wide variety of techniques in terms of the visual, the goal here is that it becomes integrated with the writing. They're working together.

So, you'll note in the specifications of the assignment that illustrations are key and the writing and the visualization are both included in the final product. They also do visual presentations in class, and that also is a chance for them to verbally and visually reinforce the writing as well. As far as the structure of the assignment, it's not necessarily a paper. I never will term it that when I'm talking about it. I call it a project. And, that's maybe a semantic separation, but for architects, the term *project* means something more than simply just one piece of a larger equation. The project encompasses all of the different tactics, mediums, strategies that we employ to solve issues. So, I call it a project.

The idea of approaching writing assignments as projects is an important aspect of the mindset needed to approach writing in architecture, and other design disciplines, because it requires representing knowledge visually, verbally, and in writing, as well as integrating the three. Later, Amir specifically describes how writing consultants help his students learn how to work with both image and word by "talk[ing] to . . . students about the position of the image, the relevance of the image, the captioning of that image and the way it's labeled." In other moments during this interview, Amir makes it clear that his students' ability to compose across modes is essential for their future work as architects.

As part of their recognition that university writing should help prepare students for workplace writing, other administrators and faculty also acknowledge that, in addition to more traditional written forms, students will likely have to compose orally and visually in their future careers. Thus, they create assignments that encourage students to practice these kinds of composing. For instance, Morgan, an assistant professor of information and logistics technology, has her upper-level, writing-intensive students work on a project that revolves around charts, graphs, and diagrams. The writing assignment takes the form of a modified IMRaD, report genre (Introduction-Methods-Results-Discussion), with a detailed appendix that includes seven different tools and methods that are constructed primarily as tables and images. Each figure in the appendix not only has to be developed, along with effective titles and captions, but also has to be written about in the IMRaD report. Although writing studies may not consider these to be complexly multimodal, they do fall on a kind of multimodal continuum, based on the coding scheme used by Grouling and Grutsch McKinney to identify to what extent student work is multimodal (2016, 59). The texts Morgan asks her students to create are not traditional, alphabetic texts, because they also have visual, numerical, and spatial components. As Joanna Wolfe notes in her 2010 *CCC* article, teaching quantitative literacy, or "rhetorical numbers" as she calls it, should be part of our writing curricula. Thus, having students learn to compose visually, orally, and in writing—the first major concept of WIP—acknowledges this focus on integrating multiple literacies in writing.

Composing Across Modes in ELET

By the start of their second semester in senior year, ELET students seem both excited and aware of what could be at stake in their writing projects. Following their first-semester senior-level ELET course, where they write individual project proposals, the second-semester course begins with five of the strongest project ideas (out of forty proposals), as chosen by the ELET faculty. Then, the second-semester students get into teams and work on creating a plan for building one of the five selected projects. This is an attempt on the part of the ELET faculty to mimic the competitiveness of the industry, according to Hannah (SRUWC administrator and project manager). As students develop these project plans, they attend four small group consultations to receive assistance in writing their project proposals and creating effective presentations. First-semester senior-level ELET 4308 students whose proposals progress to the second-semester course continue working in their groups to create the prototype, working from a small university budget and sometimes with the support of outside investors if they have them.

By the time student groups visit the writing center, they are already in teams and have draft proposals in hand. Thus, the groups spend far less time brainstorming and much more time building the projects, writing about how those projects are built, organizing and reporting on group management, and marketing their projects via oral and visual presentations, in addition to finalizing the end-of-semester report. The ELET 4208 second-semester seniors are enthusiastic about their projects and are primarily focused on creating and marketing their prototypes in ways that will attract potential investors via multimodal design elements targeted to nonexpert audiences.

Overall, ELET 4208 students seemed more familiar with the written report genre, and, thus, the seniors spend far more time discussing the particulars of the oral presentations and the PowerPoint slides as texts in themselves. This is perhaps because by the second part of the senior-level ELET course most students have already created their prototype. For instance, during their first ELET 4208 meeting, Team B had completed its project design and was in the midst of adding to the product. This team's prototype is the smartphone application iGuide, which "would benefit the SRU student body and staff throughout their daily schedules" by providing three key features:

- A live, up-to-date map of campus that is meant to replace the physical map the university uses. The map uses GPS technology and is detailed enough to help students and staff find specific classrooms and buildings.

- Real-time routing, which allows students and staff to access detailed instructions for how to get from one place on campus to another.

- Menu features that provide easy access from the main screen to building information, campus shuttle tracking, and campus restaurants.

Although they originally imagined a visually impaired user for the iGuide, Team B members realize that they will only have time to build the visual elements of the product in the timeframe of the semester. The additional audio features, they decide, could be added later.

The members of Team B spend two of the three meetings focusing on their oral presentation and their poster. SRUWC consultant Leah describes the presentation as a "snapshot of the paper," suggesting that it "should not be too technical" since it will be shared with nonexpert audience members. This is set against the more technical tone required for the entire formal report, with the exception of the newsletter section. Leah asks Team B to think about a variety of audiences for their presentation, ranging from the university (large-scale) to the individual, and tells them to think carefully about "what an outsider wants to know about the project" as they decide what to include in their fifteen-minute presentation. She also suggests that they focus on "the big picture and narrow in" without getting too specific. Again, Leah urges taking the content "directly from the paper, but putting it in layman's terms and only including what's most important." The group decides to divide up the slides so that they each design the ones that they will orally present to the group. While this conversation is obviously focused on the oral presentation, there is little discussion of how the presentation will work with the PowerPoint slides and how to utilize visuals during a presentation.

For Team B's final meeting focused on the large poster, I fill in for Leah. The group says they have no guidelines but do have access to posters from previous semesters. Team B notes the challenges involved in moving from the PowerPoint presentation to the poster. Since the size of each was very different, they cannot simply cut and paste from one to the other but have to do a lot of reformatting. Thus, we decide to discuss the poster they have already completed, but to also keep the PowerPoint in mind. Team B pulls up their poster draft and we work on it, making changes to it in real time. In particular, I review the CARP principles of design (contrast, alignment, repetition, proximity) (Williams 2014) and suggest that students work on the following:

Figure 5.1. Team B's prototype and poster

- Cut back the amount of text/information on the slide by eliminating what can be implied.
- Use more concise sentences.
- Use bullet points purposefully and consistently.
- Make sure the correct content is in the right place, and do not repeat items.
- Make sure the poster is symmetrically aligned (i.e., center the image of the prototype).
- Put the most important information (such as how it works and current features) in the center directly under the prototype since that's where your viewer's attention will be drawn. Put the less important details along the sides and corners (methods, tools, etc.).

Team B's final iGuide prototype and poster that hangs during the Undergraduate Research Symposium is shown in Figure 5.1.

As with ELET 4208 Team B, the other senior-level ELET groups seem unfamiliar with the oral and visual elements of project composition, and consultants' experiences with these modes seem to vary as well. For instance, consultants' commentary and advice center on extracting content from the written reports and reading the oral presentations as shortened versions of the alphabetic texts, rather than recognizing the presentation as a different genre with a particular set of conventions. One consultant notes that in her session, "the group brought in their oral presentation and their proposal. I read over their drafts and marked the necessary corrections." Another consultant resorts to talking about techniques they can use as they prepare for their oral presentation. She explains, "I provided tips on how to 'practice' their presentation as a group if they were unable to physically meet as a group: Google Doc flash cards, record yourself practicing to time speech, report speaking time in Google Doc to make sure no one is speaking for too long and going over time." As in Leah's group facilitation, this consultant acknowledges the presentation element of the project, but not how students should balance the oral and the visual via PowerPoint slides. Given that the SRUWC's professional development programming does not include any explicit attention to multimodal composing, this is unsurprising. Yet, this example is also indicative of students' need for support around multimodal composing, especially transferring material from one mode to another, such as from an alphabetic written report to an oral/visual presentation.

Yet, there are two consultants (Amber and Seth) who seem better prepared to work with students on visual design. For instance, they describe their time spent during the last two senior-level ELET meetings in the ways described in table 5.3. As table 5.3 indicates, both Amber and Seth seem aware of the need to shorten and condense the material included on PowerPoint slides and posters. Unsurprisingly, ELET seniors struggle with this, since they mostly cut and pasted from their final reports to create them. Seth also notes the value of having an "eye-catching" and "easy to understand" PowerPoint and poster. In particular, Seth brings to his group's attention the ways in which certain sections from the report were *not* appropriate for the poster.

While the major focus is on the multimodal elements of the ELET 4208 projects, student groups are still expected to put together a fairly extensive project report. Team B primarily composes the final report collaboratively using Google Docs, which is indicative of WIP Concept 2, team writing. The document's revision history indicates a clear primary writer for the group (Thomas), who set up the document and was the only one to go back and revise/add to others' sections. Two group members (Thomas and Jessa) revise their own sections significantly while the others make few or no changes. The group composes for just over a month, from November 1 through December 6, during a wide variety of times, including early in the morning, mid-afternoon, and late at night. The most active date/time is November 3, just a couple days

Table 5.3. Consultants' discussion of visual presentation elements

	Meeting 2	Meeting 3
Amber	I also enjoyed [the PowerPoint presentation] but recommended that they either fade out the background so that the bullet points are more easily read or that they add a white box around the wording (and keep the background as a border). Lastly, I also suggested that they reduce the length of the bullet points.	We also went over their oral presentations. Generally, it was good. We did some rearranging of the slides. We also talked about shortening their bullet points from sentences to concise phrases.
Seth	The benefits were primarily having a nontechnical eye look over things to ensure that it was (1) eye-catching, and (2) easy to understand. I think the group is generally on the right track.	I helped them with their poster, primarily. The students had significant amounts of text on the poster, so I encouraged them to represent as much information pictorially as possible. I also helped them to determine the content appropriate for the poster, such as removing a "conclusion" section, and condensing the abstract, introduction, and objectives sections. I also encouraged them to rename a couple of the poster sections, such as "hardware" and "software," where the sections included diagrams rather than actual images of hardware and software.

after the document setup, around 12:10 a.m. Four group members are active in the document at this time. Seventeen revisions are made, four of which occur with at least one person in the document at the same time. Thomas is active during fourteen of the seventeen revisions, or roughly 82 percent of the time.

The document begins with just a title and headings. Most students simply cut and paste their particular parts into the document under the correct heading on November 3 and do not make any additional changes. One team member changes the headings, but there are no additional revisions across sections, which suggests that it is unlikely that anyone went through and read the entire report, start to finish, and made changes across sections to keep them consistent and coherent. Each group member is responsible for about one or two sections, and Thomas is responsible for four. The last section to be written is the "Newsletter" portion, which seems to be the most unfamiliar given conversation during writing center consultation sessions. Thomas is the one who eventually writes this part, perhaps because the group is running out of time and someone has to do it. While the writing labor is unevenly split, conversation indicates that other group members took the lead on other parts of the project, thus making the overall labor a bit fairer. For instance, Aaron takes the lead for the PowerPoint presentation and

Nikhil organizes the poster draft. Weekly progress reports require students to keep track of how much time each group member spends on what. Thus, all group members seem very aware of distribution of labor.

WIP Concept 2: Students must learn to write in a team-based, collaborative environment that requires effective project management.

As the earlier section indicates, ELET students do nearly all of their writing in teams, and this is an attempt at mimicking the kind of writing and work they will likely do in the workplace as engineers. While some faculty have similar reasons for requiring team writing, others incorporate it primarily for workload management. First, Morgan (computer science) explains her decision to create team-based writing assignments as a necessary "survival mechanism" that the SRUWC helped her develop. Specifically, she says:

> We used to have classes around twenty to twenty-three, but then budget cuts started happening and we were basically told as a faculty, "your classes will never get smaller, they will only get larger." And, I had a big spike. I went from twenty students to thirty-five, and sometimes I had maybe forty and my goal, personal goal, is that if you have an assignment due in my class, I'm going to give you feedback within one week. So, I worked it out with [the SRUWC]—what to do? And, we decided to work in teams of two, sometimes three, [because] feedback is only as useful as it is timely.

This major shift in Morgan's approach to teaching writing was not focused on preparing students for future work-based writing but was a way for her to continue providing timely feedback. The move was also a reaction to increased class sizes, something many universities are facing, and provided Morgan with a strategy for continuing to maintain her values as a writing teacher while also keeping her workload manageable. Morgan makes her struggle with this move explicit by admitting, "I don't like that I have to give that option [of individual writing assignments] up, but it's a survival mechanism for instructors." The guilt Morgan feels is somewhat lessened in her work with the SRUWC, which helps her see that she was "just doing it more as survival" and previously hadn't "realize[d] that these are the negative effects of budget issues on the classroom."

Then, Rick (art history) discusses his work with collaborative writing and feedback through the use of Google Docs, which allows teaching assistants, professors, writing center consultants, and peers to provide writing feedback to students in one space. Like Morgan, Rick is teaching writing in a class that he describes as "too big," even though it is the only writing-intensive class in the program. The class regularly enrolls nearly fifty students, so, as Rick explains, "if it were not for the writing studio experiences and a good teaching assistant, it would be impossible." He also describes how the "writing studio," a type of SRUWC partnership where students meet in small groups to discuss their individual writing projects with peers and a writing center consultant-facilitator, significantly lowers the number of students who fail because this approach encourages students to start drafts earlier for a real audience. Rick's strong preference for the group-based peer review, rather than one-on-one, encourages a "process of discovery" that starts from where students are, rather than always revolving around a draft.

Despite these reasons for field-based writing, professional writing recognizes the need for teamwork and interpersonal skills in addition to familiarity with technology that enables working together outside of face-to-face, asynchronous settings (Anderson 2017). Writing center consultants are well positioned to support team writing, whether it be collaborative composing or group writing exchange/feedback, in part because they are technically outside the group and thus provide a more neutral perspective.

Composing Collaboratively in ELET

In the writing-intensive, ELET courses, all major writing projects are team-based. Not only are students required to complete projects and write together, but they must also track each team member's participation visually, in a Gantt chart, that is part of both the progress report and the final report. In the case of the junior-level ELET 3405 groups, the SRUWC partnership that disappeared and then makes its reappearance with a new and more specific writing assignment, team-based writing is also a way of helping students work together through a new genre.

Starting in the first meeting, writing consultant Seth helps his group divide the labor, after first helping them establish criteria for evaluating sources together. They spend some time discussing how to divide up the workload in a concrete way and discuss prioritizing the various parts of the proposal. The group agrees that the design and literature review are the most important elements and the ones to focus on first, and that two group members will focus on the design and building while the other two focus on the literature review, introduction, abstract, and other related elements of the report.

After prioritizing and dividing the labor into manageable tasks that are shared across team members, the group spends the second meeting discussing how the design and lab work will require a different kind of labor than the writing. Since I was an outsider to the discipline in many ways and was filling in for Seth during this particular meeting, I ask if the group is ready to start designing and if they have enough of an idea to start "playing around." One student explains to me that:

> Yeah, we have to work on coding. The language that we're using in this course has never been used before, so it's trial and error and going through websites and figuring it out, because you have set up all inputs and outputs and you have to figure out how to convert between binary and decimal through code.

I suggest that as the students go through this process manually, they take notes that they can later use to write up their report. Based on this and knowing that the next step for them is primarily about starting the design and writing the code, we begin to talk about plans for the next meeting and what they need to put together by next week. At least two group members take note of the work they will have ready for the next meeting: a specific breakdown of who's doing what (this is also a required part of the report itself), the beginning of a Google Doc draft that will include the literature review sources and notes so that communication is clear and they will not do too much overlapping, and some kind of writing on paper that will relate to the design and to the abstract and/or literature review (at least one of them, if both would be too much).

By the final two meetings, team members are setting goals and using their time in the writing center to help them establish deadlines. According to Seth's session notes for the third team meeting, everyone shows up and the group's Google Doc indicates that members are keeping up with the various parts of the project and completing the tasks set in the first meeting. Per the Google Doc's revision history, students do indeed get started on creating their draft later in the day on October 27 and continue to build up until the time of our meeting on November 3. By this meeting, students have drafted a project idea/concept, an abstract, a building design that became the project's "first concept," a detailed map of who would be doing what, a to-do list, a brief outline for the presentation, a list of articles and reviews for the literature review section, and a timeline with project due dates and a link to the assignment prompt.

One particular strength of how the group uses the Google Doc is the way that it enables them to keep track of who is working on what. This part of the document goes through revisions and updates, just like the other section. By the November 17 group meeting, the team members' tasks are established (table 5.4). In this session, the writing consultant's role is primarily to remind students to account for writing-specific tasks and to help them understand the time and work involved in each. Given that the focus in the class, under the direction of the TA, seems to be

Table 5.4. List of team members' tasks in Google Doc

Justin
Find sources needed to help program the project concept. I'll do some programming and work on project design. Let me know what else we need help with!

Dave
Find sources needed to work on the Literature review Assist in programming and project design

Ross
Helping with literature review and final report. Assisting with project design when possible.

Jim
I'll start working on the literature review after the sources/notes are posted on here. I'll start creating the final presentation after we have more information about our project I'll put together the Final Report when everything is complete

on research, the writing center consultant can help student writers distinguish between the two.

WIP Concept 3: Students must learn to develop clarity in their writing.

Also working from a team-based writing pedagogy, Morgan, the same assistant professor of information and logistics technology that I mentioned earlier, has been collaborating with the writing center for several years in her teaching of an upper-level, writing-intensive course focused on quality improvement methods for managing production and service operations. The purpose of the course is to introduce students to terminology and mapping processes that they can use to assess a problem, identify causes, and develop solutions for potential customers. Her major writing assignment asks students to investigate a real or fictional workplace problem through the application of Lean Six Sigma, a methodology that relies on collaborative team effort to improve performance by systematically removing waste and reducing variation. Morgan notes a difference between the kind of feedback she offered students and what the writing facilitators could provide:

> You know, when it's about the content of the class, or like how to use this quality tool, . . . [writing center facilitators] can point them back to the instructor, whereas if it's like, "I'm trying to explain this and it's not clear. Can you help me make it more clear?" well, that's in their wheelhouse, that's what the facilitator can help with.

Although she seems to overlook the relationship between content and style by separating the two, she also suggests that clarity is a general, perhaps universal, writing skill that is not specific to information and logistics technology.

Similarly, an associate dean for student affairs in the law school in her tenth year, Tara, describes the kind of generalist analytical skills in the following way:

> They really need to focus on the critical reasoning and analysis portion, and I think the rest can come, but I think the more specialized skill is what is necessary. Because even in, you know, a law review article, just with you guys, you know, you're going to state your thesis, your problem, what you're trying to address, and then, as you gather your materials—your different cases, your other articles—I mean, you're going to analyze that material against what you're trying to do, so again, you're always going to come back to that analysis, which is the meat of your project, your exam, the bar [laughs]. I mean, on the bar exam, that's what they're looking at—they're looking at how do you analyze the problem? And then they want you to come up with a definitive conclusion.

For Tara, analysis and "critical reasoning" are skills taught by English departments and writing centers—"just with you guys." Her discussion of "analysis" circles around specific elements of writing, again connected to clarity. For instance, the writer must state their thesis and end with a definitive conclusion, leaving little room for confusion or indecision.

Nevertheless, she places such emphasis on clear analysis and critical thinking because of the professionalizing aspect of her discipline. She believes that these skills will be useful beyond the university, as students write law reviews for publication and take the bar exam. She explains that the bar exam is designed to determine how students will act as lawyers in the workplace and thus determines whether or not they receive their license to practice.

Overall, university administrators and disciplinary faculty value working with the writing center because they often have students work with generalist writing consultants outside their discipline who can help students determine whether their writing is clear. The emphasis on students writing so that those outside their field can understand was an important element of "good writing" for these interviewees, pushing back against the writing across the curriculum premise that disciplinary experts are best positioned to guide discipline-specific writing, since writing is highly situated, and thus without a universal definition of what constitutes "good writing."

Recent scholarship on transfer, though, recognizes that some writing skills and habits can be taught and applied across contexts, especially when writing instructors teach intentionally for transfer and students are explicitly taught to develop a metacognitive awareness (Adler-Kassner and Wardle 2015; Anson and Moore 2016). This scholarship further corroborates the opinion of these interviewees. Further, writing center consultants in particular can help facilitate transfer by helping students make connections across assignments and contexts (Nowacek and Hughes 2015). Similarly, Thaiss and Zawacki (2006) notice some generalizable concepts of academic writing valued by faculty across disciplines, which are "persistent, open-minded" study, the valuing of "reason over emotion," and an "imagined reader who is coolly rational" (5–7). The practices of writing with a professional audience in mind at the SRU adds to this list a focus on clarity, the third concept of WIP.

Clarity beyond Correctness in ELET

The consultants who work with sophomores who are not yet used to working with the writing center or to writing in their major immediately attempt to establish credibility by positioning themselves as disciplinary outsiders who are prepared to read for clarity. For instance, writing consultant Tim's major strategy across sessions seems to be asking questions and offering his own reading and understanding of the situation or the writing, based on his outsider position. During a conversation about what kinds of search engines the students use to find research for their proposal, Tim admits that, for him, as someone who "studied humanities in school," he uses the library database. Tim also draws on his general knowledge of technical reports to guide students through the genre, commenting on clarity of ideas and organizational structure. Yet, he also admits in his consultant note, "I had to inform them that technical writing changes from discipline to discipline and that since I am not in their college, I am not qualified to tell them specifics." Tim further explains that technical writing conventions "depend on the TA, the discipline, it could be technical writing for engineering, which is a little different than technical writing for biology or math." Tim encourages students to talk with their TA about specific conventions related to format for their final report.

From his disciplinary outsider position, Tim also offers his group advice about time management and group work (WIP Concept 2), as well as writing as non-native speakers of English. For instance, Tim suggests, "all four people write [the final report], even if there's a lead writer, [and have] everyone read each section and really know, okay, what's this about, what's going on." This advice is met with a bit of laughter from two of the four group members, who explained, "we're non-native speakers, the way we're writing is like, for me, him, and him, so we can't understand, so then when we read it, some of our people may not understand, so that's why we need you." Although this is a bit confusing to follow, what the student seems to suggest is that since none of them are native English speakers, having them all read one another's work is going to result in the same kind of reading, and they will most likely not read the errors as errors.

Tim agrees that he is there to offer another reading, but then he reframes the argument in a larger context. After reminding the students that he can follow most of their ideas in the proposal, Tim tells the students, "Don't let the fact that English isn't your first language bog down your ideas, because I still knew what you wanted to say." He then explains the value of writing clearly in their future professional lives:

> You will come across times when, as seniors, or when you're working for the private sector of the government or something like that, you're going to have to write proposals for people who are outside of your field. So, if they can't follow what you're writing about, they won't fund it. That's just that. Imagine that you're writing to get money from the B-family or something like that. Those guys are in business. They're not technicians, so you want to write it in a way so that anyone ideally could understand.

Here, Tim sets the stakes for clarity in the students' writing higher. He links their ability to communicate their project clearly in writing to the likelihood that the project will be funded. Tim also attempts to get the students to think about a broader audience for their work, not only adding to his own credibility as such an outsider who can offer them advice about how to improve the clarity of their writing, but also getting them to think about how to make their writing accessible to non-specialists in their field. Here, clarity becomes something more than reaching a standard of writing and instead about communicating well enough for ideas to be understood across audiences.

WIP Concept 4: Students must learn to write in ways that are accessible to nonexpert audiences.

The across-the-curriculum emphasis on clarity stems from students' need to communicate with nonexpert audiences while drawing on their disciplinary expertise. Thus, the value of identifying other audiences or readers for student texts beyond the expert professor becomes more important. For instance, an associate dean for undergraduate business programs with over twenty years of experience in the college, Kyle explains his awareness of the difference between the kinds of writing students would likely do in the workplace versus the kind of academic writing done by faculty:

Writing in the Disciplines, if you're a biology major and you're going to do research in graduate school and publish in a respected medical professional journal, that's academic writing within the discipline. But, if you're a business student, the writing you're going to need to do would be, maybe a project analysis of why we should build a refinery in Azerbaijan, or a memo to your boss, or maybe a marketing report. And it's very different from what gets published in business journals, which is the kind of writing business professors write.

Yet, Chris, an instructional associate professor in biology, seems to approach the teaching of writing from a mindset that aligns better with Kyle's than with "academic writing within the discipline." Chris explains:

> In the sciences, just like in any sort of academic peer review, what my goal is in my class is, well certainly, I'm trying to teach my material, but really what I'm . . . trying to expose them to is, what the world is really like as a scientist. In the grand scheme of things, I know that in two years, they don't do any of the stuff that I teach them. They're going to forget about the physiology I teach, but what I do want them to know is, you know, you're going to leave here with a biology degree and you should know how to communicate as a biologist—I don't care if you're planning on medicine, I don't care if you're planning on working in a lab, I don't care if you're working at McDonald's. . . . It doesn't matter what field you're going into, you're going to have to learn to write a report, you know, a technical report.

Thus, "thinking like a biologist" is linked to communicating and writing like one. Whereas Chris emphasizes the importance of preparing students to think and communicate from the position of a professional in the field, he also shows an awareness of what Michael Carter has called "meta-genre," or the overarching genres and broader patterns of language as social action that group multiple fields together. For Chris, the value of students understanding how to write a technical report, which they learn in biology, is also something that they will likely use in other contexts, with other audiences in mind.

Nearly all university administrators and disciplinary faculty acknowledge that students will likely have to write for nonexperts in their fields, and they want their writing curricula to reflect that. This leads to both the creation of assignments with entirely new, workplace audiences (like Fernando's) and to the development of writing that can be read and understood by both experts and nonexperts alike. Thus, the fourth concept of WIP recognizes that faculty often ask students to write one text with a variety of readers in mind, something quite different from asking students to write only for academic audiences.

While the need to write for both expert and nonexpert audiences is part of discussions about clarity and composing across modes, it is especially prevalent among the senior-level ELET courses, whose writing projects have real audiences beyond peers and professors in the disciplines. For example, when Leah asks her ELET group working on the iGuide about which project guidelines include elements that are new for them, they immediately point to the "newsletter" portion of the report, where students are to imagine a nontechnical audience. Although the newsletter seems to be an odd addition to the otherwise technical report, it also represents an attempt at a kind of writing in the profession in which students will likely be expected to engage as engineers. In terms of the writing appropriate for this section, one student asks, "How do we write our opinions?" since they are not yet sure how to broadly position their work for a nontechnical audience. Leah tells Team B that including opinions, even in the newsletter section, is not appropriate for this kind of document. Instead, she suggests that the group frame what they thought of as their opinions, but are actually that which they cannot yet prove, as the "intended or potential impact." This phrase makes more sense, Leah explains, since their writing in the section "was not simply based on their opinions, but on their intentions as designers of the prototype." Leah also finds some resources for the group to use while writing up their executive summary, and she tells them they should focus their attention on writing the summary and maintaining a professional tone throughout the report itself.

WIP AND TRANSFORMATIONAL PARTNERSHIP: ELET TEAM A'S PROJECT

Although not all strategic partnerships can become transformational, writing centers will benefit most from transformational partnerships like the ELET partnership because they are the most sustainable. Drawing from service-learning partnerships, Sandra Enos and Keith Morton argue that real change is created only through partnerships that are transformational, not through those that are transactional and only focus on "get[ting] things done" (2003, 23). In particular, transformational partnerships do the following:

- Create relationships that "focus on ends beyond utilitarian exchanges"
- Work toward the goal of "mutual[ly] increas[ing] aspirations," rather than just satisfaction

- Maintain a purpose of "arous[ing] needs to create larger meanings" rather than satisfying immediate needs
- Involve partners who become "leaders" rather than managers
- "Examine institutional goals" and respond to them, instead of just accepting them
- "Transcend self-interests to create larger meanings"
- Change "group identity in [the] larger definition of community" rather than solely maintaining institutional identity
- "Engage whole institutions in potentially unlimited exchanges" rather than working within a scope limited by time, resources, and specific personnel

Rather than developing linearly, these transformational partnerships grow in a more layered fashion over time, where they may continue simple activities, in addition to reacting to the more nuanced and innovative developments that often occur unexpectedly or as the result of risk-taking. The level of depth and complexity increases over time as the partnership involves further work and new relational elements. These layers are both additive and evolutionary, depending on the partnership. For instance, a partnership could involve both one-time events and ongoing placement that leads to mutual dependence, or a one-time event could evolve into a short-term placement and eventually a transformation. When applied to interdepartmental partnerships between writing centers and departments/colleges, a transformational partnership leads to meaningful, curricular changes as well as changes across educators (instructors and consultants), student writers, and the larger community in some way, whether it be upper administration, the university itself, or larger disciplinary communities.

While the examples in this chapter show how concepts of WIP play out in particular scenarios across the four ELET/writing center partnership courses, one of the four groups created a project that strongly exemplifies what is possible in a WIP curriculum through transformational partnership. For Team A's project, facilitated by writing consultant Carly and myself, students planned for the creation of a mobile classroom with a real-world audience in mind, especially their already-committed investor. Team A is also engaged in an application for additional funds. When they arrive in the SRUWC for their first project meeting, it is clear that the group has a project leader (Wilson) and that they are all excited about their project. Wilson immediately starts explaining it to me, as he hands me a proposal draft that he is already working on and planning to submit to a national undergraduate competition called the Cornell Cup.[3]

Team A's project is to create a shipping container with solar panels that will function as a mobile classroom for children in Africa. Their goal is to create a classroom that will be "as efficient as possible and safe," keeping the harsh climate of the Mahi people's region where they would first pilot the classroom in mind as they build. Wilson also tells me that the project is already funded and that they have met with the investor a couple times this semester. Without any asking or prompting, Wilson discusses the research that still needs to be done, such as the best type of installation to use, the most efficient structure to fit the most students comfortably, the types of computers to have, and the setup of one main "supercomputer" that would hold most of the content and allow the others to work as "virtual computers." The students, chiming in to help explain, point to the images in their report that depict the mobile classrooms as they talk through the draft of their final report.

In addition, Team A members speak about the global and societal impacts and explain that while they are piloting the classroom among the Mahi people in Benin, they hope that similar models can be developed for other underserved rural communities where children have little access to safe education. The idea behind the container itself is that the classroom could be placed near remote villages to save students from the unsafe commute, during which young children have a reputation for being captured and forced to serve as soldiers in the military. The team is also planning carefully to create a sustainable model using deep cycle batteries that will provide multiple charges and a life of ten to fifteen years. The team has done substantial research and found solar panels to last thirty years and a Zuba Box Dell computer that will last ten to fifteen years and are in the process of looking into security options.

After explaining their project, the team members say that they are working on completing their application for the Cornell Cup, which is due in two weeks, and request both verbal and written feedback. Team A wants its consultant, Carly, and also me, to "point out the weak parts" and mention "any other possible ways to do it," in addition to "feedback on how a potential user might read it." This group, and Wilson in particular, has a clear idea of the kind of feedback that they need from us.

In addition to working on the formal elements of the report, Team A spends a great deal of time discussing its project budget through multiple options, tracking the time the team members spent on each part of the report via a detailed timeline of what each member did. Although this tracking is part of the ELET required assignment, Team A takes it very seriously, working constantly on updating its progress reports.

Although Carly (consultant) leads the sessions with questions about the project updates, the students themselves seem to take over leadership and often use the time to write/build within their team's live Google Doc. Team A is required to fill in and update its progress weekly, based on the actual and expected hours of work in each area. The students say that for them, splitting up the labor does not work very well and that it ends up making things "messy," causing them to "go back and redo it all as a team." In order to work on much of the project as a team, Wilson, the team leader, sets up a plan to work together via Skype twice a week, allotting additional meeting times to talk with their sponsor. They mention that the first project report seems to be a lot of work but after that, they will just need to "fill it in" with updates. Wilson admits his worry about the high word requirement, but his group members assure him that they will make it, since "we have it all, we just have to get it down in words."

Within the progress report, Team A creates a color-coded Gantt chart to provide a visual sense of how much time is spent on each part of the project and how the team members plan to spend the next semester's time. For instance, the first three months (October, November, and December), while students are enrolled in the first part of the senior-level ELET course, are primarily spent researching and ordering materials. Then, during the months of January and February when the team begins the second part of senior-level ELET, the team plans to spend time designing the interior and installing solar panels and on general and battery installation. Team A also plans for the final three months to focus on testing and finishing the product (and on finishing the interior design with final touches and improvements). What is surprisingly absent from their chart is time spent on writing. In conversation and as represented here, Team A seems to conflate "research" with "writing," even though they are two different activities that both take time and different kinds of skill.

In some ways, Team A is atypical in that they have already received funding from an investor and are looking for additional funding. In a sense, the stakes of succeeding at the project itself are higher because students are spending someone else's money and are thus expected to plan for the actual creation of a prototype that will work and use the already funded resources well. Writing a project report that will not "pass" is not really an option for Team A. In terms of the project's success within the ELET class, the faculty are already excited and supportive, since Team A has financial support for its project, and an investor who was also a medical doctor served as an additional mentor. In a sense, then, the members of Team A had already "passed," since they have the funding secured and are designing a project whose future viability had weight and meaning beyond the course.

By the end of the semester, the project changes from "Solar Classroom" to "Sachons, Sourions," a French phrase that means "Let us learn, let us smile." The final report is nine full pages and includes detailed material lists as well as background information and a cost analysis. Team A describes the project as "the creation of an Autonomous Mobile classroom . . . [and] a community-based project made for disadvantaged areas like Western Africa, focused on providing the necessary education materials for students in need." The four images from the team's final PowerPoint slides shown here include a visualization of the team's challenge and problem statement, an image of the classroom setup that the group decided on by the end of the semester, a depiction of the Edubuntu operating system features that will be used on the computers in the classroom, and a visual chart of the group's research and data collection. Figures 5.2-5.5 showcase some slides from Team A's final presentation.

Throughout the entirety of their project, these students are deeply engaged, thinking about both their writing and their presentation of the project well beyond its life in the university. Over the semester, their primary audience is not their professors but their investor, a medical doctor, who imagines their project as a pilot for a potentially large-scale endeavor. In an urban university with a strong population of underrepresented communities and at a school where immigrant and part-time students may not qualify for financial aid, the question lingers for the students: Is continuing education worth the time and expense? More often than not, these are students working multiple, low-level jobs, some even full-time, to be able to afford their tuition, fees, and textbooks. This example shows the potential of a WIP curriculum to motivate these students as they use research and writing to further their own meaningful projects that not only prepare them to be competitive in the workforce, but also keep them in school. It shows the valuable role that writing centers can play in curriculum design, as well as the importance of peer writing tutors in offering them additional writing support and encouragement in practicing agency, engagement, and transfer.

In this example, ELET's WIP curriculum is enhanced through the department's transformational partnership with the writing center. Consultants work with students to help them develop and communicate their projects across modes for a range of audiences beyond a single classroom and even the university. Working from the assumption that

Building Education

Our Objective
Overview

We plan to create an autonomous mobile computer lab that will host a classroom-like environment regulating power using a micro-controller.

Our target geographic will be Mali, a country in Africa that is known to have a poor education system and a lack of technology.

A microcontroller will be used to read the power consumption on a day-to-day basis and indicate if too much power is being consumed or if enough power has been stored.

While there may be variations of these classrooms on the market (i.e. Zubabox), our team will provide the most energy efficient platform with exceptional attention to detail and quality, while keeping costs down.

Our Challenge
Problem Statement

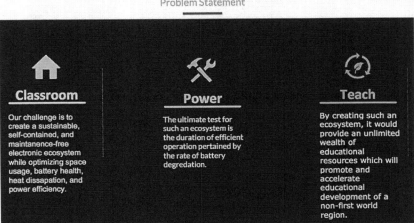

Classroom

Our challenge is to create a sustainable, self-contained, and maintenance-free electronic ecosystem while optimizing space usage, battery health, heat dissapation, and power efficiency.

Power

The ultimate test for such an ecosystem is the duration of efficient operation pertained by the rate of battery degredation.

Teach

By creating such an ecosystem, it would provide an unlimited wealth of educational resources which will promote and accelerate educational development of a non-first world region.

students are developing professional writers, consultants help writers build agency and confidence. Further, student work remains the central focus, in contrast to what career readiness programs like the "Go Pro Early" initiative likely encourage.

In terms of faculty, it is often through their work with the writing center that they begin to think about how and why they create certain kinds of writing assignments, as well as about writing as a

Figures 5.2–5.5. Selected slides from Team A's final PowerPoint presentation

developmental process, one that is both social and individual. These are important practices, regardless of course specificities. Faculty in the disciplines use WIP practices in writing center partnerships to get students to think critically about their writing in ways they can later transfer to other writing contexts, helping them understand that writing is useful beyond the university.

CONCLUSION

After ten minutes of conversation about his college's partnership with the writing center, Charley (hotel and restaurant management) confidently tells me, "We have one of the best writing centers in the country, and remember, I could be their biggest critic easily." I am not initially sure what he means. Yet, several minutes later, when I ask him about his first impression of the writing center or if he had experiences with the writing center at other universities, he explains:

> My background is [as] a horrible writer. So, I went to Purdue and Purdue had, when I was a student, an excellent writing center, but it was self-taught writing. Basically, I don't even think they did that, but 20 years ago when I got my master's, you had to have a minimal writing competency to get a master's. That was across campus. So, I spent six months in a writing lab. So, thank god I did, but that was their approach. So, I thought that approach was very effective. . . . What you would do is you would have to take timed writing exams, submit them, they graded them, you make them 300–600 words, if you made more than two mistakes you flunked it and you had to pass three papers in a row [laughs] . . . just to qualify to graduate. . . . If you got a C in either of your two [undergraduate] writing classes, you were required to go through this program, which was through the writing lab. . . . I knew every TA, I knew the director. . . . She was a dragon lady. But, she did a great job, so today, I really appreciate all that effort.

After Charley tells this to me, we both have a good laugh about how much work this was outside of a full-time master's program. While Charley was grateful for the support, I was bothered by this kind of writing center work, and it was not the first time I had heard of writing centers administering similar kinds of writing assessments. Given that he begins his story claiming the identity of a horrible writer, Charley's confidence still seems shaped by his experience over twenty years later.

As teachers of writing and directors of writing centers, we are often aware of the emotional—and often painful—experiences students have with writing before they enter our spaces. Yet, we rarely think about the kinds of writing experiences faculty may have had, and how those experiences shape their work with us. As Williams (2017) suggests, experiences with writing that are familiar often evoke an immediate emotional

https://doi.org/10.7330/9781646421770.c006

response similar to that of the previous experience (16). Unfortunately, for most students—and I would argue for at least some professors—past experiences with writing are not filled with positive emotions but instead are fraught with anxiety and insecurity. If we consider working with faculty and deans who have had negative emotional experiences as writers themselves, or who think of themselves as bad writers, we can begin to understand why and how they may: (1) seem disinterested in teaching writing; (2) teach writing in ways that emphasize easily identifiable, sentence-level mistakes over quality of ideas; and (3) look to reduce or eliminate the amount of time they spend teaching writing. This requires us to work from what Lisa Blankenship (2019) has termed *rhetorical empathy*, which she defines as both a "habit of mind" that involves "deep listening" to stories of personal experience (5) and an approach to ethical argumentation, persuasion, and language use that requires us to account for the power of emotion and pathos (25). Thus, rhetorical empathy can help inform and shape negotiated space and is connected to the work involved in establishing a rhetoric of respect.

In Charley's case, past experiences with writing encourage him to seek out the writing center. He knows that writing will be important to students in his college, especially after their early years in the field of hotel and restaurant management. Yet, Charley wants and expects the SRUWC to create the plan for the partnership, and to work one-on-one with a variety of professors in his department, some who want to teach writing and some who do not. When professors in his college are resistant to teaching writing because writing "was not their area of expertise," Charley works with the SRUWC to develop a partnership where writing consultants facilitate peer review groups multiple times over the semester during the class's actual meeting time. Charley even believes that some of the faculty are not well qualified to teach writing, and rather than trying to force them into a predetermined plan, he finds other ways to support writers in these courses.

The partnership between Charley and the SRUWC has now been going for over fifteen years. Although there is still conversation about what the partnership will look like each year, there is not talk about its continuation, or reconsideration of what other, cheaper options might be available. Yet, had the writing center been resistant to Charley's requests or the professors in his department's wide range of commitments to teaching writing, the partnership likely would not have lasted. Instead, Charley may have turned to a public-private partnership, or cut writing from the curriculum as much as possible, or turned it into something that was required without any scaffolded instruction or support.

As twenty-first-century universities continue to explore disruptive innovations and think of ways to cut costs, writing centers continue to be places well positioned to respond with alternative options that maintain a commitment to intellectual engagement and ethical pedagogy. Once they establish strategic partnerships and meaningful relationships with the writing center, faculty and administrators across campus often change their perceptions of both writing and writing center work, and their interest in avoiding or outsourcing writing instruction diminishes. As the educational landscape shifts in response to online instruction, P3s, and Go Pro Early programs, writing centers can work with administrators and disciplinary faculty to build writing support around curricular structures set by specific departments and programs. Or, in the case of Charley, the writing center can help create such curricular plans. As we work *with* various levels of the administration to ensure our sustainability, something we likely cannot do without their support, we can simultaneously protect and ensure the practice of tutoring and teaching writing within our writing centers that ultimately still allows for moments of resistance, where writing consultants and students can tactically *challenge* the corporate university in their method of practice—slowing down, emphasizing process, working collaboratively. As the writing consultants discussed in chapter 1 suggest, one-on-one and group writing conferencing within a strategic partnership's administrative framework still provides ample opportunities to center the writer's voice, respond to the violence involved when forcing translingual students into Standard Academic English, and challenge professors' guidelines or feedback when necessary.

While much of the success in building strategic partnerships at SRUWC depended on financial support from upper administrators, less-well-funded writing centers can also respond to disruptive innovations at the opportune moment via strategic partnership. One of the most important ways to do this is by thinking critically about the local context: about the needs of student writers and teachers of writing, about the university's strategic plan and mission, and about who those potential stakeholders may be. In *The Innovative University*, Christensen and Eyring account for vulnerable institutions, noting that their primary mistake is trying to emulate more elite universities rather than responding to their own specific context. These more vulnerable or less-well-funded universities benefit from asking questions to help them determine potential partners, such as: (1) From which departments/programs do most students visiting the writing center come? (2) To which departments do writing instructors who have already worked successfully with the writing center belong (e.g., through required visits, regular presentations or workshops, etc.)? (3) Which programs/departments send few or no students? Why? (4) What are the departments, programs, and/or initiatives that seem to have the administration's attention? (5) If you are turning students away due to lack of writing center funding, from which departments do those students come?

The answers to these questions may provide writing center administrators with ideas for potential partnerships within already existing writing center activity, thus requiring little to no additional funding (1 and 2); with departments who have not worked with the writing center recently or at all, perhaps due to a bad previous experience or the use of a third-party program (3 and 5); and with programs that have already received funding or that will likely have better access to support, and may be building new curricula of which writing will likely be a part (4 and 5). Since leaving SRU, in my five years as a writing center administrator at universities with little writing center support or programming, the answers to all of the above questions have helped me strategize my approach to piloting partnerships without substantial dependence on support from upper administration.

For instance, when I began my first job as a writing center coordinator at a regional state university in the Northeast, I worked with my faculty colleague, the WAC/WID (writing across the curriculum/ writing in the disciplines) coordinator, to develop strategic partnerships across campus by establishing a collaborative, course-embedded tutoring program. Our first year, we were able to use funding from her budget for a pilot, which we also holistically assessed through instructor and tutor interviews, pre- and post-semester student surveys, and writing collection and assessment. However, the following year, despite the program's success, her budget was significantly cut. In a moment of panic, we reached out to all instructors teaching writing-intensive courses to ask if they would benefit from having a course-embedded tutor. Based on those replies, we contacted department chairs and deans to see if they would be willing to support a course-embedded tutor for their particular program, at a reasonable cost of approximately $750.[1] Unanimously, across disciplines, in the midst of budget cuts, the answer was yes.

After another year of success and careful assessment of the course-embedded tutoring program, the provost again slashed my colleague's budget. At that point, our faculty partners were infuriated. So, they took it upon themselves to invite the provost to a curriculum committee meeting, at which they discussed the value of the course-embedded tutoring program and demanded that it receive support. It worked. In fact, the provost provided funding to support more course-embedded tutors than we could realistically manage administratively, especially since the WAC coordinator lost one of her administrative course releases, thus reducing the time she had to spend on the WAC program. While this example still led to support from upper administration, it also shows how, through strategic partnerships, more effective arguments to support writers and teachers of writing can be made when they come from voices across the institution. In this case, the course-embedded tutoring program was becoming integrated into the writing-intensive curriculum. We specifically sought out early partnerships with courses taught in the new Health Studies College, the College of Education, STEM disciplines, and the College of Social Work—all powerful concentrations that had already been identified by the university as priority programs. When support for writing was threatened, not only did these and other departments step up, but they also spoke out on our behalf. It was primarily the relational component of our strategic partnership that encouraged our colleagues to act this way.

In this book, I argue that creating strategic partnerships across campus is not only valuable but necessary. In doing so, I do not mean to argue for a complete shift to such a model, or that we should replace one-on-one, student-driven sessions with class- and program-specific writing support facilitated by instructors. Both kinds of writing center work are valuable and necessary. Yet, building strategic partnerships enables us to create a networked identity on campus rooted in context-specific writing support, while also reaching many students who may otherwise not interact with the writing center. And it empowers us to build relationships by teaching writing together, so that we can continue to improve our curricula and pedagogies, which, ultimately, better support student writers.

Creating successful strategic partnerships like those facilitated in the SRUWC require certain characteristics that create a context for partnership, and a tone for building relationships across campus. Developing these traits helps to position writing centers as alternative hubs for conversation around supporting and improving learning impacted by disruptive innovations in higher education, or the threat of these disruptions. In particular, building strategic partnerships requires attention to mutual benefits, stakeholder engagement, and negotiated space to become transformational rather than simply transactional.

WRITING CENTERS REQUIRE AGENCY, A RHETORIC OF RESPECT, AND VULNERABLE LISTENING TO BUILD STRATEGIC PARTNERSHIPS.

Cultivating agency within a writing center will likely look different across contexts—in part because of the many positionalities of writing centers in the university and the wide range of staffing structures (in terms of who directs and from what kind of position, as well as who does the work within the writing center), but also because of each writing center's unique history and origin story. Some writing centers may be able to develop a strong sense of agency as part of a department or larger university center or structure, while others may need to find avenues for independence, or some other way to distinguish themselves. This sense of agency is important not only for how others perceive the writing center, but also for how the writing center—and those who work within it—perceive themselves and their work. For Melissa (SRUWC director), agency was not possible until the writing center split from English. Once this happened, Melissa established her own relationship with deans and provosts that enables her to shift her focus beyond first-year writing and to hire writing consultants outside of English. More importantly, Melissa's sense of agency empowers her to exercise choice about what kinds of projects she works on and how those projects unfold.

In part because of this sense of agency and confidence in the work of the SRUWC, Melissa and her administrative staff develop relationships rooted in a "rhetoric of respect" (Rousculp 2014). Granted that Melissa set boundaries around the kinds of work they absolutely will not do (like letter-grade writing), she also says "yes" to nearly all requests for partnerships, even though the ways those partnerships would look often change in early conversations. The SRUWC's partners often explain that the partnerships work because they have relationships with the writing center staff built on trust and honesty established and maintained through listening, transparency, and talking through the process. Working from a rhetoric of respect means giving up, sometimes even resisting, the identity of "expert" and not assuming that the writing center always knows what will work best for a particular program.

In relationships (or partnerships) governed by a kind of mutual respect that is possible because of each partner's sense of agency, vulnerable listening also comes into play. Vulnerable listening stems from Shari J. Stenberg's (2015) concept of feminist repurposing, a way of challenging corporate structures that position themselves as "neutral" in order to enact change. In particular, she argues for repurposing rhetorical listening, all the while acknowledging the risks involved. Stenberg notes,

"The risk is not merely that your social position and identity may be challenged, or not merely that someone may disagree with your intellectual position, or not even that you may lose the argument; the risk is also that you may become different than you were before the argument began" (qtd. from Lynch, George, and Cooper 1997, 68). This, I would argue, is both the risk and the purpose of rhetorical listening—the risk of reading, writing, and thinking outside of a predetermined position, even as we question and rethink the positions we inevitably bring to our exchanges with others' words. (96)

If we take seriously Stenberg's recommendation of rhetorical listening, then we risk losing a sense of our own identities, our own stories, and our own ways of positioning ourselves in relation to the university. This element of rhetorical listening makes all of us vulnerable because it complicates one's stories—and one's identity—in relation to others and to the university. It may encourage us to give up certain "truths" we have about writing, and in turn requires our partners to recognize that some of their "truths" are equally wrong or limited. The risk involved with vulnerable, rhetorical listening is so high that it often keeps us academically siloed, or resistant to working with certain departments or colleagues.

Yet, in order to get to a place where this kind of listening can occur, we have to make our own sense of agency and establish a rhetoric of respect for one another. Too often, vulnerable listening is imposed, through combative explaining, upon those with whom we do not agree. Building partnerships and relationships around writing from this position does not happen. In contrast, when partnerships are created from agency and respect first, then vulnerable listening becomes less threatening. The risks and potential benefits begin to outweigh the stories and beliefs about writing that we may have to give up.

WRITING CENTERS HAVE AN IMPORTANT ROLE TO PLAY IN RESPONSE TO DISRUPTIVE INNOVATIONS IN HIGHER EDUCATION.

While disruptive innovations are not new to higher education, their presence seems to grow stronger as universities experience budget cuts and try to think creatively about how to do more with less. In a recent English Department meeting at a different university, I remember an emotionally heated conversation about the administration's decision to increase class sizes across the College of Arts and Sciences. At interdepartmental faculty meetings, colleagues in other disciplines had even offered to teach larger content classes so that writing classes could be kept smaller. Everyone seemed to see the value and need for low numbers, especially in writing classes. Even some of my colleagues in literature spoke up about their willingness to teach larger classes to keep writing courses in the department small. Yet, these perspectives did not matter; all class sizes, even writing-intensive classes, were going to see an increase. One of the other writing program administrators spoke up about her concerns specifically for our part-time instructors, who often teach three or four first-year writing courses, and how this would so negatively impact them without any increase in pay.

As a new assistant professor, I was usually quiet in department meetings, but I spoke up and said that I agreed that increasing class sizes was awful and that ideally we would keep them low, but that if we could not do that, perhaps we could find ways of supporting writing-intensive classes, especially those taught by part-time instructors, through work with the writing center, particularly through course-embedded tutoring. While some people seemed to nod as I spoke, the writing program administrator seemed annoyed, as this was not an adequate solution. It was as if my suggestion were a kind of giving up and giving in to the university's decision to increase class sizes. While I can sympathize with her perspective, it seemed to me that this was a university-wide fight that we could not win. So, then, how are we going to support student writers and faculty teaching writing in this new educational environment, where writing classes that were once capped at fifteen are now capped closer to twenty-five? If we are refused the resources necessary to create the best circumstances for the teaching of writing, then perhaps we can creatively construct alternatives, which will likely still be contingent on the availability of some additional resources but can be done with less. Such requests could be positioned as compromises that work within new constrictions while maintaining some commitment to ethical and effective writing instruction. Undergraduate peer tutoring is effective pedagogically and not as expensive as hiring instructors of record. Thus, strategic partnership provides the writing center with a way to respond to both external disruptive innovations and internal budget cuts.

These are the kinds of questions that twenty-first-century university writing centers will likely find themselves asking or perhaps departments will ask and turn to the writing center for support. These questions are especially likely in response to disruptive innovations, some of which are very workable even if perceived as being in conflict with the intellectual goals of higher education. For instance, online education is now a part of our educational landscape and can be done well, especially with support from the writing center. Similarly, stronger attention to workplace writing and finding ways of reaching writing assignments outside university settings has many benefits for student writers, yet only when improving their writing is still the focus, not industry expectations or commitments, such as those established by Go Pro Early programs. In contrast, the use of P3s is rarely the best option when it comes to writing support or assessment, even if we are still figuring out how to do writing center work well with large numbers of students.

Thus, writing centers should start thinking about how to better support writers and teachers of writing in online courses, through large-scale writing assessment, and for writing beyond the university. Although not exactly a disruptive innovation, one commonality across all three case study chapters explored in this book is that the instructors teaching in these environments are often graduate teaching assistants, many of whom need instruction about the teaching of writing. Even though each partnership has stakeholders at the programmatic or college level, graduate teaching assistants are often doing a large percentage of the teaching—in the hybrid first-year writing courses and the engineering classes, as well as in the business law and ethics course before the professor outsourced the work to Rich Feedback. Thus, writing centers can expect to work with graduate teaching assistants, especially in response to disruptive innovations. Although not directly in most writing centers' purview, we may benefit from thinking about how to support, mentor, and work with graduate teaching assistants across the disciplines, especially if little such support exists elsewhere on campus. In these scenarios, the wealth of knowledge and experience writing consultants bring can help GTAs learn more about how to effectively teach writing.

WRITING CENTERS CAN CREATE TRANSFORMATIONAL STRATEGIC PARTNERSHIPS THROUGH EARLY AND REGULAR ATTENTION TO MUTUAL BENEFITS, STAKEHOLDER ENGAGEMENT, AND NEGOTIATED SPACE.

In chapters 4–6, I explore how three specific partnerships work with attention to mutual benefits, stakeholder engagement, negotiated space, and transformational/transactional partnership qualities. Given that the partnerships studied in this book are not intentionally created to be strategic partnerships but rather evolved into a variety of kinds of partnership, early conversations to think through these concepts rarely occurred. Yet, they likely would have benefited each partnership and prevented some pitfalls. While not all (strategic) partnerships are transformational, all parties will benefit from setting a context for them to evolve into such. To engage in strategic partnership that can become transformational, writing centers should consider the following:

Establish agency, a rhetoric of respect, and an ear for vulnerable listening.
Constructing a mission statement and set of core values as a staff helps a writing center develop a sense of identity and eventually agency. Rather than simply maintaining what is on file, regularly reevaluating and adapting these documents as a team will help build confidence and community in ways that enable agency. This kind of environment, where everyone feels agency to act, make choices, and make meaning (Williams 2017), will ultimately impact conversations with student writers and with faculty who are teaching writing, too.

To develop a rhetoric of respect and an ear for vulnerable listening, writing centers should think about how other departments might view writing in ways that are different from their own. This can be done alongside a consideration of the writing center's mission statement and core values, or it could be thought of as an entirely different conversation in which the following questions are considered:

- What are the beliefs that writing centers and writing consultants hold about writing and about writers? Which of these beliefs are likely not known or held by others outside the writing center scenario?
- What do our structures and methods suggest we value? Do we hold these values?
- What do we know about how others view and understand writing, based on department policies, programs, assignment prompts, conversations with students, etc.?
- Why do others understand writing this way? What experiences might they have had that lead them to think about writing in these ways?
- Are there potential overlaps in how the writing center approaches writing and writers and in how others approach writing and writers? How might some common vocabulary be created around writing that could speak to multiple audiences?

Anticipating alternative beliefs about writing and trying to understand them help writing center administrators and consultants prepare for moments when they will be confronted with conflicts. It helps them think through the ways they might engage in conversation, while simultaneously encouraging understanding and listening.

Identify current or potential partners. Map out
stakeholders, benefits, and a negotiated space.

Most writing centers are already likely engaging in collaborations with departments and classes across the university. Early on, trying to pilot a few more robust partnerships with a range of departments and stakeholders with whom the writing center already has good relationships is important. This way, writing center administrators can start to develop a process and some methods that could be used in other contexts. Further, other departments can learn about how partnerships work from a few strong examples. Having some early success is important for securing support from upper administrators, even though some of the most transformational partnerships are likely to form with those who have not set foot in the writing center yet. Find out why they haven't.

Figure 6.1 displays the SRUWC's Partnership Process as developed in chapter 2 of this book, with added action steps based on how the three case study partnerships play out. This is one approach to work from, but other writing centers may find that a different method works for them, especially given the particularities of the writing center's staffing, structure, and size. This process offers a starting point for how writing centers might map out their active work.

From the beginning, conversations about partnership should include discussion of goals, motivations, assessment, and stakeholders (*Actions 1–4*). Creating a negotiated space requires partners to recognize a shared space in which collaborative decisions will be made, despite some differences in terms of roles, motivations, and ethical perspectives. Attention to mission statements and key terms and values will help anticipate potential conflicts across partners and/or stakeholders before they arise. In addition, partners should map out mutual benefits as well as individual partner benefits and broader university benefits. This will help identify potential stakeholders. Further, conversations about assessment should occur early and include both satisfaction-based data (e.g., were students, instructors, and tutors satisfied with how the partnership went?) as well as writing- and teaching-based data (how did writing and the teaching of writing change throughout the partnership, and how did writing and the teaching of writing differ compared with similar, non-partnership courses?). Assessment should also track whether or not the anticipated benefits are indeed fulfilled. During the first semester and year of a new partnership, these action items should be returned to and adapted regularly, as it will likely take a while to figure out how to best create negotiated space and assessment as well as the most appropriate levels of engagement across stakeholders.

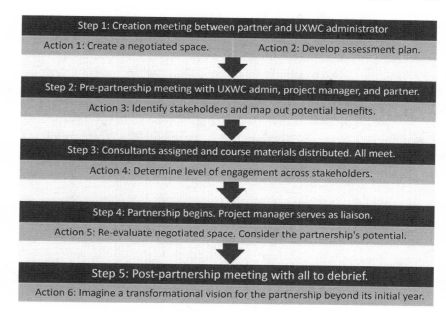

Figure 6.1. Creating strategic writing center partnership

Although none of the case study partnerships explored in this book consider student writers to be involved stakeholders in these partnerships, they absolutely should be. The absence of student voices in assessment data and in conversation among partners from both the SRUWC and the disciplines is alarming. Given that writing centers tend to primarily focus on supporting student writers, they are well positioned to bring student writers into partnership dialogue in meaningful ways beyond student satisfaction surveys. Not only are student writers' perspectives important, but additional perceptions from the writing consultants could also help shape partnerships. One simple way to make this addition would be to include both student writer and writing consultant focus group meetings in action 5, so that at the end of every semester these perspectives are taken into account before the next iteration of the partnership.

Re-evaluate the Partnership for Transformative Potential and
Imagine a Vision Beyond

Once a steady partnership has been established, partners should re-evaluate negotiated space with attention to the partnership's transformative potential and, along with that, a larger vision (*Actions 5–6*).

Although not all strategic partnerships have the potential to be transformative, many of them do. A larger vision for a partnership could involve thinking beyond a single course or semester, a single department, or even a single college. If something is working well in a single, strategic partnership, how might that partnership reach further? Are there ways to continue it beyond what it is? Are there other departments or colleges that might benefit from a similar partnership, or are there ways for students to engage with the partnership across disciplines, semesters, or courses?

* * *

While transformational partnerships are intended to have far reaching implications beyond a single course or department, strategic partnerships can have transformative elements on a small scale too. For instance, one of the most significant moments for me during this research was my conversation with Rick (art history), who is a department chair and teacher of the only writing-intensive course in the major. While this kind of writing curriculum is small, Rick's approach to the course and his thinking about teaching writing is transformed through his work with the writing center. As was the case in all interviews with disciplinary faculty, Rick turns to metaphor to help explain how he understands his partnership with the writing center:

> Have you ever read Stephen J. Gould? He was the curator of paleontology at the Museum of Natural History, but he had this very specific way of looking at evolution. He called it punctuated equilibrium, where you sort of go along, like we have for 100 years with the essay writing, and you turn in the essay at the end, and I know there have been attempts to change that, over the last century, a lot, but then, all of a sudden with the digital [era], the word processor and the networked environment, you get this completely different set of variables that have inserted themselves in this thing, and so all of a sudden, it's like I found these elements and [have] been able to bring them together in a way that I could not have imagined 15 years ago would even be interesting to me. Or, if you had talked to me 15 years ago, you would just hear—a student has to decide to work on a paper three weeks before they turn it in and then I'll give them some good feedback. That was it. And if they didn't do that, then they were just lost, I mean it was just, oh and I read so many of those lost papers. Ugh. I'd spend 30 minutes on these things, because if you flunk them, you have to tell them why, I mean it's serious stuff. And, I'm not there anymore, it's just a completely different environment. I don't have to flunk very many people.

While some of the changes Rick describes are directly connected to technology (like the use of the word processor), others seem more pedagogical, like offering students feedback throughout the writing process rather than simply to justify a bad grade. Yet now, Rick's students meet regularly in small groups with a writing center consultant to discuss their drafts. In the past year, Rick's popular writing-intensive course shifted to a hybrid format for departmental reasons, and so his partnership with the writing center also had to shift online via the use of shared Google Docs for facilitated peer review. Rick's connection between the move to scaffolded writing assignments and early, regular feedback from an experienced peer writing consultant before students submit their final drafts means that Rick does not "have to flunk very many people." Thus, the pedagogical and environmental shift of Rick's teaching through his writing center partnership has transformed how he approaches the teaching of writing and also how students receive feedback and are ultimately evaluated in his course.

As disruptive innovations like online teaching, public-private partnerships, and career readiness initiatives continue to shake higher education, the potential for sudden shifts that lead to radical change is ever present. Yet, writing centers can anticipate these shifts by building relationships via strategic partnerships, thus intervening before the teaching of writing is threatened by disruptive innovations. For some, like Rick, working with the writing center will also cause a radical change in how writing is taught, but it will be an ethical change of which instructors are deeply a part, rather than something that is outsourced.

NOTES

INTRODUCTION

1. For instance, see recent events at the University of British Columbia, the University of Alberta, and South High School.
2. For instance, see Elon 2016 and University of Virginia 2017.
3. It's important to note that, although writing centers can and often do operate according to ethical labor practices, this is not a guarantee, as Beth Towle's research on undergraduate peer tutor labor at small liberal arts colleges points out (2018).
4. This definition of agency builds from Bronwyn Williams's concept of writer agency in *Literacy Practices and Perceptions of Agency* (2018) that "implies the possibility of action and decision" as well as the "perception" that such action is possible (9).
5. In "On the Ascendance of Argument: A Critique of the Assumption of Academe's Dominant Form," Todd DeStigter argues that argument is highly privileged over other forms of writing. In particular, he claims, "the overemphasis on argumentation imposes unwarranted limits on what counts as valid thought, legitimate political subjectivity, and a feasible strategy for addressing economic inequality" (2015, 13).
6. Southern Research University stands for the university at which this research took place and is a fictious name. This anonymity was a requirement of the Institutional Review Board's approval of this research project.
7. Geller et al. define trickster as "a traveler" who "frequently breaks societal rules, blurring connections and distinctions" between binaries as well as one who crosses boundaries (2007, 15).
8. As Laura Micciche (2017) notes, *method* refers to the tools or techniques used to collect data, and *methodology* involves the theory that informs the choice to use those particular tools and approaches to analysis. Thus, I develop qual-RAD as both method and methodology, or what I call "method(ology)," to recognize both aspects.
9. For a map of the Writing Center, see chapter 2 of this book.
10. The replication of Grutsch McKinney's research questions was also done by Andrea Scott (2015) in her research about writing centers in Germany. These questions include: (1) In your own words, what is a writing center? (2) How do you describe the role of the writing center to others at SRU? (3) In what ways do you think the SRUWC is different from other writing centers? (4) In what ways do you think the SRUWC is similar to other writing centers?
11. For a description of Grutsch McKinney's writing center grand narrative, see page 49 of this book.
12. Since part of this project was to replicate Grutsch McKinney's four questions, I did make sure that all questions were asked during the interview or via a follow-up interview.
13. For an example of an interview log that follows these rules, see Appendix A.

14. Clifford Geertz's seminal 1973 *The Interpretation of Cultures* presents "thick description," a new theory of culture that emphasizes interpretation and which was groundbreaking in the field of American anthropology at the time.

15. For an explanation of this kind of relationship, see Muriel Saville-Troike's *The Ethnography of Communication: An Introduction* and Margaret Diane LeCompte's *Researcher Roles and Research Partnership*

16. Although I struggled with not providing more "thick description" in these instances, the scope of the project and the primary subject (the SRUWC) made it impossible for me to provide extensive context for each participant.

CHAPTER 1: ESTABLISHING AGENCY

1. Jeremy explained that by "old days," he meant when he was a consultant, around 2010–2011.

2. During my research, someone else explained to me that the reason for having initials, rather than names, on the scheduler was because when the scheduler did include names, students were not making appointments with consultants who had non-American sounding names.

3. In addition to this physical move in 2012, the SRUWC also experienced an institutional move from under the leadership of the dean of the College of Arts and Social Sciences to a position under the vice provost and dean of Undergraduate Student Success.

4. Melissa gave me a copy of this article after one of our interviews.

5. For an example of a "cost estimate," see chapter 5.

6. Rather than tracking the number of students seen, the SRUWC measures its activity in terms of "student interactions" or the number of times each student interacts with a consultant in a one-on-one or group setting. For the GENB 4350 (Business Writing Tutorial), which consisted of individual consultations, there were 683 interactions in fall 2013 and 618 in spring 2014, according to the WC's 2014 annual report. More details about this partnership are described in the faculty interview with Dean Kyle in chapter 2.

7. As of 2015, the SRUWC had worked with eleven of the university's twelve colleges.

8. In using the term *middle-administrator*, I intentionally evoke the concept of "middle managers" as developed in James Paul Gee, Glynda Hull, and Colin Lankshear's *The New Work Order: Behind the Language of the New Capitalism*. Gee et al. describe "middle managers" as team leaders who work as project directors and consultants who supervise themselves. Yet, based on the work these administrators do, I use the term *project manager* throughout this chapter because it more specifically describes the kind of work they do. Figure 2.2 presents the 2015 SRUWC's organizational structure per the annual report.

9. It's worth noting that these two writing center environments, homey/comfortable and intellectual/professional, are not necessarily mutually exclusive, as Williams 2018 points out.

10. Although I originally intended to interview consultants (and did conduct some interviews), I found greater value in observing the reading groups as a way of understanding the consultants collectively. Since this year there were more new consultants than experienced ones, I worried that one-on-one interviews about the SRUWC may be uncomfortable and perhaps seem premature to newer members of the SRUWC staff.

11. The idea of tutors forming a "community of practice" draws from Etienne Wenger's sense of the phrase developed in *Communities of Practice: Learning, Meaning, and*

Identity (1998). Geller et al. (2007) apply this concept to writing center studies in *The Everyday Writing Center: A Community of Practice.*

CHAPTER 2: COUNSELORS, TSUNAMIS, AND WELL-OILED MACHINES

1. In saying this, I do not mean to suggest that architecture is the only field that values or emphasizes these particular writing conventions. Amir himself refers to architecture as a "design discipline," thus suggesting that there are other similar disciplines within that broader category. However, I do mean to argue that the writing knowledge suggested here is particular to architecture and may not apply to other disciplines such as business, biology, English, or political science.
2. I worked as the consultant for the Marketing 8397 partnership between the Bauer Business School and the writing center for three consecutive summers in 2013, 2014, and 2015.
3. For a more developed account of my co-teaching with Carol, see Hallman, "Re-envisioning Course-Embedded Programs."

CHAPTER 3: REWORKING WITH THE ENGLISH DEPARTMENT

1. In addition to facilitating online groups for English, I also led face-to-face studios for a section of art history and a section of human resource development. About 80 percent of my work and that of the other GTFs in my cohort was rooted in the WC/English Department partnership.
2. Megan is the pseudonym for Miley, whose research on this program is referenced throughout this chapter.
3. Molly is the pseudonym for Gray, whose research is referenced in this chapter.
4. The WC facilitator, Casey, participated in this conversation as well. Yet, the students seemed to ignore her in favor of responding to one another, so I did not include her response here.
5. While this conversation eventually became somewhat productive for the students, the emotional labor likely experienced by Casey (the facilitator) deserves some acknowledgment. Casey was also learning how to best navigate the online studio space for the first time and lacked power in the course's structure and workload, all of which was established by the FYW program and WC. Yet, she was the one on the other end when the student lashed out. Because the hybrid instructor and the WC are both more likely to be perceived as administrators and thus more threatening, it seemed unsurprising that students would feel most comfortable voicing frustrations in the studio space to the facilitator.

CHAPTER 4: ENGAGING CHALLENGES

1. This chapter does not include a participant matrix because there are no new interviewees. For Sam's bio, see chapter 2. For Kyle's bio, see chapter 3.
2. According to the previous assistant director of Writing in the Disciplines at the SRUWC, most of the graders were actually undergraduate peer tutors, and the course size was approximately 600 students per course.
3. Although both Edumetry and Rich Feedback were used interchangeably in the texts and by the people included in this chapter, I've decided to use Rich Feedback throughout to maintain consistency.

4. Kyle mentioned during our interview that Rich Feedback has an initial machine score/reading of the essay before it's graded by a human, and then the two scores are compared.
5. See chapter 4 of this book for discussion of stakeholder engagement.

CHAPTER 5: NAVIGATING WORKPLACE REALITIES

1. TAs at SRU are different from teaching fellows (TFs) in that they are not fully responsible for course design and curriculum but rather assist the primary professor and often act as graders who also provide oversight of lab classes.
2. Although ELET faculty and administrators were contacted with a request for an interview, they were unresponsive and thus never met for an interview. However, these partners seemed to have little involvement in the teaching of the courses themselves, which were instead led by TAs.
3. The Intel-Cornell Cup is a college-level embedded design competition "created to empower student teams to become the inventors of the newest innovative applications of embedded technology." Teams have the opportunity to win up to $7,500.

CONCLUSION

1. This amount enabled us to paid course-embedded tutors at a slightly higher hourly rate than general tutors.

REFERENCES

Adams Wooten, Courtney, Jacob Babb, and Brian Ray, eds. 2018. *WPAs in Transition: Navigating Educational Leadership Positions.* Logan: Utah State University Press.

Adler-Kassner, Linda, and Elizabeth Wardle. 2015. *Naming What We Know: Threshold Concepts of Writing Studies.* Logan: Utah University Press.

Alexander, B., S. Adams Becker, and M. Cummins. 2016. *Digital Literacy: An NMC Horizon Project Strategic Brief* 3, no. 3. Austin, TX: The New Media Consortium.

Allen, Elaine I., and Jeff Seaman, with Doug Lederman and Scott Jaschik. 2012. "Conflicted: Faculty and Online Education, 2012." The Babson Survey Research Group and *Inside Higher Ed.*

Alvarez, Nancy, Francia Brito, Cristina Salazar, and Karina Aguilar. 2016. "Agency, Liberation, and Intersectionality among Latina Scholars: Narratives from A Cross-Institutional Writing Collective." *Praxis: A Writing Center Journal* 14, no. 1.

American Counseling Association. 2022. "What is Professional Counseling?" American Counseling Association. https://www.counseling.org/aca-community/learn-about-counseling/what-is-counseling#.

Anderson, Daniel. 2008. "The Low Bridge to High Benefits: Entry-Level Multimedia, Literacies, and Motivation." *Computers and Composition* 25, no. 1: 40–60.

Anderson, Janna, Jan Lauren Boyles, and Lee Rainie. 2012. *Main Findings: Higher Education's Destination by 2020.* Washington, DC: Pew Research Center.

Anderson, Paul V. 2017. *Technical Communication: A Reader-Centered Approach.* Boston: Cengage Learning.

Anderson, Paul, et al. 2015. "The Contributions of Writing to Learning and Development: Results from a Large-Scale Multi-Institutional Study." *Research in the Teaching of English* 50, no. 2 (November): 199–235.

Anson, Chris M., and Jessie L. Moore, eds. 2016. *Critical Transitions: Writing and the Question of Transfer.* Perspectives on Writing. Fort Collins: The WAC Clearinghouse and University Press of Colorado.

Appleby, Drew C. 2017. "The First Step to Overcoming Procrastination: Know Thyself." *Psychology Student Network* (January).

Association of American Colleges and Universities. 2018. "Falling Short? College Learning and Career Success."

Babcock, Rebecca Day, and Terese Thonus. 2012. *Researching the Writing Center: Towards an Evidence-Based Practice.* New York: Peter Lang.

Babson Survey Research Group. 2018. *Higher Education Reports: Online and Distance Education.* https://www.babson.edu/academics/faculty/babson-survey-research-group/.

Bagehot. 2017. "Jeremy Corbyn, Entrepreneur." *The Economist* 53 (June 15, 2017).

Baker, Anthony, Karen Bishop, Suellynn Duffey, Jeanne Gunner, Richard Miller, and Shelley Reid. 2005. "The Progress of Generations." *WPA: Writing Program Administration* 29, nos. 1/2: 31–57.

Balester, Valerie, Nancy Grimm, Jackie Grutsch McKinney, Sohui Lee, David M. Sheridan, and Naomi Silver. 2012. "The Idea of a Multiliteracy Center: Six Responses." *Praxis: A Writing Center Journal* 9, no. 2.

Banks, Clare, Birgit Siebe-Herbig, and Karin Norton. 2016. *Global Perspectives on Strategic International Partnerships: A Guide to Building Sustainable Academic Linkages.* New York: Institute of International Education.

https://doi.org/10.7330/9781646421770.c007

Barnett, Robert W., and Jacob S. Blumner. 1999. *Writing Centers and Writing Across the Curriculum Programs: Building Interdisciplinary Partnerships.* Santa Barbara: Praeger.

Barrow, Clyde. 1990. *Universities and the Capitalist State: Corporate Liberalism and the Reconstruction of American Higher Education, 1894–1928.* Madison: University of Wisconsin Press.

Bartholomae, David. 1986. "Inventing the University." *Journal of Basic Writing* 5, no. 1 (Spring 1986): 4–23.

Bartholomae, David, and Anthony Petrosky, eds. 2010. *Ways of Reading: An Anthology for Writers.* Boston: Bedford/St. Martin's.

Bawa, Papia. 2016. "Retention in Online Courses: Exploring Issues and Solutions—A Literature Review." *SAGE Open* 1, no. 11.

Beason-Abmayr, Beth, and Jennifer Shade Wilson. 2018. "Building a Partnership with a Campus Communication Center." *Journal of Microbiology and Biology Education* 10, no. 1.

Beaufort, Anne. 1999. *Writing in the Real World: Making the Transition from School to Work.* New York: Teachers College Press.

Bell, Lisa. 2011. "Preserving the Rhetorical Nature of Tutoring When Going Online." In *The St. Martin's Sourcebook for Writing Tutors,* edited by C. Murphy and S. Sherwood, 326–334. Boston: Bedford/St. Martin's Press.

Berlin, James. 1996. *Rhetorics, Poetics, and Cultures: Refiguring College English Studies.* Urbana: National Council of Teachers of English.

Best Colleges. 2017. *2017 Online Education Trends Report.* Best Colleges.

Birkenstein, Cathy, and Gerald Graff. 2016. *They Say/I Say: The Moves That Matter in Academic Writing.* New York: W. W. Norton & Company.

Bishop, Wendy. 1999. *Ethnographic Writing Research: Writing It Down, Writing It Up, and Reading It.* Portsmouth, NH: Boynton/Cook Publishers.

Blankenship, Lisa. 2019. *Changing the Subject: A Theory of Rhetorical Empathy.* Logan: Utah State University Press.

Blumner, Jacob, and Pamela Childers. 2011. "Building Better Bridges: What Makes High School–College WAC Collaborations Work?" *The WAC Journal* 22: 91–101.

Bok, Derek. 2003. *Universities in the Marketplace: The Commercialization of Higher Education.* Princeton, NJ: Princeton University Press.

Book, Cassandra A. 2018. "Preparing Students for Writing Futures: New Possibilities for Transfer in TA Education." Watson Conference, University of Louisville, 2018.

Boquet, Elizabeth H. 1999. "'Our Little Secret': A History of Writing Centers, Pre– to Post–Open Admissions." *College Composition and Communication* 50, no. 3: 463–482.

Bosson, J. K., Amber B. Johnson, Kate Niederhoffer, and William B. Swann. 2006. "Interpersonal Chemistry Through Negativity: Bonding by Sharing Negative Attitudes About Others." *Personal Relationships* 13: 135–150.

Bousquet, Marc, Tony Scott, and Leo Parascondola, eds. 2004. *Tenured Bosses and Disposable Teachers: Writing Instruction in the Managed University.* Carbondale: Southern Illinois University Press.

Bowie, Jennifer L., and Heather A. McGovern. 2013. "De-Coding Our Scholarship: The State of Research in Computers and Writing from 2003–2008." *Computers and Composition* 30: 242–262.

Brammer, Charlotte, and Mary Rees. 2007. "Peer Review from the Students' Perspective: Invaluable or Invalid?" *Composition Studies* 35, no. 2 (Fall): 71–85.

Brandt, Deborah. 2001. *Literacy in American Lives.* Cambridge: Cambridge University Press.

Brewer, Meaghan. 2020. *Conceptions of Literacy: Graduate Instructors and the Teaching of First-Year Composition.* Logan: Utah State University Press.

Bridgeford, Tracy, and Kirk St.Amant, eds. 2015. *Academy-Industry Relationships and Partnerships: Perspectives for Technical Communicators.* Amityville: Baywood Publishing Company.

Brizee, Allen, and Jaclyn M. Wells. 2016. *Partners in Literacy: A Writing Center Model for Civic Engagement.* Lanham: Rowman & Littlefield Publishers.

Brodkey, Linda. 1987. "Writing Ethnographic Narratives." *Written Communication* 4, no. 1: 25–50.

Brooks, Kevin, Michael Tomanek, Rachel Wald, Matthew Warner, and Brianne Wilkening. 2006. "What's Going On? Listening to Music, Composing Videos." *Computers and Composition Online.* Special Issue on Composing with Sound (Fall).

Brown, Renee, Brian Fallon, Jessica Lott, Elizabeth Matthews, and Elizabeth Mintie. 2007. "Taking on Turnitin: Tutors Advocating Change." *The Writing Center Journal* 27, no. 1: 7–28.

Brown, Stephen Gilbert, and Sidney I. Dobrin, eds. 2004. *Ethnography Unbound: From Theory Shock to Critical Praxis.* Albany: State University of New York Press.

Brown, Stuart C., and Theresa Enos, eds. 2002. *The Writing Program Administrator's Resource: A Guide to Reflective Institutional Practice.* Mahwah: Erlbaum.

Brueggemann, Brenda Jo. 1992. "Still-Life: Representations and Silences in the Participant-Observer Role." In *Methods and Methodology in Composition Research*, edited by Gesa Kirsch and Patricia A. Sullivan, 17–39. Carbondale: Southern Illinois University Press, 1992.

Bruner, Jerome. 1991. "The Narrative Construction of Reality." *Critical Inquiry* 18 (Autumn): 1–21.

Bruner, Jerome. 2003. *Making Stories: Law, Literature, Life.* Boston: Harvard University Press.

Buck Sutton, Susan. 2016. "Mutual Benefit in a Globalizing World: A New Calculus for Assessing Institutional Gain through International Academic Partnerships." In *Global Perspectives on Strategic International Partnerships: A Guide to Building Sustainable Academic Linkages*, edited by Clare Banks, Birgit Siebe-Herbig, and Karin Norton, 175–186. New York: Institute of International Education.

Bugdal, Melissa, and Ricky Holtz. 2014. "When Writing Fellows Become Reading Fellows: Creative Strategies for Critical Reading and Writing in a Course-Based Tutoring Program." *Praxis: A Writing Center Journal* 12, no. 1.

Busteed, Brandon. 2019. "This Will Be the Biggest Disruption in Higher Education." *Forbes,* April 30, 2019.

Carillo, Ellen C. 2014. *Securing a Place for Reading in Composition: The Importance of Teaching for Transfer.* Logan: Utah State University Press.

Carino, Peter. 1992. "What Do We Talk About When We Talk About Our Metaphors: A Cultural Critique of Clinic, Lab, and Center." *Writing Center Journal* 13, no. 1 (Fall): 31–43.

Carlson, Scott. 2019. "The Outsourced University: How Public-Private Partnerships Can Benefit Your Campus." *Chronicle of Higher Education* (April).

Carpenter, Russell. 2015. "Engagement through Emerging Technologies: A Humanistic Perspective on Academe-Industry Relationships and Partnerships." In *Academy-Industry Relationships and Partnerships: Perspectives for Technical Communicators*, edited by Tracy Bridgeford and Kirk St.Amant, 141–156. Amityville: Baywood Publishing Company.

Carpenter, Russell, and Sohui Lee, eds. 2016. "Pedagogies of Multimodality and the Future of Multiliteracy Centers." *Computers and Composition* 41: 1–78.

Carpenter, Russell, Scott Whiddon, and Kevin Dvorak, eds. 2014. "Special Double Issue on Course-Embedded Writing Support Programs in Writing Centers." *Praxis: A Writing Center Journal* 12, no. 1.

Carter, Michael. 2007. "Ways of Knowing, Doing, and Writing in the Disciplines." *College Composition and Communication* 58, no. 3: 385–418.

Cashman, Ray. 2008. *Storytelling on the Northern Irish Border: Characters and Community.* Bloomington: Indiana University Press.

Caswell, Nicole I., Jackie Grutsch McKinney, and Rebecca Jackson. 2016. *The Working Lives of New Writing Center Directors.* Logan: Utah State University Press.

Cauthen, Randy. 2010. *Black Letters: An Ethnography of a Beginning Legal Writing Course.* New York: Hampton Press.

Chapelle, Carol A., Elena Cotos, and Jooyoung Lee. 2015. "Validity Arguments for Diagnostic Assessment Using Automated Writing Evaluation." *Language Testing* 32, no. 3: 385–405.

Chemishanova Polina, and Robin Lynne Snead. 2017. "Reconfiguring the Writing Studio Model: Examining the Impact of the PlusOne Program on Student Performance and Retention." *Engineering*.

Chen, Michelle. 2017. "The Higher-Education Crisis Is a Labor Crisis." *The Nation*, May 9, 2017.

Child, Robert. 1991. "Tutor-Teachers: An Examination of How Writing Center and Classroom Environments Inform Each Other." In *The Writing Center: New Directions*, edited by Ray Wallace and Jeanne Simpson, 169–183. Garland Publishing, 1991.

Chiseri-Strater, Elizabeth. 1991. *Academic Literacies: The Public and Private Discourse of University Students*. Portsmouth: Heinemann, 1991.

Christensen, Clayton M., and Henry J. Eyring. 2011. *The Innovative University: Changing the DNA of Higher Education from the Inside Out*. San Francisco: Jossey-Bass.

Christensen, Clayton M., Michael B. Horn, and Curtis W. Johnson. 2008. *Disrupting Class: How Disruptive Innovation Will Change the Way the World Learns*. New York: McGraw-Hill.

Christensen, Clayton M., Michael E. Raynor, and Rory McDonald. 2015. "What Is Disruptive Innovation?" *Harvard Business Review* (December).

Cintron, Ralph. 1998. *Angels' Town: Chero Ways, Gang Life, and Rhetorics of the Everyday*. Boston: Beacon Press.

Clark, Irene. 1988. "Collaboration and Ethics in Writing Center Pedagogy." *The Writing Center Journal* 9, no. 1: 3–12.

Clifford, James, and George E. Marcus, eds. 2010. *Writing Culture: The Poetics and Politics of Ethnography*. Oakland: University of California Press, 2010.

Conference on College Composition and Communication. 2009. Statement on Assessment.

Coogan, David. 2001. "Towards a Rhetoric of On-line Tutoring." In *The Allyn and Bacon Guide to Writing Center Theory and Practice*, edited by Robert W. Barnett and Jacob S. Blumner 555–560. Boston: Allyn and Bacon.

Cooke-Sather, Alison, Catherine Bovill, and Peter Felten. 2014. *Engaging Students as Partners in Learning and Teaching: A Guide for Faculty*. San Francisco: Jossey-Bass.

Corbett, Steven J., Michelle LaFrance, and Teagan E. Decker, eds. 2014. *Peer Pressure, Peer Power: Theory and Practice in Peer Review and Response for the Writing Classroom*. Southlake: Fountainhead Press.

Corbett, Steven J., and Michelle LaFrance. 2017. *Student Peer Review and Response: A Critical Sourcebook*. Boston: Bedford/St. Martin's.

Cotos, Elena. 2011. "Potential of Automated Writing Evaluation Feedback." *CALICO Journal* 28, no. 2: 420–459.

Cotos, Elena, and Nick Pendar. 2008. "Automated Diagnostic Writing Tests: Why? How?" In *Towards Adaptive CALL: Natural Language Processing for Diagnostic Language Assessment*, edited by C. A. Chapelle, Y. R. Chung, and J. Xu, 65–68. Ames: Iowa State University, 2008.

Cox, Geoffrey M. 2019. "Can Starbucks Save the Middle Class? No. But It Might Ruin Higher Education." *The Chronicle of Higher Education*, August 1, 2019.

Cox, Michelle, Jeffrey R. Galin, and Dan Melzer, eds. 2018. *Sustainable WAC: A Whole Systems Approach to Launching and Developing Writing Across the Curriculum Programs*. Urbana: National Council of Teachers of English.

Crowley, Sharon. 1998. *Composition in the University: Historical and Polemical Essays*. Pittsburgh: University of Pittsburgh Press.

Cushman, Ellen. 1998. *The Struggle and the Tools: Oral and Literate Strategies in an Inner City Community*. Albany: State University of New York Press.

de Certeau, Michel. 2011. *The Practice of Everyday Life*. Berkeley: The University of California Press.

Deitering, Anne-Marie, and Beth Filar Williams. 2018. "Make It Work: Using Service Design to Support Collaboration in Challenging Times." *International Information & Library Review* 50, no. 1: 54–59.

DeLoach, Scott, Elyse Angel, Ebony Breaux, Kevin Keebler, and Kathleen Klompien. 2014. "Locating the Center: Exploring the Roles of In-Class Tutors in First Year Composition Classrooms." *Praxis: A Writing Center Journal* 12 no. 1.

Denny, Harry. 2010. *Facing the Center: Toward an Identity Politics of One-To-One Mentoring.* Logan: Utah State University Press.

Denny, Harry, John Nordlof, and Lori Salem. 2018. "'Tell Me Exactly What It Was that I Was Doing That Was So Bad': Understanding the Needs and Expectations of Working-Class Students in Writing Centers." *The Writing Center Journal* 37, no. 1: 67–100.

Denny, Harry, Robert Mundy, Liliana Naydan, Richard Severe, and Anna Sicari, eds. 2019. *Out in the Center: Public Controversies and Private Struggles.* Logan: Utah State University Press.

Devet, Bonnie. 2012. "Using Metagenre and Ecocomposition to Train Writing Center Tutors for Writing in the Disciplines." *Praxis: A Writing Center Journal* 11, no. 2.

Devet, Bonnie. 2015. "The Writing Center and Transfer of Learning: A Primer for Directors." *The Writing Center Journal* 35, no. 1 (Fall/Winter): 119–151.

DeStigter, Todd. 2015. "On the Ascendance of Argument: A Critique of the Assumption of Academe's Dominant Form." *Research in the Teaching of English* 50, no. 1: 11–34.

Dias, Patrick, Aviva Freedman, Peter Medway, and Anthony Par. 1999. *Worlds Apart: Acting and Writing in Academic and Workplace Contexts.* New York: Routledge.

Dingo, Rebecca, Rachel Riedner, and Jennifer Wingard. 2005. "Disposable Drudgery: Outsourcing Goes to College." In *Transnational Writing Program Administration*, edited by David Martins, 265–288. Logan: Utah State University Press, 2015.

Dinitz, Susan, and Diane Howe. 1989. "Writing Centers and Writing-Across-the-Curriculum: An Evolving Partnership." *The Writing Center Journal* 10, no. 1: 45–51.

Douglas-Gabriel, Danielle. 2016. "The Real Crisis in Higher Education Is about a Lot More Than Debt." *The Washington Post,* August 11, 2016.

Downing, David B., Claude Mark Hurlbert, and Paula Mathieu, eds. 2002. *Beyond English Inc.: Curriculum Reform in a Global Economy.* Portsmouth: Boyton/Cook Heinemann.

Driscoll, Dana, and Sherry Wynn Perdue. 2012. "Theory, Lore, and More: An Analysis of RAD Research in *The Writing Center Journal,* 1980–2009." *The Writing Center Journal* 32, no. 2: 11–39.

Duggan, Lisa. 2003. *The Twilight of Equality? Neoliberalism, Cultural Politics, and the Attack on Democracy.* Boston: Beacon Press.

Dvorak, Kevin, and Shanti Bruce, eds. 2008. *Creative Approaches to Writing Center Work.* New York: Hampton Press.

Dynarski Susan, C. J. Libassi, Katherine Michelmore, and Stephanie Owen. 2018. "Closing the Gap: The Effect of a Targeted, Tuition-Free Promise on College Choices of High-Achieving, Low-Income Students." *AEAWeb,* December 3, 2018.

Eicher, Bobbie, Lalith Polepeddi, and Ashok K. Goel. 2018. "Jill Watson Doesn't Care If You're Pregnant: Grounding AI Ethics in Empirical Studies." *AIES '18: Proceedings of the 2018 AAAI/ACM Conference on AI, Ethics, and Society,* 88–94. New York: Association for Computing Machinery.

Enos, Sandra, and Keith Morton. 2003. "Developing a Theory and Practice of Campus-Community Partnerships." In *Building Partnerships for Service-Learning,* edited by Barbara Jacoby, 20–41. San Francisco: Jossey-Bass, 2003.

Eodice, Michele. 2003. "Breathing Lessons, or Collaboration Is . . ." In *The Center Will Hold: Critical Perspectives on Writing Center Scholarship,* edited by Michael A. Pemberton and Joyce Kinkead, 114–129. Logan: Utah State University Press, 2003.

Essid, Joe, and Brian McTague, eds. 2020. *Writing Centers at the Center of Change.* New York: Routledge.

Eubanks, Philip. 2011. *Metaphor and Writing: Figurative Thought in the Discourse of Written Communication.* New York: Cambridge University Press.

Faber, Brenton D. 2002. *Community Action and Organizational Change: Image, Narrative, Identity.* Carbondale: Southern Illinois University Press.

Fain, Paul. 2020. "CUNY's Move on Corporate Tuition Benefits." *Inside Higher Ed,* February 17, 2020.

Fallon, Brian. 2011. "Why My Best Teachers Are Peer Tutors." National Conference on Peer Tutoring in Writing.

Ferer, Elise. 2012. "Working Together: Library and Writing Center Collaboration." *Reference Services Review* 40, no. 4: 543–557.

Fitzgerald, Lauren, and Denise Stephenson. 2012. "Directors at the Center: Relationships Across Campus." In *The Writing Center Director's Resource Book,* edited by Christina Murphy and Byron Stay, 115–125. New York: Routledge.

Geertz, Clifford. 1973. *The Interpretation of Cultures.* New York: Basic Books.

Geller, Anne Ellen, Michele Eodice, Frankie Condon, Meg Carroll, and Elizabeth H. Boquet. 2007. *The Everyday Writing Center: A Community of Practice.* Logan: Utah State University Press.

Gentile, Francesca. 2014. "When Center Catches in the Classroom (and Classroom in the Center): The First-Year Writing Tutorial and the Writing Program." *Praxis: A Writing Center Journal* 12, no. 1.

George, Dianna. 1999. *Kitchen Cooks, Pate Twirlers, and Troubadors: Writing Program Administrators Tell Their Stories.* New Hampshire: Boynton/Cook-Heinemann.

Gere, Anne Ruggles, Sarah C. Swofford, Naomi Silver, and Melody Pugh. 2015. "Interrogating Disciplines/Disciplinarity in WAC/WID: An Institutional Study" *College Composition and Communication* 67, no. 2 (December): 243–266.

Giroux, Henry. 2002. "The Corporate War against Higher Education." *Workplace: A Journal for Academic Labor* 9: 103–117.

Goel, Ashok K., and Lalith Polepeddi. 2016. "Jill Watson: A Virtual Teaching Assistant for Online Education." In *Design and Intelligence Laboratory.* Design and Intelligence Laboratory, School of Interactive Computing, Georgia Institute of Technology.

Gordon, Layne. 2014. "Beyond Generalist vs. Specialist: Making Connections Between Genre Theory and Writing Center Pedagogy." *Praxis: A Writing Center Journal* 11, no. 2.

Gray, Mary. 2018. "Something Gained: The Role of Online Studios in a Hybrid First-Year Writing Course." In *The Writing Studio Sampler: Stories about Change,* edited by Mark Sutton and Sally Chandler, 185–206. Fort Collins, CO: The WAC Clearing House.

Greenfield, Laura. 2019. *Radical Writing Center Praxis: A Paradigm for Ethical Political Engagement.* Logan: Utah State University Press.

Grego, Rhonda C., and Nancy S. Thompson. 2008. *Teaching/Writing in Thirdspaces: The Studio Approach.* Carbondale: Southern Illinois University Press.

Griffin, Frank. 2001. "The Business of the Business Writing Center." *Business and Professional Communication Quarterly* 64, no. 3.

Grouling, Jennifer, and Jackie Grutsch McKinney. 2016. "Taking Stock: Multimodality in Writing Center Users' Texts." *Computers and Composition* 41: 55–67.

Grutsch McKinney, Jackie. 2009. "New Media Matters: Tutoring in the Late Age of Print." *The Writing Center Journal* 29, no. 2: 28–51.

Grutsch McKinney, Jackie. 2013. *Peripheral Visions for Writing Centers.* Logan: Utah State University Press.

Hall, R. Mark. 2010. "A Social Capital View of a Writing Center-WAC Partnership." *Praxis: A Writing Center Journal* 7, no. 2.

Hall, R. Mark. 2017. *Around the Texts of Writing Center Work: An Inquiry-Based Approach to Tutor Education.* Logan: Utah State University Press.

Hallman, Rebecca. 2014. "Re-envisioning Course-Embedded Programs at the Graduate-Level: A Tutor's Experience in a Doctoral Translingual Marketing Class." In "Special

Double Issue on Course-Embedded Writing Support Programs in Writing Centers," edited by Russell Carpenter, Scott Whiddon, and Kevin Dvorak. *Praxis: A Writing Center Journal* 12, no. 1.

Hallman Martini, Rebecca. 2016. "Rejecting the Business-Model Brand: Problematizing Consultant/Client Terminology in the Writing Center." *Open Words: Access and English Studies*. Fort Collins: WAC Clearinghouse.

Hallman Martini, Rebecca, and Travis Webster. 2017. "What Online Spaces Afford Us in the Age of Campus Carry, 'Wall-Building,' and Orlando's Pulse Tragedy." In *Handbook of Research on Writing and Composing in the Age of MOOCs*, edited by Elizabeth Monske and Kristine Blair, 278–293. Hershey: IGI Global, 2017.

Hallman Martini, Rebecca, and Travis Webster, eds. 2017. *Writing Centers as Brave/r Spaces*, Special Issue of *The Peer Review* 1, no. 2.

Harrington, Susanmarie, Steve Fox, and Tere Molinder Hogue. 1998. "Power, Partnership, and Negotiations: The Limits of Collaboration." *WPA: Writing Program Administration* 21, nos. 2–3: 52–64.

Harris, Muriel. 1995. "Talking in the Middle: Why Writers Need Writing Tutors." *College English* 57, no. 1 (January): 27–42.

Harris, Muriel, and Michael Pemberton. 2001. "Online Writing Labs (OWLs): A Taxonomy of Options and Issues." In *The Allyn and Bacon Guide to Writing Center Theory and Practice*, edited by Robert W. Barnett and Jacob S. Blumner, 521–540. Boston: Allyn and Bacon.

Harrison, Rebecca L., and Brooke Parks. 2017. "How STEM Can Gain Some STEAM: Crafting Meaningful Collaborations Between STEM Disciplines and Inquiry-Based Writing Programs." In *Writing Program and Writing Center Collaborations: Transcending Boundaries*, edited by Alice Johnston Myatt and Lyneé Lewis Gaillet, 117–139. London: Palgrave Macmillan.

Haswell, Richard H. 2005. "NCTE/CCCC's Recent War on Scholarship." *Written Communication* 22, no. 2: 198–223.

Haviland, Carol P., Carmen M. Fye, and Richard Colby. 2001. "The Politics of Administrative and Physical Location." In *The Politics of Writing Centers*, edited by Jane Nelson and Kathy Evertz, 85–98. Portsmouth: Boyton/Cook.

Healy, Dave. 1995. "From Place to Space: Perceptual and Administrative Issues in the Online Writing Center." *Computers and Composition* 12, no. 2: 183–193.

Heath, Shirley Brice. 1983. *Ways with Words: Language, Life and Work in Communities and Classrooms*. Cambridge: Cambridge University Press.

Hegelheimer, Volker, Ahmet Dursun, and Zhi Li. 2016. "Automated Writing Evaluation in Language Teaching: Theory, Development, and Application." *Computer Assisted Language Instruction Consortium* 33, no. 1: i–v.

Helms, Robin. 2016. "Emerging Priorities: Strategic Planning and Dealing with Ethical Dilemmas." In *Global Perspectives on Strategic International Partnerships: A Guide to Building Sustainable Academic Linkages*, edited by Clare Banks, Birgit Siebe-Herbig, and Karin Norton, 203–216. New York: Institute of International Education.

Hemmeter, Thomas. 1990. "The 'Smack of Difference': The Language of Writing Center Discourse." *Writing Center Journal* 11, no. 1: 35–49.

Hennelly, Robert. 2016. "The Job Crisis We Must Not Ignore: Employment for Young Americans Remains Staggeringly Low." *Salon*, September 2, 2016.

Hewett, Beth. 2016. *The Online Writing Conference: A Guide for Teachers and Tutors*. Boston: Bedford/St. Martin's.

Hewett, Beth, and Rebecca Hallman Martini. 2018. "Educating Online Writing Instructors Using the Jungian Personality Types." *Computers and Writing* 47, no. 1 (March): 34–58.

Hillocks, George, Jr. 1999. *Ways of Thinking, Ways of Teaching*. New York: Teachers College Press.

Horn, Michael B., and Heather Staker. 2015. *Blended: Using Disruptive Innovation to Improve Schools*. San Francisco: Jossey-Bass.

Huisman, Bart, Nadira Saab, Jan van Driel, and Paul van den Broek. 2018. "Peer Feedback on Academic Writing: Undergraduate Students' Peer Feedback Role, Peer Feedback Perceptions, and Essay Performance." *Assessment and Evaluation in Higher Education* 43, no. 6: 955–968.

Inoue, Asao B. 2019. *Labor-Based Grading Contracts: Building Equity and Inclusion in the Compassionate Writing Classroom.* Fort Collins: The WAC Clearinghouse.

Jackson, Holly A. 2017. "Collaborating for Student Success: An E-mail Survey of U.S. Libraries and Writing Centers." *The Journal of Academic Librarianship* 43, no. 4: 281–296.

Jackson, Rebecca. 2008. "Resisting Institutional Narratives: One Student's Counterstories of Writing and Learning in the Academy." *Writing Center Journal* 28, no. 1 (Fall/Winter): 23–41.

June, Audrey Williams. 2010. "Some Papers are Uploaded to Bangalore to Be Graded." *Chronicle of Higher Education,* April 4, 2010.

Kastman Breuch, Lee-Ann M., and Sam J. Racine. 2000. "Developing Sound Tutor Training for Online Writing Centers: Creating Productive Peer Reviews." *Computers and Composition* 17, no. 3: 245–263.

Kebritchi, Mansureh, A. Lipschuetz, and Lilia Satiague. 2017. "Issues and Challenges for Teaching Successful Online Courses in Higher Education." *Journal of Educational Technology Systems* 46, no. 1.

Kinkead, Joyce. 2011. "Undergraduate Researchers as Makers of Knowledge in Composition in the Writing Studies Major." In *The Changing of Knowledge in Composition: Contemporary Perspectives,* edited by Lance Massey and Richard C. Gebhardt. Logan: Utah State University Press.

Kirklighter, Cristina, Joseph Moxley, and Cloe Vincent, eds. 1997. *Voices and Visions: Refiguring Ethnography in Composition.* Portsmouth: Heinemann.

Kovach, Jamie, Michelle Miley, and Miguel Ramos. 2012. "Using Online Studio Groups to Improve Writing Competency: A Pilot Study in a Quality Improvements Methods Course." *Decision Sciences Journal of Innovative Education* 10, no. 3: 363–387.

Lerner, Neal. 2012. "Of Numbers and Stories: Quantitative and Qualitative Assessment Research in the Writing Center." In *Building Writing Center Assessments that Matter,* edited by Ellen Schendel and William J. Macauley Jr., 108–114. Logan: Utah State University Press.

Lillis, Theresa. 2008. "Ethnography as Method, Methodology, and 'Deep Theorizing': Closing the Gap between Text and Context in Academic Writing Research." *Written Communication* 25, no. 3: 353–388.

Lindahl, Carl. 2004. "Thrills and Miracles: Legends of Lloyd Chandler." *Journal of Folklore Research* 41, nos. 2–3 (May–December): 33–171.

Lindahl, Carl, ed. 2003. *American Folktales: From the Collections of the Library of Congress.* New York: Routledge Press.

Lindquist, Julie. 2002. *A Place to Stand: Politics and Persuasion in a Working-Class Bar.* Oxford: Oxford University Press.

Lockett, Alexandria. 2018. "A Touching Place: Womanist Approaches to the Center." In *Out in the Center: Public Controversies and Private Struggles,* edited by Harry Denny, Robert Mundy, Liliana Naydan, Richard Severe, and Anna Sicari. Logan: Utah State University Press.

Lunsford, Andrea A., and Karen J. Lunsford. 2008. "'Mistakes Are a Fact of Life': A National Comparative Study," *College Composition and Communication* 59, no. 4 (June): 781–791.

Macauley, William J., and Nicholas Mauriello, eds. 2007. *Marginal Words, Marginal Works? Tutoring the Academy in the Work of Writing Centers.* Cresskill: Hampton Press.

Mackiewicz, Jo, and Isabelle Thompson. 2014. *Talk About Writing: The Tutoring Strategies of Experienced Writing Center Tutors.* New York: Routledge.

MacPhail, Theresa. 2015. "The Importance of Writing Skills in Tech-Related Fields." *Chronicle Vitae*, July 23, 2015.

Madhani, Naureen. 2016. "Faculty Experiences of International Partnerships: Perspectives from South Africa." In *Global Perspectives on Strategic International Partnerships*, edited by Clare Banks, Birgit Siebe-Herbig, and Karin Norton, 217–230. New York: Institute of International Education.

Mahala, Daniel. 2007. "Writing Centers in the Managed University." *The Writing Center Journal* 27, no. 2: 3–17.

Marks, Jonathan. 2019. *The Perils of Partnership: Industry Influence, Institutional Integrity, and Public Health*. Oxford: Oxford University Press.

Martinez, Aja Y. 2016. "Alejandra Writes a Book: A Critical Race Counterstory About Writing, Identity, and Being Chicanx in the Academy." *Praxis: A Writing Center Journal* 14, no. 1: 56–61.

McCall, William. 1994. "Writing Centers and the Idea of Consultancy." *Writing Center Journal* 14, no. 2 (Spring): 163–171.

McCleese Nichols, Amy, and Bronwyn T. Williams. 2019. "Centering Partnerships: A Case for Writing Centers as Sites of Community Engagement." *Community Literacy Journal* 13, no. 2 (Spring): 88–106.

McDonald, Terrence T. 2016. "Plans for NJCU Writing Tutoring Center Anger Students, Staff." *NJ.com*, June 27, 2016.

McKinney, Lyle, Heather Novak, Linda Serra Hagedorn, and Maria Luna-Torres. 2017. "Giving Up on a Course: An Analysis of Course Dropping Behaviors Among Community College Students." *Research in Higher Education* 60: 184–202.

Micciche, Laura R. 2017. *Acknowledging Writing Partners*. Fort Collins: The WAC Clearinghouse and University Press of Colorado.

Mila-Schaaf, Karlo, and Maui Hudson. 2009. "The Interface Between Cultural Understandings: Negotiating New Spaces for Pacific Mental Health." *Pac Health Dialog* 15, no. 1 (March): 113–119.

Miley, Michelle. 2018. "Writing Studios as Countermonument: Reflexive Moments from Online Writing Studios in Writing Center Partnerships." In *The Writing Studio Sampler: Stories about Change*, edited by Mark Sutton and Sally Chandler, 167–183. Fort Collins, CO: The WAC Clearing House.

Miley, Michelle, and Doug Downs. 2017. "Crafting Collaboricity: Harmonizing the Force Fields of Writing Program and Writing Center Work." In *Writing Program and Writing Center Collaborations: Transcending Boundaries*, edited by Alice Johnston Myatt and Lyneé Lewis Gaillet, 26–46. London: Palgrave Macmillan.

Miley, Michelle L. 2013. "Thirdspace Explorations in Online Writing Studios: Writing Centers, Writing in the Disciplines and First Year Composition in the Corporate University." PhD diss., University of Houston.

Monske, Elizabeth A., and Kristine L. Blair, eds. 2017. *Handbook of Research on Writing and Composing in the Age of MOOCs*. Hershey: IGI Global.

Monty, Randall. 2019. "Undergirding Writing Centers' Responses to the Neoliberal Academy." *Praxis: A Writing Center Journal* 16, no. 3.

Monty, Randall W. 2016. *The Writing Center as Cultural and Interdisciplinary Contact Zone*. London: Palgrave Pivot.

Moore, Jessie L., and Randall Bass, eds. 2017. *Understanding Writing Transfer: Implications for Transformative Student Learning in Higher Education*. Sterling: Stylus Publishing.

Mortensen, Peter, and Gesa E. Kirsch, eds. 1996. *Ethics and Representation in Qualitative Studies of Literacy*. Urbana: National Council of Teachers of English.

Moss, Beverly. 2002. "Ethnography and Composition: Studying Language at Home." In *Methods and Methodology in Composition Research*, edited by Gesa Kirsch and Patricia A. Sullivan. Carbondale: Southern Illinois University Press.

Myatt, Alice J., and Lyneé L. Gaillet, eds. 2017. *Writing Program and Writing Center Collaborations.* London: Palgrave Macmillan.

Myers-Breslin, Linda, ed. 1999. *Administrative Problem-Solving for Writing Programs and Writing Centers: Scenarios in Effective Program Management.* Urbana: National Council of Teachers of English.

Nall, Stacy, and Kathryn Trauth Taylor. 2013. "Composing with Communities: Digital Collaboration in Community Engagements." *Reflections: A Journal of Public Rhetoric, Civic Writing, and Service Learning* 12, no. 2 (Spring): 9–26.

Naydan, Liliana. 2018. "Transitioning from Contingent to Tenure-Track Faculty Status as a WPA: Working toward Solidarity and Academic-Labor Justice through Hybridity." In *WPAs in Transition: Navigating Educational Leadership Positions,* edited by Courtney Adams Wooten, Jacob Babb, and Brian Ray, 284–296. Logan: Utah State University Press.

Nelson, Cary, and Stephen Watt. 1999. *Academic Keywords: A Devil's Dictionary for Higher Education.* New York: Routledge.

Nichols, Melissa. 2015. "Can WPAs Align Their Beliefs with Their Practices?" *Axis: The Blog of Praxis: A Writing Center Journal,* August 11, 2015.

North, Stephen M. 1984. "The Idea of a Writing Center." *College English* 46, no. 5: 433–446.

Nowacek, Rebecca S., and Bradley Hughes. 2015. "Threshold Concepts in the Writing Center: Scaffolding the Development of Tutor Expertise." In *Naming What We Know: Threshold Concepts of Writing Studies,* edited by Linda Adler-Kassner and Elizabeth Wardle, 171–185. Logan: Utah State University Press.

Ohmann, Richard M. 1976. *English in America: A Radical View of the Profession.* New York: Oxford University Press.

Pagnac, Susan, Shelley Bradfield, Cyndi Boertje, Elizabeth McMahon, and Gregory Teets. 2014. "An Embedded Model: First-Year Success in Writing and Research." *Praxis: A Writing Center Journal* 12, no. 1.

Paiz, Joshua. 2018. "Expanding the Writing Center: A Theoretical and Practical Toolkit for Starting an Online Writing Lab." *The Electronic Journal for English as a Second Language* 21, no. 4: 1–19.

Pemberton, Michael A. 1995. "Rethinking the WAC/Writing Center Connection." *Writing Center Journal* 15, no. 2 (Spring): 116–133.

Peterson, Patricia Webb. 2001. "The Debate About Online Learning: Key Issues for Writing Teachers." *Computers and Composition* 18, no. 4: 359–370.

Phillips, Tallin. 2013. "Tutor Training and Services for Multilingual Graduate Writers: A Reconsideration." *Praxis: A Writing Center Journal* 10, no. 2.

Phillips, Talinn, Paul Shovlin, and Megan L. Titus. 2018. "'An Exercise in Cognitive Dissonance': Liminal WPA Transitions." In *WPAs in Transition: Navigating Educational Leadership Positions,* edited by Courtney Adams Wooten, Jacob Babb, and Brian Ray, 70–86. Logan: Utah State University Press.

Poe Alexander, Kara. 2013. "Material Affordances: The Potential of Scrapbooks in the Composition Classroom." *Composition Forum* 27 (Spring).

Powell, Beth, Kara Poe Alexander, and Sonya Borton. 2011. "Interaction of Author, Audience, and Purpose in Multimodal Texts: Students' Discovery of Their Role as Composer." *Kairos: A Journal of Rhetoric, Technology, and Pedagogy* 15, no. 2.

Prior, Paul. 2018. "How Do Moments Add Up to Lives: Trajectories of Semiotic Becoming vs. Tales of School Learning in Four Modes." In *Making Future Matters,* edited by Rick Wysocki and Mary P. Sheridan. Logan, UT: Computers and Composition Digital Press.

Proctor, Douglas. 2016. "Stakeholder Engagement for Successful International Partnerships: Faculty and Staff Roles." In *Global Perspectives on Strategic International Partnerships: A Guide to Building Sustainable Academic Linkages,* edited by Clare Banks, Birgit Siebe-Herbig, and Karin Norton. New York: Institute of International Education.

Protopsaltis, Spiros, and Sandy Baum. 2019. "Does Online Education Live Up to Its Promise? A Look at the Evidence and Implications for Federal Policy." *George Mason University* (January).

Racia-Klotz, Helen, Christopher Giroux, Christina Montgomery, Ka Vang, Crystal Brinson, Zach Gibson, Taeler Singleton, and Kramer Stoneman. 2014. "'Developing Writers': The Multiple Identities of an Embedded Tutor in the Developmental Writing Classroom." *Praxis: A Writing Center Journal* 12, no. 1.

Ramage, John D., John C. Bean, and June Johnson, eds. 2012. *Writing Arguments: A Rhetoric with Readings.* New York: Pearson.

Readings, Bill. 1996. *The University in Ruins.* Cambridge, MA: Harvard University Press.

Reich, Nicholas. 2018. "Queering the Air: Increasing LGBTQ+ Inclusivity in the Writing Center." *Cultural Rhetorics, Writing Centers, and Relationality: Constellating Stories,* Special Issue of *The Peer Review* 2, no. 2 (Spring).

Reid, E. Shelley, and Heidi Estrem, with Maria Belcheir. 2012. "The Effects of Writing Pedagogy Education on Graduate Teaching Assistants' Approaches to Teaching Composition." *WPA: Writing Program Administration* 36, no. 1 (Fall): 32–73.

Reinheimer, David A. 2005. "Teaching Composition Online: Whose Side Is Time On?" *Computers and Composition* 22, no. 4: 459–470.

Restaino, Jessica. 2012. *First Semester: Graduate Students, Teaching Writing, and the Challenge of Middle Ground.* Carbondale: Southern Illinois University Press.

Rickert, Thomas. 2007. *Acts of Enjoyment: Rhetoric, Zizek, and the Return of the Subject.* Pittsburgh: University of Pittsburgh Press.

Riddick, Sarah, and Tristin Hooker, eds. 2019. *Race and the Writing Center,* Special Issue of *Praxis: A Writing Center Journal* 16, no. 2.

Riessman, Catherine. 2007. *Narrative Methods for the Human Sciences.* New York: SAGE Publishing.

Rose, Jeanne Marie. 2012. "Writing Time: Composing in an Accelerated World." *Pedagogy: Critical Approaches to Teaching Literature, Language, Composition, and Culture* 12, no. 1 (Winter): 45–67.

Rousculp, Tiffany. 2014. *Rhetoric of Respect: Recognizing Change at a Community Writing Center.* Urbana: National Council of Teachers of English.

Runciman, Lex. 1990. "Defining Ourselves: Do We Really Want to Use the Word *Tutor*?" *The Writing Center Journal* 1, no. 11: 27–34.

Russell, Scott. 1999. "Clients Who Frequent Madam Barnett's Emporium." *The Writing Center Journal* 20, no. 1 (Fall/Winter): 61–72.

Ryan, Leigh, and Lisa Zimmerelli. 2015. *The Bedford Guide for Writing Tutors.* Boston: Bedford/St. Martin's.

Santana, Christina, Shirley K. Rose, and Robert LaBarge. 2018. "A Hybrid Mega-Course with Optional Studio: Responding Responsibly to an Administrative Mandate." In *The Writing Studio Sampler: Stories about Change,* edited by Mark Sutton and Sally Chandler, 97–114. Fort Collins, CO: The WAC Clearing House.

Schendel, Ellen, and William J. Macauley Jr. 2012. *Building Writing Center Assessments that Matter.* Logan: Utah State University Press.

Seidman, Irving. 2012. *Interviewing as Qualitative Research: A Guide for Researchers in Education and the Social Sciences.* New York: Teachers College Press.

Selfe, Cynthia L. 2007. *Multimodal Composition: Resources for Teachers.* New York: Hampton Press.

Seltzer, Rick. 2017. "Net Price Keeps Creeping Up." *Inside Higher Ed,* October 25, 2017.

Sewell, Thomas R. 2016. "Student Outcomes in Traditional, Hybrid, and Online Courses in Community College Career and Technical Education Programs." *Electronic Theses and Dissertations,* Paper 3101.

Seyler, Dorothy U. 2014. *Read, Reason, Write.* New York: McGraw-Hill Education.

Shah, Rachael W. 2020. *Rewriting Partnerships: Community Perspectives on Community-Based Learning.* Logan: Utah State University Press.

Sheridan, David M., and James A. Inman, eds. 2010. *Multiliteracy Centers: Writing Center Work, New Media, and Multimodal Rhetoric.* New York: Hampton Press.

Shermis, Mark D., and Ben Hamner. 2013. "Contrasting State-of-the-Art Automated Scoring of Essays." In *Handbook of Automated Essay Evaluation: Current Applications and New Directions,* edited by Mark D. Shermis and Jill Burstein, 313–346. New York: Routledge.

Shull, Anthony J. 2016. "A Positive Breakup: Managing a Soft Landing with Strategic International Partnership Termination." In *Global Perspectives on Strategic International Partnerships: A Guide to Building Sustainable Academic Linkages,* edited by Clare Banks, Birgit Siebe-Herbig, and Karin Norton, 67–74. New York: Institute of International Education.

Simpkins, Neil, and Virginia Schwarz. 2015. "Queering RAD Research in Writing Center Studies." *Another Word,* November 9, 2015.

Simpson, Steve. 2013. "Building for Sustainability: Dissertation Boot Camp as a Nexus of Graduate Writing Support." *Praxis: A Writing Center Journal* 10, no. 2.

Slaughter, Sheila, and Larry L. Leslie. 1997. *Academic Capitalism: Politics, Policies, and the Entrepreneurial University.* Baltimore: Johns Hopkins University Press.

Slaughter, Sheila, and Gary Rhoades. 2004. *Academic Capitalism and the New Economy: Markets, State, and Higher Education.* Baltimore: Johns Hopkins University Press.

Smith, L., T. Hudson, M. Hemi, S. Tiakiwai, R. Joseph, A. Barrett, and M. Dunn. 2008. "The Negotiated Space." Unpublished paper, Te Hau Mihi Ata: Matauranga Maori, Science and Biotechnology. Hamilton, NZ: Waikato University.

Snart, Jason. 2015. "Hybrid and Fully Online OWI." In *Foundational Practices of Online Writing Instruction,* edited by Beth L. Hewett and Kevin Eric DePew. Fort Collins: The WAC Clearinghouse and Parlor Press.

Soules, Aline, Sarah Nielsen, Danika LeDuc, Caron Inouye, Jason Singley, Erica Wildy, and Jeff Seitz. 2014. "Embedding Multiple Literacies into STEM Curricula." *College Teaching* 62, no. 4: 121–128.

Spangler, Dalton. 2019. "Making the Grade: Classes Students Are Most Likely to Pass or Fail." *The Stallion.* Abraham Baldwin Agricultural College, February 12, 2019.

Stay, Byron L., Christina Murphy, and Eric Hobson, eds. 1995. *Writing Center Perspectives.* Emmetsburg: NWCA Press.

Stenberg, Shari J. 2015. *Repurposing Composition: Feminist Interventions for a Neoliberal Age.* Logan: Utah State University Press.

Sutton, Mark, and Sally Chandler, eds. 2018. *The Writing Studio Sampler: Stories About Change.* Fort Collins: The WAC Clearing House.

Sutton, Susan Buck. 2016. "Mutual Benefit in a Globalizing World: A New Calculus for Assessing Institutional Gain Through International Academic Partnerships." In *Global Perspectives on Strategic International Partnerships: A Guide to Building Sustainable Academic Linkages,* edited by Clare Banks, Birgit Siebe-Herbig, and Karin Norton. New York: Institute of International Education.

Tardy, Christine. 2009. *Building Genre Knowledge.* Anderson, SC: Parlor Press.

Terlip, Laura, and Jeffrey Brand. 2015. "STEM Education, Ethics and Communication." *Conference on Ethics in Higher Education* 14.

Thaiss, Christopher, and Tara Porter. 2010. "The State of WAC/WID in 2010: Methods and Results of the U.S. Survey of the International WAC/WID Mapping Project." *College Composition and Communication* 61, no. 3 (February): 534–570.

Thaiss, Christopher, and Terry Myers Zawacki. 2006. *Engaged Writers and Dynamic Disciplines: Research on the Academic Writing Life.* Portsmouth: Heinemann.

Thompson, Isabelle. 2009. "Scaffolding in the Writing Center: A Microanalysis of an Experienced Tutor's Verbal and Nonverbal Tutoring Strategies." *Written Communication* 26, no. 4: 417–453.

Titus, Megan, Jenny L. Scudder, Josephine R. Boyle, and Alison Sudal. 2014. "Dialoging a Successful Pedagogy for Embedded Tutors." *Praxis: A Writing Center Journal* 12, no. 1.

Towle, Beth. 2018. "Understanding (and Advocating for) Peer Tutor Labor through Empirical Research." International Writing Centers Association Conference. Atlanta, October 2018.

Van Horne, Sam. 2012. "Situation Definition and the Online Synchronous Writing Conference." *Computers and Composition* 29, no. 2: 93–103.

VanLehn, Kurt. 2011. "The Relative Effectiveness of Human Tutoring, Intelligent Tutoring Systems, and Other Tutoring Systems." *Educational Psychologist* 46, no. 4: 197–221.

Vygotsky, Lev S. 1962. *Thought and Language.* Cambridge: The MIT Press.

Walsh, Lynda, and Andrew B. Ross. 2015. "The Visual Invention Practices of STEM Researchers: An Exploratory Topology." *Science Communication* 37 (January 21, 2015): 118–139.

Wang, Pei-ling. 2015. "Effects of an Automated Writing Evaluations Program: Student Experiences and Perceptions." *Electronic Journal of Foreign Language Teaching* 12, no. 1: 79–100.

Warnock, Scott. 2009. *Teaching Writing Online: How and Why.* Urbana: National Council of Teachers of English.

Warschauer, Mark, and Paige Ware. 2006. "Automated Writing Evaluation: Defining the Classroom Research Agenda." *Language Teaching Research* 10, no. 2: 1–24.

Webster, Travis. 2021. *Queerly Centered: LGBTQA Writing Center Directors Navigate the Workplace.* Logan: Utah State University Press.

Wenger, Etienne. 1998. *Communities of Practice: Learning, Meaning, and Identity.* Cambridge: Cambridge University Press.

Williams, Bronwyn. 2017. *Literacy Practices and Perceptions of Agency: Composing Identities.* New York: Routledge Press.

Williams, Robin. 2014. *Non-Designer's Design Book.* San Francisco: Peachpit Press.

Wilson, Julie. 2018. " 'Not Alone in the Process': Designing Equitable Support for First-Year Writers in the Writing Center." *Praxis: A Writing Center Journal* 15, no. 2.

Wisniewski, Carolyn. 2018. "Looking through Narrow Windows: Problem-Setting and Problem-Solving Strategies of Novice Teachers." *Writing Program Administration* 42, no. 1: 36–55.

Wolfe, Alexandra. 2016. "Clayton Christensen Has a New Theory." *Wall Street Journal,* September 30, 2016.

Wolfe, Joanna. 2010. "Rhetorical Numbers: A Case for Quantitative Writing in the Composition Classroom." *College Composition and Communication* 61, no. 3 (February): 452–475.

Zebroski, James T. 1999. "The Expressivist Menace." In *History, Reflection, and Narrative: The Professionalization of Composition, 1963–1983,* edited by Mary Rosner, Beth Boehm, and Debra Journet. Vol. 3, *The Perspectives on Writing: Theory, Research, Practice,* 99–113. Stamford, CT: Ablex Publishing Corporation.

INDEX

Note: page numbers followed by *f* and *t* refer to figures and tables respectively. Those followed by n refer to notes, with note number (and chapter number where needed).

ABOUT THE AUTHOR

Rebecca Hallman Martini is assistant professor of English and director of the Writing Center at the University of Georgia, where she teaches courses in composition theory, digital storytelling, and academic writing. She is a recipient of both the International Writing Centers Association (IWCA) Ben Rafoth Graduate Research Grant and the IWCA Research Grant and has been awarded national and local grants for her work in community engagement and experiential learning. She is the founding editor of IWCA's *The Peer Review* and her work has been published in *Across the Disciplines, WPA, Praxis, Computers and Composition,* and *ROLE.*